50 INNOVATI\
THE CONSUMP

EMOTIONAL CAPITAL
FOR THE TRIPLE WIN

ELENA V. AMBER

First published in Great Britain by Practical Inspiration Publishing, 2025

© Elena V. Amber, 2025

The moral rights of the author have been asserted.

ISBN 978-1-78860-701-8 (paperback)
      978-1-78860-700-1 (hardback)
      978-1-78860-703-2 (epub)
      978-1-78860-702-5 (Kindle)

All rights reserved. This book, or any portion thereof, may not be reproduced without the express written permission of the publisher.

Every effort has been made to trace copyright holders and to obtain their permission for the use of copyright material. The publisher apologizes for any errors or omissions and would be grateful if notified of any corrections that should be incorporated in future reprints or editions of this book.

EU GPSR representative: LOGOS EUROPE, 9 rue Nicolas Poussin, LA ROCHELLE 17000, France Contact@logoseurope.eu

Want to bulk-buy copies of this book for your team and colleagues? We can customize the content and co-brand *Emotional Capital for the Triple Win* to suit your business's needs.

Please email info@practicalinspiration.com for more details.

Contents

Part 1: Emotional capital for the triple win 1
1. What is this book about? 3
2. Consumption revolution: A call for change 9
3. Intersection of sustainable consumption and impulsive buying behavior 25
4. Triple win: Sustainable consumption strategy 41
5. Creating conditions where others can thrive 63
6. Emotional Capital for the Triple-Win framework 81

Part 2: 50 innovative ways to lead the consumption revolution 99
7. Create sustainable awareness 101
    1. Create impulsive buying awareness 101
    2. Educate about the consequences of impulsive buying 102
    3. Educate about emotional reasons for overconsumption 103
    4. Educate about the value of well-being over welfare 104
    5. Embrace personal values and the true meaning of self-care 105
    6. Promote health benefits related to sustainable consumption 107

- 7. Leverage diverse personal values for sustainable consumption 108
- 8. Embrace individual actions and help to make informed choices 109
- 9. Don't be trapped by cultural polarization of individualism and collectivism 111
- 10. Create better stories for the collective compass 113

8. Foster triple-win mindset 117

- 11. Stand with people: share ultimate responsibility 117
- 12. Employ values of impact and activism 119
- 13. Deal with uncertainty with straightforwardness 120
- 14. Understand sustainable degrowth 121
- 15. Support sufficiency 122
- 16. Promote voluntary simplicity 123
- 17. Showcase anti-consumption effects 124
- 18. Promote minimalism 126
- 19. Actively support zero-waste movement 127
- 20. Promote sharing economy 131

9. Create impact, becoming a positive force for people and the planet 133

- 21. Base on those customers who care about sustainable consumption and social stability 133
- 22. Be aware of lifestyle, the unique way values and beliefs are behaviorally expressed 135
- 23. Support local communities 136
- 24. Build knowledge communities 137
- 25. Cultivate a "being more human" approach 138
- 26. Mind social consciousness phenomenon 140
- 27. Understand the influencing direction of social networks 140

28. Invite key opinion leaders, not merely influencers 142
29. Promote pro-social behavior 143
30. Promote pro-environmental behavior 144

10. **Empower by transferring knowledge, skills, and practices** 149

    31. Warn about the role of the survival mode in overconsumption 149
    32. Educate about "green consumerism" 151
    33. Help to build long-term emotional regulation 152
    34. Link sustainable consumption with positive emotions 153
    35. Foster mindfulness 154
    36. Suggest taking a pause 156
    37. Take an active part in finance planning and education 158
    38. Enhance consumers' sustainable consumption attitudes 160
    39. Embrace customers with pro-environmental self-identity 161
    40. Promote consumer self-efficacy 163

11. **Advocate for a triple win (and help others)** 167

    41. Mind consumer engagement paradox 167
    42. Evolve business strategy for a triple win: for people, the planet, and prosperity for all 169
    43. Provide customers with trustworthy information 170
    44. Embrace the role of marketing communication in promoting sustainable consumption 172
    45. Use a post-growth marketing mix 173
    46. Don't use patronizing messaging, but suggest practices and direct benefits 176
    47. Don't build on vulnerabilities 177

48. Blacklist sales based on stress, fear, or negative emotions..178
49. Promote long-term sales, don't stimulate impulsive buying related to material purchases 180
50. Innovate as a crazy and search for new opportunities.. 181

12. Custodians of existence and stewards of life equilibrium 185

Notes 195

Index 217

PART 1
EMOTIONAL CAPITAL FOR THE TRIPLE WIN

1

What is this book about?

You don't need me to tell you the world is entering the middle of the unknown. Our climate is shifting, planetary resources are drained faster than they can replenish, and countries routinely exceed agreed regenerative boundaries. Waves of waste continue to grow while social inequalities, conflicts, and climate-forced migrations remain ever-present. Underpinning all these is a root discussion about the central causing factor: unlimited economic growth. And while fears of overpopulation have subsided, concerns are shifting to behaviors like impulsive buying that keep fueling this endless growth. Researchers have found that impulsive purchases make up as much as 90% of all buying decisions. Could reimagining their relationship with consumers enable businesses to find a more effective sustainable approach than the greenwashing we have seen so far? Could they shift away from fueling this impulsivity to something more meaningful? Could this change lead to a deeper alignment—one that benefits consumers, businesses, and the planet? These aren't just abstract questions. That's what the research suggests, and in this book, I aim to demonstrate how that research translates into actionable business strategies.

Initial post-growth response based on making products more sustainable has proven insufficient. Decades of political economy propositions, social movements such as degrowth, models and practices involving commons, agroecology, and cooperatives advocating for life simplification, sufficiency, and economic slowdown appeared very slowly. We do not even have a clear common ground on what sustainability or sustainable consumption is. This book describes multiple types of it, with all types pointing to different directions. Arguing over whether technology or reduced economic growth serves the current situation best stops us from focusing on real change, which can only happen with the active participation of the critical mass of the population involved.

Concerns about impulsive buying highlight a rarely discussed issue: the sharp conflict between traditional business goals and new consumption methods emphasizing minimalism, voluntary simplicity, and anti-consumption. Can you imagine any business plan based on "degrowing" sales numbers? It is never feasible. Instead, can you consider not buying all those things last Black Friday? It sounds very realistic and beneficial for your wallet. However, any business owner is a customer, too, and we should not stand on the different sides of the wall. How could businesses navigate this consumption challenge? To what extent can we degrow without collapsing the existing system? The destruction of it will harm many, beginning with the most vulnerable populations we have long strived to protect from poverty and hunger. Can we navigate change without the need to rebuild everything from scratch? Radical changes have proven to be painful, challenging, and lengthy in recovery for generations involved.

How can we align with natural resources and operate within planetary boundaries instead? Will the sharing economy and new offerings from the experience economy also be beneficial? What are alternatives for degrowth, and is there any new role for business systems? These crucial questions should be addressed openly and collaboratively rather than shifting responsibility among governments, businesses, and consumers. This book discusses all these vital issues in detail, highlighting that while unlimited economic growth is impossible and degrowth offers an immediate solution, there is a third way forward. The third way provides a sustainable and long-term path through a triple-win approach: for people, the planet, and prosperity for all. However, it requires a social transformation: we must change from consumerists to caring and responsible managers of natural resources with long-term regeneration goals and solutions.

An emerging scientific stream worth exploring offers strong potential for development. It suggests that our lifestyle is driven by overconsumption; not caused solely by the overpopulation previously assumed, but rather heavily influenced by buying habits. Impulsive purchasing refers to unnecessary buying, meaning reducing consumption doesn't have to impact essentials. This raises an important question: what drives this behavior? Studies suggest it is not confined to the global North or individualistic cultures, as widely promoted; it is also prevalent in collectivist and developing countries, highlighting consumerism's global nature. Similarly, it's challenging to attribute impulsive buying solely to personal impulsivity traits, as initial research suggested. Given the high numbers, it implies either we all possess these traits or are overlooking the real influences behind it.

Impulsive buying can be beneficial or necessary, supported by our daily investments, and previous research suggests it serves as a self-regulation mechanism to help meet our psychological needs. To prevent further harm, we must understand the complex scientific details behind overconsumption and confront the truth about our current lifestyle. A systematic investigation reveals that businesses significantly influence impulsive buying, while consumers widely embrace impulse purchases, with majority of studies referring to internal factors. This supports the idea that we address our emotional and mental challenges through external purchases, whether to enhance status, self-respect or escape daily troubles affecting us all. We may feel uncomfortable without external boosts of confidence, safety, and psychological relaxation. Therefore, sustainable consumption progress is impossible without personal effort and inner change. Embracing a post-growth mindset requires not only an idealistic vision but a fundamental shift in our insatiable needs.

While we should acknowledge issues in foundational concepts of past systems or ideas, we can certainly build upon them. Historically, business has played a significant role beyond money or transactions. It originated from trade, which served a largely forgotten purpose: fostering social connections. Trade existed long before formal economies, uniting people into larger communities rather than isolated tribal groups. Rather than competing for resources, they began exchanging and enhancing them. Trade symbolized collective connections, enabling mutual empowerment through social exchange and sharing. I found this idea compelling, and businesses can fulfill this role by transforming their core to support a sustainable future, acting as aggregators of existing resources and becoming a source of positive change rather than a limitation. Using the United Nations Sustainable Development Goal 12 (SDG 12)—which calls for sustainable consumption and production—as a focus of our research, this book proposes business strategies for societal transformation to achieve sustainable consumption patterns.

Nearly half of the navigated academic propositions in our research highlight the importance of cultural and educational change as significant factors needed to achieve sustainable consumption. This necessitates substantial lifestyle changes, social connection adjustments, and time to cultivate new values, making discussions on self-transformation a priority. Marketing and business practices that serve consumers' needs must be terminated as exploiting consumers' emotional vulnerabilities for profit. Instead, new business leaders should seek every possibility to empower people and help them realize their full potential. The current crisis affects everyone, yet it also makes us need each other more than ever. Mutual support is crucial in an era of ongoing shifts toward a sustainable future where businesses can change direction and stand with people, invest in the power of informed decisions, and drive collective actions.

This book is grounded in extensive academic research, with transparent citations that provide access to original sources for further details and deeper insights from environmental studies, marketing, social sciences, and psychology. It presents 50 innovative strategies for new business leaders and innovators to drive the consumption revolution through access to a unique type of capital. Emotional capital is the active resource that emerges through social interactions when we invest in the common good, build shared values and enhance communities. Decision-making leaders should harness the genuine ability sensing others and investing in social cohesion rather than solely relying on emotional intelligence protocols, which, while helpful, do not initiate social change. There is a novel perspective on empathy, enabling the empowerment of others by sharing knowledge, skills, and practices.

This book presents sustainable transformations as an exciting, inspiring, and practical possibility, offering leadership ideas for a new mindset and discovering an unprecedented role for business. The first five chapters focus on researching and analyzing emerging science behind impulsive buying behavior related to empowerment and social transformation, and summarizing key information to save executive time. These chapters help business leaders understand overconsumption with essential nuances and encourage redefining leadership for a "triple-win" approach—benefiting people, the planet, and universal prosperity. Businesses are encouraged to shift from simply meeting customer needs to empowering them: *stop selling* for people and *start building a future together*. The book's second part provides detailed descriptions for each of the 50 strategies summarized across five dimensions of emotional capital, each with a *specific role for businesses* to apply and leadership skills to employ, offering a strong foundation for a sustainable future.

After discovering this information, I see opportunities for actions beyond simply addressing overpopulation or relying on quick fixes. The ideas in this book can inspire significant progress, from entrepreneurial startups to boardrooms, helping to ensure a more abundant future for everyone. By combining *science*, *business*, and *collective action*, we can empower individuals, not just policymakers, to *drive real change*. I want to explore this path with you—connecting what we already know to practical business strategies that move beyond superficial greenwashing toward real, lasting sustainability. Let's ask the tough questions, challenge our assumptions, and imagine what's truly possible together.

2

Consumption revolution: A call for change

This chapter gives business leaders and changemakers a clear summary of the current crisis and the economic discussions around it, focusing on the key factors at play. It explains why sticking to "business as usual" is no longer an option and sets the stage for understanding the consumption revolution and the value of investing in social transformation.

Multiple crises have shifted priorities for everyone

As emphasized by Amber et al.,[1] multiple crises have shifted priorities across the global economy. The COVID-19 pandemic disrupted supply chains, geopolitical conflicts unsettled energy markets, and policy changes like Brexit and the US–China trade dispute impacted global trade. Meanwhile, decarbonization goals for 2030 and 2050 have pushed sustainability to the forefront. Additionally, Lynas et al.,[2] highlight a growing agreement among scientists that *endless economic growth* and *overproduction*, driven by human activity, are not sustainable within the Earth's planetary boundaries.

The mismatch between current practices and environmental sustainability is causing serious problems like environmental damage, climate crises, resource depletion, and biodiversity loss. As Hagens[3] points out, Earth's limited resources and strained resilience call for new priorities that balance the environment and economy. With growing awareness of overconsumption and overdevelopment, more people are supporting the idea of "prosperity without growth." Solutions like Green Growth, A-growth, and Degrowth offer different approaches to tackle these urgent challenges.

Balderjahn and Appenfeller[4] highlight that the global population currently consumes 70% more resources than the Earth can sustainably replenish, with private consumption playing a significant role in this imbalance. The initial push for more sustainable products led to what is known as the *"greening of the economy,"* an effect that has reappeared in policy discussions every decade since the early 1970s. However, green consumption does not necessarily advocate for reduced consumption and is often viewed as just another market offer. Podoshen and Andrzejewski[5] raise concerns that green consumption can sometimes reward consumers and even promote growth through consumption.

One of the first marketing scholars who started a discussion on the need to decrease consumption was George Fisk,[6] who discussed responsible consumption. Haider et al.[7] point out that businesses often promote impulsive buying, which can make their claims of corporate social responsibility seem like *"greenwashing."* While consumers may want to reduce impulse purchases, Key et al.[8] argue that retailers have little motivation to help, leading to criticism of marketing as *"consumption engineering."* Palminhas[9] highlights that mainstream sustainable development policies have done little to change this unsustainable trajectory. To explore how sustainable communication marketing could drive sustainable consumption, Kilbourne[10] emphasizes the importance of examining how businesses encourage consumption and the outcomes of these efforts.

The challenge of achieving sustainable consumption in for-profit businesses

Adam Smith famously stated that consumption is the *"sole end and purpose of all production."* In business, growth is a major goal, especially when it comes to entering new markets or expanding internationally. However, as Hickel et al.[11] highlight that modern growth often ignores its impact on climate change and environmental damage. Overconsumption, driven by *consumerism* and materialism, leads to ecological, social, and personal imbalances. Research shows that reducing consumption can improve human well-being. Lorek and Spangenberg[12] emphasize that sustainable development means living *within ecological limits* while meeting everyone's needs. This involves encouraging sustainable habits, reducing impulsive purchases, educating consumers on the harm of overbuying, and promoting the environmental benefits of green purchasing.

The idea of sustainable consumption has drawn significant attention both in international academic circles and among business practitioners worldwide, with extensive research examining it from multiple perspectives. However, Amber et al.[13] point out that businesses and marketing researchers have often *overlooked the issue of overconsumption*, assuming that a shift toward eco-friendly products would mitigate their harmful environmental impact. Green consumption has come under increased scrutiny for potentially sustaining consumption levels rather than reducing them. It has also been criticized for misleading consumers into believing they are contributing to sustainability. Kalaniemi et al.[14] emphasize that achieving environmental sustainability isn't just about technological advancements or better products—it also requires cutting back on consumption and making significant lifestyle changes. Similarly, Sheth et al.[15] point out that while greening the economy is a step in the right direction, rising levels of consumption could cancel out any progress toward sustainability. These findings underline the need to address overconsumption and adopt more mindful consumption habits to achieve lasting environmental sustainability.

Today, businesses face the challenge of balancing traditional growth goals with new approaches to consumption, such as anti-consumption, sufficiency, minimalism, and voluntary simplicity. These ideas question marketing's usual role of driving demand by encouraging the purchase of material goods and services. To address this, businesses need to explore innovative strategies that support sustainable consumption. Let's begin by exploring the growth-degrowth nexus, which is essential for understanding these challenges.

Comprehending the growth-degrowth nexus

The concept of sustainability gained prominence with the publication of "Limits to Growth," a report commissioned by the Club of Rome in 1972, which introduced the idea of ecological limits on global population and economic growth. Later, in 1987, the Brundtland Commission released "Our Common Future," a report that outlined how sustainability can be achieved by meeting the needs of the present without compromising the ability of future generations to meet their own needs. This raises a critical question: what quantities of our current resources must be preserved to ensure future generations can thrive? The sustainability concept faces the challenge of reconciling with the demand for *endless economic growth*—a notion deeply embedded in the foundation of *industrial society*.

Economic growth has long been associated with an improved standard of living, as evidenced by data. A study of 46 countries in sub-Saharan Africa from 1972 to 1997 found a strong connection between economic growth and poverty reduction. When local economies stagnate, job losses lead to increased poverty and hunger. However, the World Bank's "Poverty and Shared Prosperity Report 2018"[16] shows that about 736 million people still live in extreme poverty, primarily in sub-Saharan Africa and South Asia. Consequently, the belief that economic growth can effectively address social issues like poverty or hunger has raised questions.

Moreover, "global asymmetric resource flows" highlight how wealthier nations often exploit materials, energy, land, and labor from poorer regions, leading to unequal exchange relations. Research by Hornborg and Martinez-Alier[17] indicates that industrialized countries in Western Europe, the United States, and Japan heavily rely on material imports, shifting environmental burdens onto other nations. This phenomenon not only exacerbates environmental degradation but also perpetuates economic inequalities and social injustices. The exploitation of resources in poorer regions without fair compensation further widens the gap between the haves and the have-nots, challenging the notion that economic growth alone can address the complex web of social and environmental issues we face.

Economic growth also contributes to climate change through large-scale production processes. Swedish scientist Svante Arrhenius first identified this link in his 1896 work, "On the Influence of Carbonic Acid in the Air upon the Temperature of the Ground".[18] Maintaining current levels of economic activity also requires protecting the resilience of critical ecosystems and natural systems. However, ecological economists argue that this is not being achieved.

The Stiglitz-Sen-Fitoussi Commission highlighted the need to move beyond relying solely on economic growth and GDP to assess a country's well-being. Instead, they called for a broader set of indicators that focus on factors like the distribution of well-being and sustainability. The OECD's new Well-being Framework reflects this shift by helping track societal progress "beyond GDP" and promoting policies that are people-focused and integrated across key areas affecting individuals, the planet, and future generations. This framework helps us understand changes in human well-being, particularly during ecological and digital transitions, and identifies key areas for improvement. The report "How's Life?"[19] provides detailed charts showing whether life is improving in 37 OECD countries and four partner countries. It includes updated data from over 80 indicators, measuring current well-being, inequalities, and resources for the future.

In 2024, De Schutter, the United Nations Special Rapporteur on Extreme Poverty and Human Rights, wrote an important article critiquing the pursuit of unlimited economic growth: "Obsession with Growth is Enriching Elites and Killing the Planet. We Need an Economy Based on Human Rights".[20] The article is based on De Schutter's report, "Ending Poverty by Looking Beyond Growth," where he argues that the current approach to economic growth is flawed. As he stated on LinkedIn: "For decades we have been following the same, tired recipe: grow the economy first, then use the wealth to combat poverty. This is not only misguided, it is dangerous. In the name of GDP we are pushing our planet and its people to the brink".[21] This work offers a powerful critique of the idea of limitless economic growth.

A growing movement is challenging traditional growth models, calling for urgent change. It focuses on reducing consumption and promoting *sufficiency*, aiming for a lifestyle that balances energy, materials, land, and water use within the planet's limits. Martínez-Alier et al.[22]

define sustainable degrowth as both a concept and a social movement, rooted in ecological economics, social ecology, economic anthropology, and environmental activism. Similarly, Sekulova et al.[23] describe degrowth as a collective process that seeks to fairly reduce overall production and consumption. The goal is to create a socially just and ecologically sustainable framework, often referred to as "post-development." While degrowth is increasingly seen as a path to sustainability, many economists agree that an organized shift toward degrowth will be politically challenging.

Understanding growth and degrowth is not simple, though degrowth may be a necessary short-term solution. Does this mean we will need to permanently change our way of life, and to what extent? The answer is linked to a third option: focusing on better understanding and managing our natural resources, or *natural capital*.

Enhancing understanding of natural capital

Economists have traditionally focused on three key factors of production for economic development: land, labor, and capital. However, this perspective has evolved with the introduction of socio-environmental systems and the concept of natural capital. British economist Schumacher[24] first introduced the idea of natural capital to distinguish it from man-made capital, which includes things like machinery, infrastructure, factories, and technology. Unlike man-made capital, which is non-renewable, natural capital is renewable and plays a unique role in economic systems.

Natural capital, as emphasized by ecological economists, includes various elements and processes within ecosystems. Douglas[25] highlights that contemporary literature often uses the term *renewable resources* interchangeably with *renewable energy*; however, water, soil, wildlife, forests, plants, and wetlands are also types of renewable resources. Natural capital includes all abiotic and biotic components of ecosystems, as well as the ecosystems themselves, taking a broad, holistic view. A key feature of natural capital is its *capacity for renewal*. Intricately linked to the fundamental natural principle of multiplication, this capacity is compellingly described in indigenous Quechua thought, as explored by Gary Urton in his work on Quechua ontology of numbers and arithmetic philosophy, "The Social Life of Numbers".[26] Urton references two words: "mira, miray," which denote reproductive force connected to the creative powers of "mama"—the origin of numbers and ordinal sequences, and "askhayay," akin to multiplication, as in "from one, many appear," such as the propagation of many plants from one seed or numerous potatoes from one, similar to numerical multiplication. "Miray" refers to the pluralization characteristic of humans and animals—adult reproductive females—and serves as a base for indigenous idea about nature as a maternal source.

Understanding natural capital has helped ecological economics expand traditional economists' understanding of key factors in economic development, opening the door to new discussions. Sustainable development, based on renewable resources, creates opportunities for new connections between natural, social, and economic systems. To achieve this, human activity must shift from focusing solely on maximizing profits to creating a balanced, regenerative relationship that benefits everyone. While man-made capital is non-renewable, the circular economy emphasizes reducing, reusing, and recycling it. Unlike man-made capital, natural capital can recover, regenerate, and multiply—but only if used within the limits of the system's ability to renew and restore itself.

As Rockström et al.[27] highlight, regeneration is not infinite because nine environmental ceilings define the planet's clear boundaries; crossing these boundaries leads to severe environmental damage and potential tipping points in Earth's systems. Persson et al.[28] note that humanity has already exceeded some of these boundaries, particularly with pollutants and "novel entities," like plastics. The real question is: can we find a way to restore balance? That requires understanding of sustainability as a system of interconnected pillars.

Adopting a systems approach to sustainability

The early literature considers the pillars of sustainability—such as environmental, economic, and social—split broadly between those who view the three pillars of sustainability as inter-connected yet distinct perspectives and those who take a *balanced systems approach*. The system's view is rooted in the notion that sustainability represents *interdependent parts* in transitioning from an unsustainable state to a sustainable one. This refers to an important systemic characteristic called *resilience*.

The discussion on resilience types is crucial, covering environmental, economic, and social domains within the broader sustainability framework. A dichotomy exists between conventional and ecological economists' perspectives, influencing the characteristics of sustainability systems and manifesting as two types: *engineering* and *ecological resilience*. The discussion hinges on whether the state *resisting change* or *transforming for a new order* is fundamental for the ongoing global polycrisis.

When examining the single global equilibrium state of the system, we must consider *engineering resilience*, which restores the system to its natural state after each intervention, regarded as a shock. Gunderson[29] explained that this definition implies that the system exists near a *single global equilibrium condition*. Engineering resilience assumes only one regime and considers whether the system can resist at the very bottom of the regime. It is more about resistance, which allows the system to bounce back after each shock event. Think of this ability as crucial for *short-term change*, which will pass by, and everything will come back to the norm. This type often relies on recovery based on *additional external resources* needed to bring the system to the same state again.

Holling[30] referred to resilience as a *natural system's ability*, which is different from engineering resilience. It allows the system's *self-regeneration* but does not necessarily keep it the same, allowing it to *transform under new conditions*. This type of resilience, known as *ecological resilience*, reflects the system's dynamics and refers to an alive ecosystem's capacity to cope with change via the effect of "*self-organization.*" It refers to the coping capacity in which the *internal ability* of the system allows a quick re-organization and resolving disruptions *without external resources*. Interactions between disturbances and resources in ecological resilience will reconfigure the existing system, eventually establishing a new and more *optimal reference state* that deviates from a steady equilibrium. That means old, well-known norms will no longer exist, and the system will establish the new norm, striving to find a new balance and becoming reorganized. Consequently, resilience can be viewed as comprising *multiple equilibria*, wherein the magnitude of disturbance that can be absorbed before the system redefines its structure serves as a measure of resilience. Think of this ability as *transformation*, a result of *adaptability* needed for *long-term change* when a system needs to transform to fit a new reality.

As per Gunderson, this notion supports the system's *dynamic characteristics*, which are influenced by manipulating the variables and processes governing its behavior and should be complemented by resource utilization, investment allocation, technological advancement, and institutional transformation. Tri et al.[31] made a notable comparison between engineering and ecological resilience. Table 1 presents a summary based on their findings:

Table 1. The main differences between engineering and ecological resilience

	Engineering resilience is presented by stability near one regime equilibrium returning after every shock	**Ecological resilience** is presented by multiple regimes equilibria far from a single condition where any changes are learning opportunities without a need to come back after every change
Viewpoint on resilience	Resilience is resistance and ability for recovery	Resilience is the ability to adapt, transform, keep tolerance, and make reorganization
Main characteristic	Protect the existing configurations of the system	Explore modifications of the system
Main qualities	Robustness, redundancy	Self-organization, adaptive capacity

Although there have been many advances in non-equilibrium thermodynamics in recent decades, including self-organizing, open, dissipative, far-from-equilibrium systems, applying network science concepts and methods to economic systems, I want to underline the ecological equilibrium approach as a base for understanding resilience applied to socio-ecological systems. Fath et al.[32] referred to new methods as powerful for understanding and predicting behavior in socioeconomic systems yet underlined that systemic ecological and economic health requires a balance of efficiency and resilience to be maintained within a particular *"window of vitality."* This simply means we found it logical to remain part of the system after any changes, and we should not expect the system to thrive without human involvement.

Considering *socio-ecological resilience* when discussing long-term changes that apply to living systems is of utmost importance because it is an approach in which humans and nature are studied as an integrated whole, not as separated parts. To Folke et al.,[33] *socio-ecological resilience* is the capacity of the ecosystem to cope with change. According to Biggs et al.[34] it is the ability to adapt to changes in socio-ecological systems, especially unexpected ones, in ways that continue to support *human well-being*. The social and ecological systems are linked in *coupled human-environment systems*.

Research on human-made capital and *engineering resilience* for optimal profit maximization, alongside natural capital and *socio-ecological resilience* for renewable capacity regeneration and cooperative sustainability, underpin the development of two critical economic approaches to sustainability: *weak* and *strong sustainability*.

Differentiating between weak and strong sustainability

Weak and *strong* approaches to sustainability hold different views on unlimited growth on a planet with limited natural resources. The origin of the *weak sustainability concept* is related to the theory of neoclassical economic development. The methodological features of the concept were created by Solow.[35] This prevailing economic paradigm, viewing all forms of capital solely as resources for optimal allocation, faced a challenge where the simplistic outlook of humans harvesting resources rather than engaging in mutual development needs to be altered.

A *strong sustainability* approach, which highlights constraints of economic growth, posits that sustainable development relies on environmental responsibility. This perspective is increasingly recognized as a vital prerequisite for achieving economic efficiency and fostering social cohesion. Advocates of *strong sustainability* questioned the simplistic view of the world where humanity consumes without integral development. The ability to *self-regenerate*, or *socio-ecological resilience* in our discussion, is only possible within planetary boundaries. Such a change should be *coupled with the exploitation of resources, direction of investments, orientation of technological development*, and *institutional change*. Strong sustainability proponents vote for the *significance of cooperation between human and nature households*, leading to the implementation of several appropriate actions fostering such collaboration between humanity and the environment, mitigating unlimited economic growth.

Hobson[36] pointed out that such a weak and strong dichotomy presents a starkly polarized view of approaches to sustainability that, in reality, often intersect and overlap depending upon the aims, methods, and desired outcomes being suggested. In their view, a *weak consumption approach* enhances the efficiency of the production–consumption nexus through technological innovation and voluntary interventions, aiming for economic growth and improved socioeconomic well-being. A *strong sustainable consumption approach* focuses on shifting from growth-centric concepts to nonconsumption practices, driven by grassroots movements, aiming for sociopolitical transformation and well-being without relying solely on economic growth. These two approaches hold different views on types of technological advancement, too.

Shaping the future: the impact of technological advancements

Weak sustainability advocates consider the environmental sustainability pillar with a possibility to trade-offs to other elements of the whole system. They state that such environmental trade-off could be carried out with the economic aspect of the system in a way so that *technological development decouples the social pillar from dependency on natural resources.*

However, Biely et al.[37] refers to instances of contentious technological advancements, such as the *decoupling of agricultural land from agricultural production*, which has resulted in significant trade-offs, including substantial increases in fertilizer, pesticide, energy, and water usage. Hautakangas[38] highlights that bioeconomy interventions have been scrutinized, directly pertain to enhancing resource productivity, and fall under the scope of *Green Economy* alongside *Clean Tech* and *Circular Economy*. As noted by Daly and Farley,[39] although cross-breeding of biology and economy sounds healthy and we all use its simple products in everyday life, utilizing fermentation to produce and preserve bread and wine, a key component of bioeconomy created a mass opposition movement. Helm[40] noted that use of biotechnologies, which includes transgenics and gene editing, had enormously negative social feedback against *Frankenstein food* (genetically modified food—GMO) for family tables. Wunderlich and Gatto[41] suggest that although consumers worldwide are displaying limited understanding, misconceptions, and even unfamiliarity with GMO food products, it seems that the green revolution is less preferable for humans than green evolution.

As an exemplification, the IFIC Foundation[42] conducted research on labels proposed by the U.S. Department of Agriculture's Agricultural Marketing Service with the purpose of disclosing information about "bioengineered" foods. The findings indicate a significant increase in consumer concerns, particularly related to human health. Despite the limited knowledge, 47% of individuals claimed to avoid GMO foods to some extent. Among those who refrain from GMOs, the majority (85%) do so out of concerns for human health, while concerns about the environment (43%), animal health (36%), and agriculture/farming (34%) are of lesser importance. The primary objective of the bioeconomy is the enhancement of the resources utilized, which demands both technological and ethical development over time. Careful implementation of substitution management strategies should be based on the provided solutions, taking into consideration the hidden costs of fossil fuels as an important lesson for humanity. In light of the difficulties met by technological-based solutions for natural capital scarcity, more and more voices are voting for *natural adaptation solutions* based on nature's *self-regeneration* mechanisms.

It has been proposed that advancements in technical *resource productivity* serve as potential alternatives to the exponential growth of the economy. However, Daly,[43] in his acclaimed work "Beyond Growth," expounds on the notion that improving resource productivity is a prudent approach, as long as it does not conflict with other capital and labor productivity. Consequently, *strong sustainability advocates* argue about the trade-off possibility between the elements of a sustainability system because there are variations in the extent to which people are allowed to destroy the environment. To them, as underlined by Wilderer et al.,[44] it would be illogical to employ the same (technological) mechanisms for a solution as those by which the problem was created.

This points to the fact that technological development during industrialization has already led to exponential pollution growth, climate change, and resource scarcity. Biely et al.[37] even state that *weak sustainability* could, therefore, be considered illegitimate. Gunderson[29] stated that maintaining constancy of production (*economic pillar of sustainability*) proves counterproductive, as it leads to a decrease in the resilience of ecosystems (*environmental pillar of sustainability*). The proponents of *strong sustainability* do not fundamentally oppose technological advancement. However, their argument is grounded in the notion that allocating natural resources toward technological development aimed at reducing future generations' reliance on resources may inadvertently lead to increased environmental pressures.

Consumption revolution: a call for change

Let's summarize why do we need to reconsider the way we consume. Toth and Szigeti[45] emphasized that population growth has always been the main driver in biosphere transformation, but there has been a stronger one: accelerating consumption. They pointed out that instead of a "population bomb," we should speak about an "overconsumption detonator" of environmental disaster. We not only exceed sustainable consumption levels, but even those who identify themselves as environmentalists and conscious consumers often make unsustainable choices. Researchers have found that although the majority of consumers indicate a preference for greener, healthier, and more sustainable products, their actual purchasing behaviors frequently deviate from these stated preferences, resulting in an *attitude-behavior gap*. For example, Ismael and Ploeger[46] reported that while many acknowledge that consuming organic food enhances their well-being, they often overlook the implications of the misalignment between their intentions and actual behaviors. Pereira Heath and Chatzidakis[47] revealed that most respondents distanced themselves from those who purchase excessively when challenged about their behavior. Nevertheless, the "attitude-behavior gap" persists.

At the same time, multiple academic research suggests up to 90% of consumers are impulsive purchasers, and up to 80% of individual consumption is based on impulsive buying behavior when a consumer experiences a persistent urge to buy something immediately. For example, Amos et al.[49] point out two studies: the research by Coca-Cola which shows that impulsive buying accounts for more than 50% of all their grocery purchases, and the National Endowment for Financial Education study which found that more than 87% of American adults admit to impulsive buying. Wang et al.[50] referred to a report that shows that 68% of online purchases in China are impulsive. Kacen et al.[51] noted that impulsive buying accounts for almost 80% of purchases in certain product categories. Husnain et al.[52] found it represents between 40% and 80% of overall purchases. Spiteri Cornish[53] observes that, be it positive or negative, hedonic or utilitarian, individual or social, any of our impulsive choices are well-known to businesses and intricately woven into the fabric of retail success. It has been suggested that encouraging spur-of-the-moment purchases becomes a symphony of urgency, social influence, and retail design. Considerable academic attention has been devoted to exploring ways to enhance sustainable consumption by reducing impulsive buying.

Consequently, businesses face unprecedented challenges in identifying where to direct their efforts, given that there is a strong call for wealthy economies to: abandon growth of gross domestic product (GDP) as a goal, scale down destructive and unnecessary forms of production, reduce energy and material use, and focus economic activity around *securing human needs* and *well-being*. This book explores the question, "What should for-profit firms consider when developing strategies that align with sustainable consumption?" with three primary objectives:

First, Chan et al.[54] emphasized that research remains inconclusive regarding whether sustainable consumption policies should prioritize *altering consumer behavior* (and to what extent) or ensuring the accessibility of *sustainable products* for the general population. Therefore, this study investigates what the current academic opinion on that matter within literature is at the *intersection of sustainable consumption and impulsive buying behavior*.

Second, grasping a sustainable consumption subject can be difficult without a shared understanding of overall sustainability, particularly when examining the behavioral dimensions of sustainable consumption—a continual challenge. Therefore, the aim is to systematically review existing research to shed light on the complex nature of *sustainable consumption*.

Third, the United Nations Sustainable Development Goal 12 (hereinafter SDG 12) calls to ensure sustainable consumption and production patterns. A key point of criticism due to van Driel et al.[55] is the gap between the ambitious transformation implied by the goal's core headline and the actual targets and indicators adopted. Following that gap, this book aims to indicate *actionable business propositions* for businesses using a comprehensive systematic review approach based on identified sustainable consumption insights.

Can brands build a highly sustainable reputation and image to encourage reduced consumption and shift demand patterns? If so, my task is to compile and provide *actionable business propositions* that influence sustainable consumption and enhance business strategies and actions.

Consumption revolution: a call for change: key takeaways

- Multiple crises have shifted priorities for everyone, prompting us to challenge our current way of life.
- The pursuit of sustainable consumption in for-profit businesses challenges the traditional goal of serving seemingly insatiable consumer needs.
- Understanding the growth-degrowth relationship provides insights into the meaning and history of economic development.
- The concept of natural capital, with its unique regenerative abilities, offers an alternative path.
- Adopting a systems approach to sustainability helps differentiate between short-term and long-term solutions.
- Distinguishing between weak and strong sustainability is crucial for understanding the debate over long-term goals like continued economic growth and non-consumption-based well-being.
- Shaping the future: how technological advancements impact resource allocation.
- Consumption revolution: a call for change making social transformation inevitable.

3

Intersection of sustainable consumption and impulsive buying behavior

Sustainable consumption isn't just something for economists and environmentalists to think about—it's also tied to how we, as consumers, behave. Ecological economists talk about two approaches: "weak" sustainable consumption, which mainly focuses on product changes, and "strong" sustainable consumption, which is all about cutting down consumption overall. Either way, the message is clear: we need to rethink how we consume. This chapter includes some insights from the manuscript submitted for publication, "A Multi-Country SLR of Sustainable Consumption in Impulsive Buying: Actionable Marketing Propositions for Multinational Companies and Conceptualization," by Amber et al.[1]

The intersection of sustainable consumption and impulsive buying behavior emerged in 2012

There has been an increasing frequency of publications since 2012, indicating a burgeoning intersectional field. To understand whether academia recognizes the intersection, a comparative analysis of publications on sustainable consumption in impulsive buying behavior is presented, with a summary shown in Figure 1. These findings, presented through infographics by decade and year, highlight a growing yet fragmented interest in this area, signaling promising directions for future interdisciplinary studies. Over the past decade, more publications have started to recognize and directly explore the connection between sustainable consumption and impulsive buying behavior.

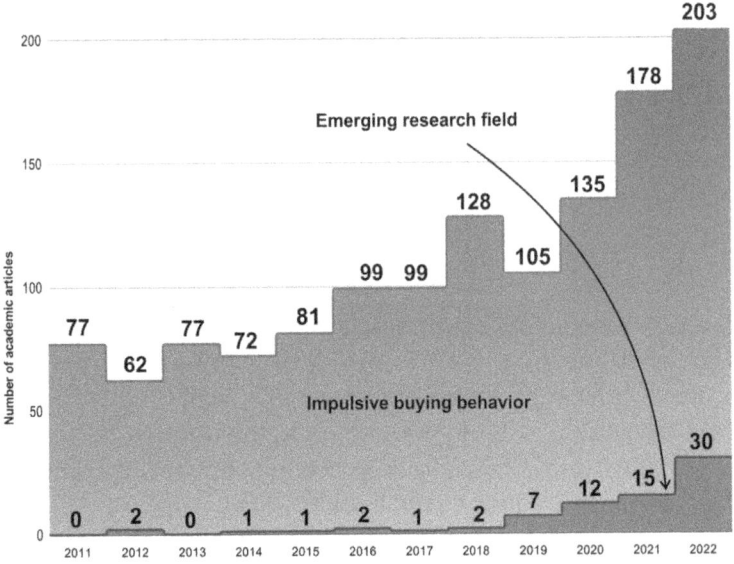

Figure 1. Emerging research field in sustainable consumption, adapted from Amber et al.[1]

There is not only a link between sustainable consumption and impulsive buying; the same factors that help stop impulsive buying might also encourage more sustainable habits. That's why it makes sense to connect consumer behavior (something studied in psychology and social sciences) with economics and environmental studies. This study is the first of its kind and identifies the emerging field at the crossroads of sustainable consumption and impulsive buying behavior from 2012. Exploring this fascinating intersection inspired practical goals and a desire to find directions and opportunities for businesses during current times of complex change. The research includes a summary and pulls together key trends, wrapping it all up into a few simple chapters identified from more than 200 researchers' voices, compactly presented in just a few chapters.

Sustainable consumption at the nexus with impulsive buying is studied globally

Reflecting on the authorship characteristics of each article led to insightful data on the global distribution of contributors. As shown in Figure 2, the authors come from different countries, showing a good geographical spread. Interestingly, Chinese institutions lead the way, contributing almost a quarter of the research articles. They are followed by the United States and the United Kingdom at about 10% each, with Germany and India close behind at the level of about 7% each. Canada and Korea round things out, each with about 4%.

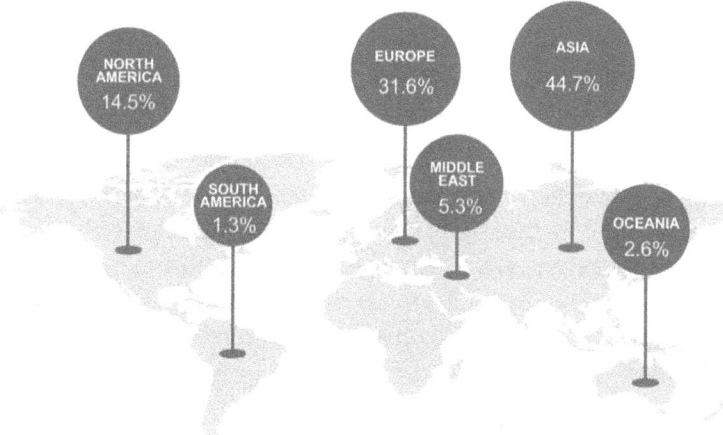

Figure 2. Authorship analysis, adapted from Amber et al.[1]

Looking at where these authors come from, Asia is leading with almost half of the research articles considered and showing strong involvement in the subject of sustainable consumption. Europe represented one-third of the sample, followed by North America, the Middle East, Oceania, and South America (Brazil). The lack of contributions from African and Nordic/Scandinavian countries highlights untapped research opportunities, especially when it comes to understanding the complex dynamics in the global North–South context. Many social comments and scientific discussions today refer to energy overconsumption in the global North, where detailed research on other consumers' products in both regions could be highly beneficial.

Nearly half of the articles reviewed are published in open-access journals, which allow anyone to read them for free. These journals play a key role in sharing research and making it accessible to everyone. However, they often face criticism, mainly due to the perception that articles from highly ranked, paid scientific journals are more reliable and reputable. This belief can create resistance to new ideas and make it harder for emerging research fields to gain acceptance—especially in areas like business and marketing, where conflicts of interest may arise around topics like voluntary simplicity consumption, sufficiency, and anti-consumption. Despite these challenges, open-access journals remain vital platforms for sharing innovative research, promoting the free exchange of information, and fostering the exploration of new ideas.

Chinese researchers comprise about 40% of articles in open-access journals like *Sustainability* and *PLOS ONE*. Much of their work focuses on food and e-commerce, especially health and mobile health services. Later, we will dive into some academic tips for businesses communicating about sustainable consumption, but for now, it's interesting to note that China is pioneering in linking sustainable products to *personal benefits*, especially in health and food, which are hot public topics. It turns out that using environmental messages is not cutting it to get people on board with sustainable consumption.

The analysis also revealed that most papers are authored by three individuals from the same countries. This pattern is particularly noteworthy as it suggests that a small proportion of research on sustainable consumption at the intersection with impulsive buying behavior involves international collaborative teams. These findings indicate the potential for increased cross-border collaborations to expand the scope and impact of future studies.

Interdisciplinary approach to sustainable consumption and impulsive buying behavior

Next, the analysis reveals a substantial concentration of research in four fields: *environmental science, marketing, social sciences*, and *psychology*. Linking consumer behavior with economic data analysis is exactly what's needed to explore the connection between sustainable consumption and impulsive buying. It underscores the growing importance of understanding how individual choices affect both the environment and the economy. By examining this relationship, we can uncover valuable insights to guide smarter decisions and create effective strategies for promoting more sustainable consumer habits. Figure 3 illustrates this complex relationship, serving as a helpful guide for further exploration and analysis.

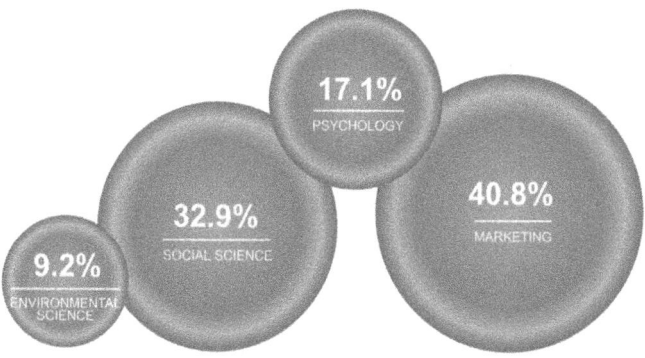

Figure 3. Fields of research based on the selected articles, aggregated view

Marketing dominates with 40.8% of the articles, highlighting the crucial role of marketing strategies and consumer engagement in studying sustainable purchasing patterns. *Social sciences* closely follow, with 32.9% emphasizing the significance of social norms and cultural contexts in shaping buying behavior. The field of *psychology* contributes 17.1% of the articles, providing valuable insights into the cognitive processes that influence consumer choices. *Environmental science* comprises only 9.2% of the literature, highlighting the potential for studies on the environmental impact of consumer habits. For example, a recent study by Tian et al., "Keeping the Global Consumption within the Planetary Boundaries,"[56] which includes research across 168 countries and up to 201 consumption groups, investigates distribution of six environmental footprints. The complementary nature of these research areas, exploring the nexus of impulsive buying behavior within the realm of sustainability, demonstrates their interconnected and complex relationship.

Understanding consumer responsibility in sustainable consumption

It has been stressed that consumers often do not accept sustainable consumption responsibility but frequently consume excessively. Liu et al.[48] highlighted that altering individual habits is essential for achieving sustainable consumption and has been widely recognized. Purvis et al.[57] underlined that unlimited economic development encompasses social concerns, whereas sustainable development requires fundamental changes, including *individuals*. However, in their article, "'Blame it on Marketing': Consumers' Views on Unsustainable Consumption," Pereira Heath and Chatzidakis[47] revealed that many consumers do not perceive that their daily choices significantly impact the environment. Another study by Lorek and Fuchs[58] indicates that sustainable consumption involves industry, government, but also *household consumption patterns*. To make it simple, all three levels of consumption are usually reflected as follows:

1. **Micro-level** sustainable consumption research aims at individual or household consumption. This is precisely the focus of this book.

2. **Meso-level** sustainable consumption research aims at private organizations or groups.

3. **Macro-level** sustainable consumption research aims at the structures of systems, such as government consumption or aggregated industries' consumption.

Fischer et al.[59] revealed that the predominant discourse in sustainable consumption research (documented in roughly two-thirds of all journal articles reviewed in their research) posits *individual behavioral changes* as the primary route toward sustainability, with the majority of studies (three-quarters) focusing directly on the consumer to alter private or household habits for a more sustainable consumption system. What does research state on individual consumption?

Academic verdict: more than 60% of articles suggest a need for a consumption decrease

Two analysis steps were implemented to comprehend the academic point of view better. First, each article was categorized according to its primary research argument, which formed four distinct groups. Next, four groups were analyzed, and the types of sustainable consumption were mainly discussed.

Classification of articles based on the *main research argument* identified are presented in Table 2.

Table 2. Main research argument

The main research argument in the academic discussion	Consumption	Impulsive Buying behavior	%
Need to increase consumption and impulsive buying behavior	Increase	Increase	11
Need to decrease consumption and impulsive buying behavior	Decrease	Decrease	54
Need to change for sustainable products discussed; impulsive buying is ok	Change and increase	Increase	28
Need to change to sustainable products and decrease impulsive buying	Change and decrease	Decrease	8

The consolidated result of the main research argument analysis is presented in Figure 4. The results show two radically opposite main research arguments almost equal in size, such as *Increase consumption and impulsive buying behavior* which equals 11% and *Change consumption products and decrease impulsive buying behavior* with a sum of 8%.

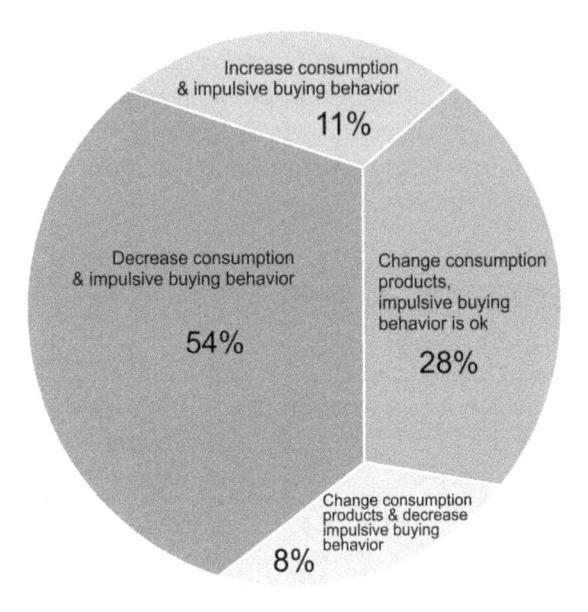

Figure 4. Analysis of the main research argument in relation to impulsive buying behavior, adapted from Amber et al.[1]

Next, the argument, *Change consumption products and impulsive buying behavior is ok*, accounts for 28%, contrasting with the more prevalent *Decrease consumption and impulsive buying behavior* at 54%. The result supports the prior argument by Markauskaitė and Rūtelionė[60] of two major paths in academic discussions: one is to consume *products that are environmentally friendly*, and the other is the *anti-consumption*.

This research identified that only 35.5% of the literature focuses on environmentally friendly products directly via *green consumption* (14.3% cases) or *indirectly* via discussions regarding change for more sustainable products. These discussions include categories such as *need to change for sustainable products, impulsive buying is ok* (28%) and *need to change for sustainable products and decrease impulsive buying* (8%). It could be concluded that greening, or changing products to be more sustainable, is not a target topic within the research studies' scope. Research focus number one is the decrease in consumption and impulsive buying behavior.

What kind of studies suggest impulsive buying needs to increase?

Additionally, the analysis of academic arguments was done for the group of 11%, which voted for an *increase in consumption and impulsive buying behavior*. It was done in order to understand the obtained research results in relation to the prior research trends identified. This trend highlights academic opinions, such as those of Spiteri Cornish,[53] who assert that impulsive buying is crucial for the long-term success of many retailers. Consequently, Wei Jie et al.[61] recommend encouraging impulsive purchases, while Lee and Wan[62] emphasize creating urgency to motivate immediate orders. Additionally, Zafar et al.[63] suggest designing a positive social climate to stimulate impulsive buying.

There is evidence from Um et al.[64] regarding impulsive buying arguments that drive sales. Wei Jie et al.[61] emphasize that retailers should focus on impulse purchasing by investing more in online shop design. Cho et al.[65] highlight the importance of creating an attachment to products, enhancing interactions among existing followers, and attracting new individuals to brand communities, which can ultimately trigger impulsive buying, as noted by Zafar et al.[63]

However, additional analysis reveals that these arguments were put forth within the literature sample directly (62.5%) or indirectly (by publications between 2019–2020) related to COVID-19. First, it was linked to poor sales outcomes during the pandemic in severely affected sectors from the HoReCa (hotel, restaurant, and café/catering) market segment, contributing to a decline in sales due to government restrictions on travel and large gatherings in connection with the need for CO_2 emission reductions and safety requirements. Second, research has underscored the essential increase in health and sports-related products during the pandemic. Sajid et al.[66] point out that the *fear of the coronavirus* has driven the purchase of green products, such as organic food. Chiu et al.[67] note that it significantly influences impulsive buying decisions, which prioritizes health, safeguards emotions, and enhances overall *consumer well-being*.

The literature review investigates the question, "How does impulsive buying positively influence sustainable consumption?" The results are presented in Table 3.

Table 3. *Samples of a positive influence of impulsive buying*

Samples of a positive influence of impulsive buying	Effect	Reference
Increase organic purchases, which is good for personal health	+	57
Signaling interpersonal warmth and comforting	+	64
Help to overcome anxiety and perceived threats such as scarcity or severity	+	65
Help to relax, enhance perceived self-efficacy, and enable interaction with others	+	58
Help to regain a sense of equilibrium once under stress and worry	+	66
Increase good mood and enjoyment and repair psychological state for some time	+	48
Help to beat death anxiety, threats, and uncertainly	+	67

Create a sense of life satisfaction and produce positive effects due to goal attainment and investment into enacting marketplace roles (consumers)	+	68
Increase work engagement by recovering	+	69

These research considerations enable us to infer that impulsive purchasing behavior is considered or deemed acceptable and even favorable when associated with sustainable products or health-related items that significantly influence the *quality of human life*, ultimately aiding in alleviating adverse psychological consequences at the individual level. It is also considered a tool aiding sales degrowth during an economic crisis related to pandemic circumstances. Therefore, this study results do not relate to impulsive buying as essential for the long-term success of many retailers,[53] but resulting in a short-term solution for aiding COVID-19's unprecedented circumstances and being essential for the psychological health of consumers themselves.

However, the reasoning for impulsive purchases regarding the overall *well-being of consumers* via health-related products is very intriguing. This fact is very important for the following discussion regarding the phenomenon of impulsive buying behavior and its adverse or favorable potential, where research results related to well-being will be separately presented in the following chapters, forming a significant research trend.

What types of sustainable consumption relate to arguments for reduced consumption or product changes to become more sustainable?

Further analysis was done regarding relations of the main research argument, research focus, and types of sustainable consumption as presented in Table 4.

Table 4. Analysis of relations between types of sustainable consumption researched, main research argument, and focus

Main argument in relation to impulsive buying behavior	Research literature	The main types of sustainable consumption discussed
Increase consumption and impulsive buying behavior	11%	90% sustainable consumption (not specified), 10% unneeded consumption
Decrease consumption and impulsive buying behavior	54%	Various, except green and sharing types of consumption
Change consumption products. Impulsive buying behavior is ok	28%	Within 30.4% papers, focusing more on to impulsive buying behavior, almost half (is general sustainable (not specified) consumption. Within 69.6% focused on sustainable consumption a bit more than a half is green consumption. Saring consumption discussed only within this category
Change consumption products and decrease impulsive buying behavior	8%	20% focused more to impulsive buying behavior is arguing for voluntary simplicity. 80% related to sustainable consumption has half as green consumption and half as various types, each of one

There are few distinct trends that have been identified and partly published by Amber et al.[1]:

1. Of the research papers, 54% fall into the category "Decrease consumption and impulsive buying behavior," focusing equally on how to make consumption more sustainable (50%) and how to mitigate impulsive buying behavior (50%). Green consumption is not seen as a solution here, being mentioned only by 3.1% of articles in this category. Instead, this group is based on environmentally and socially driven consumption.

2. Only 14.3% of current research actively promotes *green consumption* despite a longstanding call for greening the economy, assuming that shifting toward eco-friendly products could offset any rise in consumption impacts.

3. When research discusses an increase in impulsive buying behavior, it usually refers to general sustainable consumption type without any specifications.

4. Of the considered literature scope, 36% supports the shift toward more sustainable products via the categories *"Change consumption products and impulsive buying is ok"* and *"Change for sustainable products and decrease impulsive buying"*.

5. There is a literature scope that discusses *both impulsive buying and voluntary simplicity-like types of consumption* (which is 23.4% of this research), and those articles related to the main research argument *change consumption products and decrease impulsive buying behavior*, where research tries to identify how is it possible to achieve sustainable consumption by mitigation of impulsive buying.

6. When research literature discusses the change of consumption products without a decrease in numbers, it usually refers not only to *green sustainable consumption* but also to sharing consumption, which is discussed only within this category.

Understanding the types of consumption strategies and arguments offered is imperative, not only for the sake of academic advancement but also because this is the academic foundation for practical application proposals. Managers are alerted to the advantages of maintaining a sustainable business focus. To White et al.,[68] these benefits include the identification of new products and markets, leveraging emerging technologies, and motivating and retaining employees. However, it is impossible to consider sustainable consumption without individual consumer behavior and its socio-ecological impact. This book provides not only unique insights and a comprehensive understanding of various types of sustainable consumption at the nexus with impulsive buying behavior, but also includes exhausting analyses of practical (managerial) propositions, which are discussed further.

Intersection of sustainable consumption and impulsive buying behavior: key takeaways

- The intersection of sustainable consumption and impulsive buying behavior emerged in 2012 and steadily developed over a decade.

- Sustainable consumption in impulsive buying behavior is studied globally, yet more focus is needed on global North and South consumers' products and items beyond energy.

- Open-access journals are pioneering the field with China as a leading publication country, especially on personal sustainable benefits related to health and food.

- Understanding consumer responsibility in sustainable consumption is essential as this gives us the power to take action.

- Academic verdict: more than 60% of articles suggest a need for a consumption decrease, and most of them state that products must become sustainable. That means we need to change our current lifestyle.

- What kind of studies suggest impulsive buying needs to increase? The case points to business dynamics that seek recovery during a pandemic.

- Green consumption is no longer a primary focus. What forms of sustainable consumption are most necessary? While most studies agree on the need for sustainable products, the emphasis is on reducing consumption levels and curbing impulsive buying behavior.

4

Triple win: Sustainable consumption strategy

This chapter looks at sustainable consumption in-depth, breaking down multiple types identified in academic research. It introduces a transparent model for a triple-win approach that balances three key areas: environmentally driven consumption, socially driven consumption, and economically driven consumption. Understanding these different types is crucial for building a clear view of sustainable consumption and helping business leaders create strategies that align with these dynamics. Instead of making all consumers the same, the focus is on recognizing and valuing the diversity of consumer preferences, which vary depending on the business and its goals. The chapter also examines what drives these consumer groups, what inspires them, and what limits them, offering data to help companies make informed decisions. This chapter draws on material from the forthcoming academic book chapter, "Leveraging SDG12 for Marketing Communication and Consumer Trust: Theoretical Elucidations and Practical Recommendations," by Amber et al.[13]

A need for a balance: the optimal solution

Let's delve into nuances as soon as we understand the need for sustainable consumption and mitigating impulsive buying behavior. First, it is essential to grasp the concept of sustainable consumption itself. The articles reviewed don't consistently define sustainable consumption, but I have compiled a summary that not only clarifies this concept but also presents diverse viewpoints, allowing readers to appreciate its complexity. This understanding is beneficial for productive discussions among all stakeholders and highlights the need to avoid oversimplifying sustainable consumption and the topic of sustainability in general. Following the advice of Areias et al.,[69] we should treat sustainability as a complex issue. Why is this important? This perspective is crucial because we seek long-term, intricate solutions rather than superficial quick fixes following the idea that we must embrace change instead of wasting energy, time, and resources battling symptoms to resist it.

For instance, while green consumption may lack a strong reputation, there is no denying our need for more sustainable products. Although we aim to change our lifestyle, we still require better technological solutions. I support the notion that we must explore all possible opportunities during times of change. Given the significant environmental pressures, like the climate crisis and resource limitations, we must cease power struggles and focus on understanding the nuances. The optimal solution lies not in dominating leading opinion but in balance, which we must identify and maintain for long-term change. This process may be challenging, much like incorporating physical exercise into a daily routine, but the overall health and immunity benefits are crucial. Therefore, I encourage you to explore the diverse range of sustainable consumption options, each contributing unique insights into sustainable pathways. As you read this, try to envision what suits your business situation best, what is preferable, and what seems unsuitable. Identifying a unique position for each business and entrepreneur is essential, as there should not be a single best solution but rather a balanced blend of many.

What is sustainable consumption, anyway?

Since the term "sustainable consumption" was formally introduced by the Oslo Symposium in 1994, it has attracted growing academic and media attention. Yet, Vergragt et al.[70] pointed out that sustainable consumption is relatively new and still lacks a well-defined structure, with its boundaries remaining fluid. In their study, Liu et al.[48] charted the evolution of sustainable consumption research, highlighting the initial focus on consumption behavior, public policy, social factors, and economics from 1995–2005 and noting a shift from 2006 to 2014 toward exploring the environmental impact of consumer behavior, aiming to bridge the gap between attitudes and behavioral intentions by deciphering the central factors influencing sustainable consumption. Dimitrova et al.[71] confirm that earlier studies focused on attempts to understand the sustainable consumption phenomenon and the environmental impact of individual actions. Figueroa-García et al.[72] remind us that from the theory standpoint, sustainable consumption is rooted in ethical consumer research, and studies still concentrate on its core – attitudes, values, and norms as per our literature review results, which will be presented further. Later, it was noticed that sustainable consumption is more than ethical.

As discussed in Chapter 1, economic research embraced two main concepts: *weak sustainable consumption*, which aims for *continued economic growth* alongside improved socio-ecological well-being, and *strong sustainable consumption*, which calls for multi-level sociopolitical transformation to *prioritize nonconsumption-based well-being*. Yet the topic of sustainable consumption is much more complex. There are numerous types of sustainable consumption to consider, such as mindful, responsible, and green consumption; voluntary simplicity; and anti-consumption. This diversity makes the topic of sustainable consumption particularly appealing. Researchers, like Gossen et al.,[73] highlight methods such as *downshifting*—reducing overall consumption to enhance life satisfaction by consciously deciding to work less and decrease personal consumption due to lower income. They also mention *slow consumption*, which involves producing less waste and using fewer resources by avoiding excessive consumption and rapid production cycles, trends, and inferior quality. Fischer et al.[59] revealed integration challenges arising from the disciplinary diversity and fragmentation characteristic of sustainability communication.

Haider et al.[7] conducted a comprehensive academic literature review from 1976 to 2021, published in the journal *Sustainability*, in social studies. This body of work investigates various micro-level (individual) modalities of sustainable consumption. For the purpose of this research, I succinctly encapsulated their findings in Table 5 to have a better viewpoint for sustainable consumption diversity.

Table 5. Types of sustainable consumption, summarized from Haider et al.[7]

Consumption	Characteristics in academic literature
Responsible consumption	Webster defined a socially responsible consumer as someone who "takes into account the public consequences of his or her private consumption" through efficient resource usage, due to a regard for the needs of the whole human race.
	Roberts categorized responsible consumption into societal and environmental dimensions, meaning that a socially responsible consumer will always consume products that have a minimal effect on society and the environment.
	Responsible consumers will always feel liable for the social and environmental consequences of consumption choices.
	Responsible consumption is a broad concept that comprises purchasing products with minimum societal or environmental impact, engaging with a specific company as a support for its philanthropic efforts, boycotting an unethical company or product, willingly trading off quality, prestige, or convenience for an extra cost or lower performance.
	Responsible consumption covers green and ethical consumption; green consumption is more concerned with the environmental impact of consumption, whereas ethical consumers care about consumption's moral consequences.

Green consumption	Green consumption means to choose products causing minimum ecological impact, moderate their consumption, be more conscious of the produced waste, engage with companies making the minimum environmental impact, recycle frequently, and opt for clean or renewable energy.
Green consumers are willing to bear the extra cost and effort of green consumption by refining their consumption practices if it contributes to environmental sustainability while maintaining their current lifestyle.
The emphasis of green consumption is more on ecological sustainability than social sustainability, and uses consumption as a means of identity creation.
As green products and services are just another market offer, they are criticized for perpetuating consumption rather than inhibiting it to sell more products.
Green products are also blamed for giving consumers a false belief that they are being pro-sustainability by spending more, failing to challenge the dominant social paradigm (DSP).
Ethical consumption	There is a clear distinction between the ethics of consumption and ethical consumption.
The ethics of consumption question the morality of modern consumerism to challenge it, whereas ethical consumption uses consumerism by expressing moral commitments.
Klein, Smith, and John described ethical consumption as being "against selfish interests for the good of others," where consumption is used as a means for social good.

	Ethical consumptions are norms-driven and depend on socioeconomic factors, which is why ethical consumption decisions are based on moral standards (in the individual or the group) that guide consumption behaviors.
Ethical consumption is not always sustainable as it can be motivated by diverse factors like human rights, the environment, fair trade, and political orientations.
Ethical consumption movements like Fairtrade and "buy local" can encourage overconsumption to help the producers; they are, thus, criticized for not contributing to sustainable consumption.
Anti-consumption	Anti-consumption intentionally and meaningfully avoids consumption by rejecting or refusing material goods acquisition or by reusing once-acquired goods.
Anti-consumption is a financially independent and intentional nonconsumption behavior, manifested through practices like frugality and voluntary simplicity, creating a "resistance" identity.
Frugality is the action of restricting acquisition voluntarily, with the resourceful usage and thoughtful disposal of economic goods to avoid waste and save material resources, making it a monetary-based anti-consumption behavior with few environmental concerns.
For a frugal person, saving material resources and reducing waste is virtuous and a source of pleasure.

	Due to its highly materialistic nature, frugality can have a negative correlation with green consumption and is yet to develop as a real anti-consumerism phenomenon.
Voluntarily simplicity	Voluntary simplicity is a non-monetary-motivated anti-consumption activity wherein the primary goal is a good life based on non-material consumption.
	Voluntary simplifiers are economically stable but not frugal. Their satisfaction stems from the non-material values they cultivate to live soulful, conscious, simple, and "inwardly rich" lives for inner peace and psychological well-being.
	Elgin and Mitchell consider material simplicity, the desire for small human-scale institutions, self-determination, ecological awareness, and personal/inner growth as the five core values of voluntary simplicity.
Mindful consumption	Mindfulness implies an awareness of, or an enhanced focus on, experiences, feelings, and thoughts to be a conscious part of everyday mundane activities like eating food or interacting with family or friends.
	Mindfulness encourages more pro-environmental behavior by inducing benevolent attitudes and compassion toward others and by inhibiting materialistic hedonic values.
	Mindfulness promotes subjective well-being, a sustainability behavior pre-condition, and positively moderates intentions into actual behaviors.

The advantage of mindfulness is that it can be cultivated for ecological well-being on an individual and societal level.

There is no clear operationalized definition of mindfulness, resulting in a fragmented and weak objective observation that is missing the robust and empirically proven causal effects of mindfulness on sustainable consumption.

Sheth et al.'s model of mindful consumption is viewed as the link between a person's mindset and behavior. It affects how one cares about oneself, the community, the environment, and subsequent consumption behaviors (repetitive, acquisitive, aspirational). Sheth et al. want sustainability efforts to be (1) more customer-centric, (2) holistic, (3) targeting the mindset as well as behavior, and (4) making consumers, businesses, and policymakers all responsible for sustainability.

The "mind" part connects self well-being with community and nature well-being for mindful resource extraction and waste disposal. Consumption temperance involves acquiring goods and services within the bounds of needs and capacity, breaking the recursive shopping cycle for new fashion or technology, and being non-conspicuous about consumption.

Mindfulness can potentially change compulsive, impulsive, habitual, and addictive consumption behaviors.

Sharing	As one of the three ways to acquire goods, sharing is a non-reciprocal and social act of giving to others that which is ours for their use and getting from others things for our use.

For Belk, the non-reciprocal dimension of sharing is essential as it gives joint ownership, creating an extended self that is connected to those with whom we share. He explains the benefits of sharing via the examples of mothering and "share-consuming" resources within a household, a behavior that creates bonds and connections and breaks interpersonal barriers, contributing to well-being.

Sharing activities also include a picnic with others at a beach or a park, using public infrastructure, e.g., roads and streetlights, sharing advice, jokes, opinions, photos, and comments, and voluntary social work.

Sharing a meal, a car, or communal laundry all bring about sustainability by decreasing resource usage and waste while enhancing personal well-being.

This quality has evolved the idea of sharing from an individual- and family-level concept into meso- and macro-level phenomena of collaborative consumption for collaborative, access-based consumption and a sharing economy.

As the sufficiency economy, the sharing economy also garnered much academic and managerial interest, as indicated by the increase in the volume of research articles.

Sufficiency	Fuchs and Lorek defined sufficiency as "changes in consumption patterns and reductions in consumption levels."

> Sufficiency is the reconfiguring of consumption practices by consuming material goods for an extended period, decreasing demand levels, keeping conspicuous consumption at a minimum, enjoying nonmaterial experiences, and developing an "enoughness" mindset and behavioral shift.
>
> The "sufficiency turn" of social corporate responsibility (SCR) can be considered SCR's third evolutionary phase at the individual level, although it also moves sustainability toward the societal level to challenge the dominating social paradigm.
>
> Sufficiency can be on an individual, community, or societal level.

Inspired by these discussions, I conducted an academic literature review to better understand the academic perspective from a mix of four disciplines: *marketing*, *social sciences*, *psychology*, and *environmental studies*.

Multiverse of sustainable consumption

I found and examined multiverse of sustainable consumption types in the academic discourse within the chosen intersection: at the nexus of sustainable consumption and impulsive buying behavior. The most discussed type is *General sustainable consumption*, without any specifications, signaling further theory development potential with deeper differentiation. Notably, *Green consumption* holds second place with about half of the general sustainable consumption share. Haider et al.[7] explained that green consumption means choosing products that cause minimum ecological impact, being more conscious of the produced waste, engaging with companies making the minimum environmental impact, recycling frequently, and opting for clean or renewable energy. It was pointed out by Testa et al.[74] that academics focus on product qualities within green consumption. Some studies have examined a broad category of green products, while other scholars have focused on specific product categories like apparel, personal care items, electric cars, ecological paper products, green detergents, and remanufactured products. Current research includes articles such as Jakubowska and Sadilek,[75] which discusses organic products and the influence of product knowledge and psychological consumer behavior on sustainable green food purchases, as in the study by Mazhar et al.[76] Other topics include consumer materialistic and green value conflict explored by Markauskaitė and Rūtelionė,[60] the impact of social and environmental sustainability awareness on green trust by Khalil and Khalil,[77] and the effects of fear or similarity during COVID-19 on green purchase behavior. Third place holds a group of *Voluntary simplicity*-related studies. This group receives significant support from the proponents of the "prosperity without growth" movement, which advocates for lifestyles of *sufficiency*. The level of degrowth is suggested to be within a sustainable scale of resource use, which can be defined as a scale that does not require a physical volume of throughput that might put carrying capacity or ecosystem services at risk. Prior systematic literature review and analysis by Fitzpatrick et al.[78] explored degrowth policy proposals and summarized consumption degrowth as follows: by discouraging luxury consumption (for example, through boycotts, flying quotas, progressive taxes on consumption, taxes on secondary houses, sports cars, yachts, and private jets) and encouraging voluntary simplicity with bike infrastructures, co-housing, shared utilities, repair cafes, and decommodified hobbies. Other types include *sufficiency*, *frugality*, or *anti-consumption*. Altogether, these consumption types advocate for a decrease in consumption and a change in consumer lifestyle.

Next, various types of sustainable consumption related to social requests—such as *ethical consumption, responsible consumption, mindful consumption, sharing consumption, social consumption,* and *conscious consumption*—have been identified. The latter group comprises *luxury consumption, excessive consumption, indulgent consumption,* and *unneeded consumption*, where the discussion primarily revolves around impulsive buying behavior and *psychological well-being*. Few studies have referenced *healthy food consumption*. While there are no clear distinctions between certain consumption types, which often intersect and complement each other, it happens that aggregation is possible.

Triple-win sustainable consumption model

Featuring three core pillars of sustainability, such as "environmental," "economic," and "social," Amber et al.[13] present the **triple-win sustainable consumption model**. Three distinct groups of this model reflected the following groups of consumption: *"economically driven," "environmentally driven,"* and *"socially driven."* The model builds on similarities and differences between types of consumption and their corresponding attributes. This approach is notable for balancing two quite polarized economic viewpoints on sustainable consumption with a third, "socially driven" perspective emphasizing access to social support. Three distinct groups aggregated by the triple-win sustainable consumption model are illustrated in Figure 5.

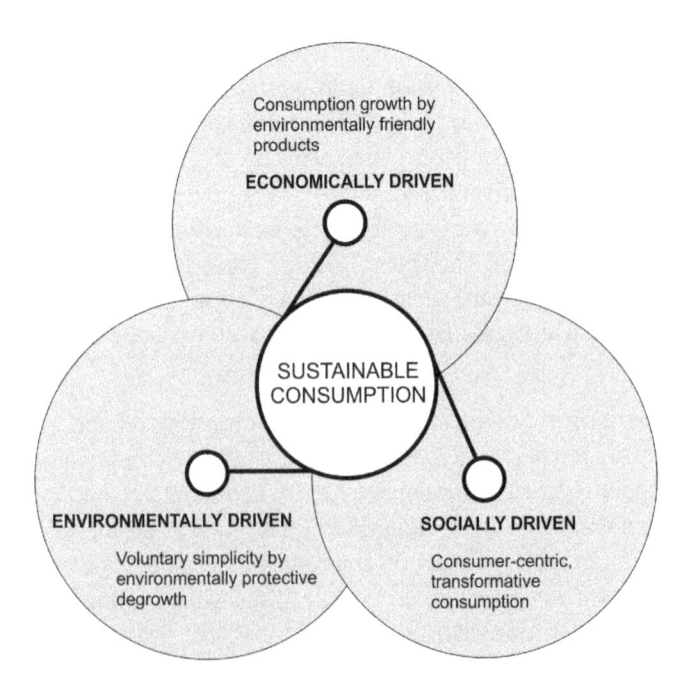

Figure 5. Triple-win sustainable consumption model adapted from Amber et al.[13]

The socially driven consumption group seems a valuable addition to Markauskaitė and Rūtelionė[60] reflections on two possible pathways: one is to consume *environmentally friendly products*, and the other is to implement *anti-consumption*. It points to the fact that, to embrace decreased consumption or any other significant lifestyle changes, we must remember that it is connected with the social domain, without which nothing will be changed. The triple-win sustainable consumption model identified a promising new possibility on the horizon that could redefine our future and economic outcome. A new academic discussion of the *socially driven consumption* group has been revealed. This group is larger than the one encompassing voluntary simplicity and related concepts advocating for the social direction of sustainability research demand. It does not complement growth or degrowth so much but stands alone for *socially driven transformation*. Thus, the model complements the prior opinion of researchers, including Fischer et al.,[59] which suggested that *individual behavior changes* are crucial to achieving sustainability. Consequently, the economic viewpoint clearly benefits from a multidisciplinary framework for sustainable consumption. It can be enriched by considering the current social impact of impulsive buying behavior, which affects up to 90% of all purchases. Playing currently as a warning factor it holds significant transformative potential through its direct connection with social factors. This third pathway of *socially driven transformation* is a powerful force that can reshape consumption, not only through degrowth policy proposals but also by enhancing it with the human desire for sustainable living and the subsequent *inner transformation*.

Moving toward a sustainable society necessitates adopting a broader mindset, including the idea that an ongoing increase in material consumption could harm the environment to the extent that net gains are negative. Therefore, green consumption practices and reducing consumption through degrowth-related viewpoints should be considered and implemented as complementary rather than opposite approaches. Still, it also highlights the need for inner transformation because it involves *social action*. As shared by Lorek and Spangenberg,[12] the transition to sustainability requires sustainable production and consumption patterns and—as enshrined in the 1992 Rio Principles and Agenda 21—more justice and democracy, empowerment of marginalized groups, and international collaboration to solve global environmental and social problems.

Let's examine each consumption group individually.

Economically driven consumption group: general sustainable, green and healthy food

This group focuses on promoting consumption growth but with a sustainable twist. It includes consumption types like *general sustainable*, *green*, and *healthy food* choices. Figure 6 presents the *economically driven consumption* group.

Cultivate consumer trust
Keep promoting individual benefits of green product
Implement reward system
Support local business
Influence consumer's values
Focus on emotional connection

General sustainable, green, healthy food

Consumption growth by environmentally friendly products

Economically driven

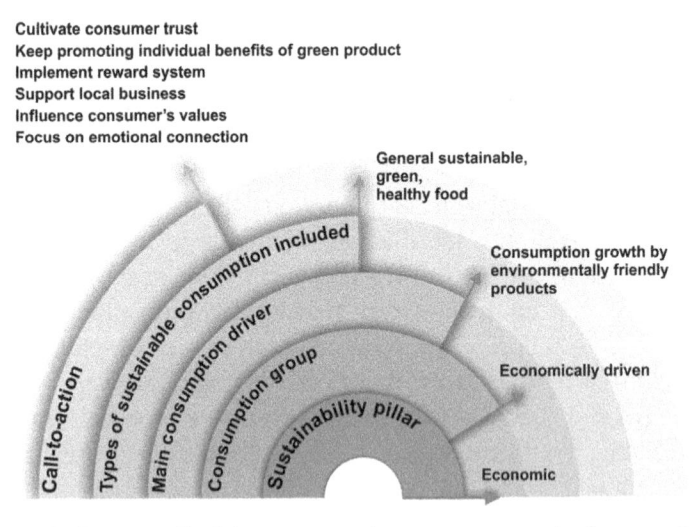

Economic

Call-to-action
Types of sustainable consumption
Main consumption driver
Consumption included
Consumption group
Sustainability pillar

Figure 6. Economically driven consumption group summarized as per Amber et al.[13]

With a strong focus on the environment, this group is about choosing products with less ecological impact, embracing new technologies, and being conscious about waste. Supporters of this approach are often those optimistic about working with local communities, recycling, and switching to clean energy. Green consumers, who are happy to pay a bit more for sustainable and healthy products, are expected to back these efforts and even make some changes to their routines. In real life, however, it is not always the case. For example, on February 9, 2025, Switzerland was set to vote on an "environmental responsibility" initiative. While it didn't lay out specific limits or actions, the goal was clear: to curb pollution and resource use driven by the economy in order to protect life on Earth. At the vote, 69.75% rejected the initiative, as announced in various media.[79]

A primary critique dynamic for this consumption group is the concern of "greenwashing." Studies found it is crucial to emphasize clear and trustworthy communication about sustainable products, companies' sustainability efforts, informative certifications, and effective monitoring systems. Another critique trend is the argument that green products perpetuate consumption rather than curb it. They may create a false sense of pro-sustainability without challenging the dominant social paradigm. Lastly, concerns remain about green products not always being available and their high prices, which require retailers' attention and adjustments. These concerns are from followers of healthy food consumption type, requiring retailers' attention and price adjustments. This sector holds the potential to surpass traditional food consumption and relate to other health-related products and services.

As pointed out by Amber et al.,[13] businesses that support this group utilize *traditional marketing strategies*, with a strong trend toward focusing on *consumer emotions*, *immersive experiences*, and *emotional engagement*. Recent studies suggest various *emotional strategies to boost sales*: building connections to encourage impulse buys, engaging emotions like nostalgia or boredom for compensatory consumption, leveraging FOMO (fear of missing out) and loss for retail sales, and using coronavirus-related fears to influence green product purchases. In Chapter 2, I analyzed 11% of the study sample, directly focused on the need for increasing impulsive buying behavior, which includes *exploiting emotions*. It has been found that this case is related to health and sports products and is significantly influenced by COVID-19 industries like HoReCA. However, there's much more emphasis on *emotional engagement* beyond that. This trend raises questions about *how marketing communication might contribute to overconsumption* and

Environmentally driven consumption group: voluntary simplicity, sufficiency, frugality, minimalism, and anti-consumption

creating demand, which needs more exploration to understand its impact better.

This group advocates for decreased consumption through consumer lifestyle changes and include voluntary-simplicity like types: *voluntary simplicity, sufficiency, frugality, minimalism,* and *anti-consumption*.

Figure 7 summarizes key research findings on the *environmentally driven consumption group*.

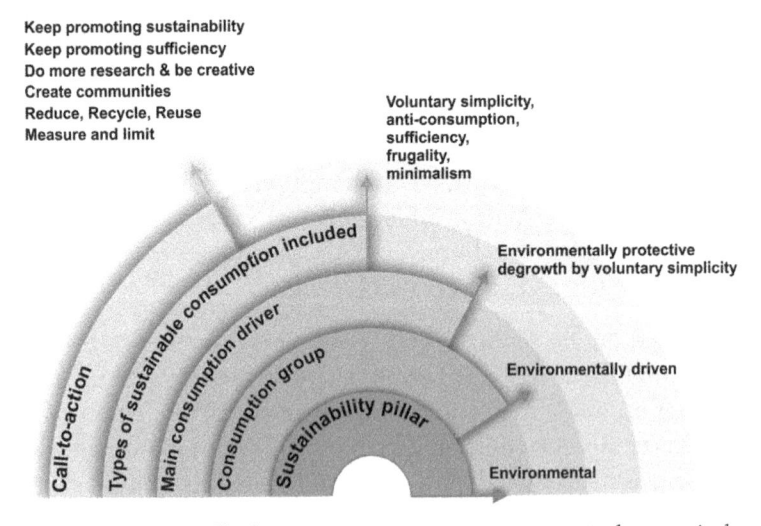

Figure 7. Environmentally driven consumption group, summarised as per Amber et al.[13]

The supporters of this group believe our current economic system is unsustainable. They argue that our planet's resources are limited and continuous economic growth harms the environment. They promote degrowth, advocating for reduced consumption and production to preserve resources for the future. Individuals can practice degrowth by living simply, reducing waste, and supporting local businesses. They encourage boycotting companies with unsustainable practices. Researchers suggest public policies to limit advertising and regulate resource extraction. Degrowth aims for a sustainable society through conscious consumption and policy changes. Amber et al.[13] point out that this group is keenly aware of human vulnerability regarding sophisticated marketing campaigns and suggest *transparency and proactive consumer defense strategies*. For example, researchers like Pellegrino et al.[80] have recommended implementing public policies to measure and limit the spread of deceptive marketing campaigns that target vulnerable audiences.

There are subtle variations within proposed consumption types that can be seen as complementary. For instance, *anti-consumption* deliberately avoids acquiring material goods by rejecting or reusing items. It embodies financially independent behaviors like frugality and voluntary simplicity, promoting a "resistance" identity. *Frugality* involves voluntarily limiting acquisitions, using resources in the maximum possible way, and disposing thoughtfully to save resources, with a *focus on monetary aspects rather than environmental concerns*. Saving resources and reducing waste are seen as virtuous and pleasurable for frugal individuals. Despite its materialistic nature, frugality has not fully evolved into an anti-consumerism movement. *Minimalism* follows its own philosophy, focusing on style and the art of life, emphasizing simplicity to create maximum impact.

Sufficiency involves reconfiguring consumption practices by decreasing demand for material goods over time, minimizing conspicuous consumption, embracing nonmaterial experiences, and fostering an "enoughness" mindset and behavioral shift. Sufficiency can manifest on individual, community, or societal levels. *Voluntary simplicity* is a non-monetary-motivated anti-consumption activity. The primary aim is to achieve a good life through nonmaterial consumption. Voluntary simplifiers, economically stable but not frugal, find satisfaction in cultivating nonmaterial values. Their goal is to lead soulful, conscious, simple, and "inwardly rich" lives for inner peace and *psychological well-being*.

We can incorporate elements of all these styles, such as adopting a minimalist fashion style, applying anti-consumption to specific food products or during fasting periods, simplifying the pace of life to what is naturally comfortable for us, and even deciding to say "enough" to certain habits. All these consumption styles will be explained further with practical propositions.

This book, pointing through the triple-win sustainable consumption model, underlines that moving forward with environmental propositions without *inner consumer transformation is impossible*. Folke et al.[81] remind us that resilience should be considered a *socio-ecological quality*, where humans and nature is an integrated whole rather than as distinct entities. Therefore, this group should be closely connected and coordinate actions with activists from the *socially driven consumption group*. This group's proponents play a crucial role in addressing the discrepancy between attitudes and actions, known as the *"attitude-behavior gap,"* where individuals who consider themselves environmentally conscious consumers may choose unsustainable options. Overconsumption is anchored in impulsive buying behavior, and post-growth proponents must heed Daly's[43] reminder that human needs are seemingly insatiable. Therefore, I suggest they dedicate energy, time, research efforts, and activist actions to carefully examine mitigation of impulsive buying and its unconscious factors, especially when it comes to material purchases.

Socially driven consumption group: ethical, responsible, sharing, mindful, social, and conscious

As explained by Amber et al.,[13] this group incorporates *ethical, responsible, sharing, mindful, social,* and *conscious consumption*. Being a socially responsible consumer involves considering private consumption's public impact, using resources efficiently, and caring for the global community. This includes selecting products with minimal societal and environmental effects, taking responsibility for consumption choices, and supporting efforts to help vulnerable groups. *Ethical consumption* is all about sticking to our values and making choices that benefit society. It puts human rights, environmental sustainability, and fair trade first rather than just focusing on what we want. *Being mindful* helps us pay attention to our daily actions, encouraging us to adopt eco-friendly habits and improve our well-being. This way of thinking connects how we feel with what we do, supporting *responsible consumption* and sustainability efforts.

The socially driven consumption group warns consumers to be more conscious of their spending patterns and control their impulsive buying tendencies. It advises marketers to continue educating customers about the negative aspects of impulsive buying. It primarily aims to prioritize consumer *well-being and happiness*, as presented in Figure 8.

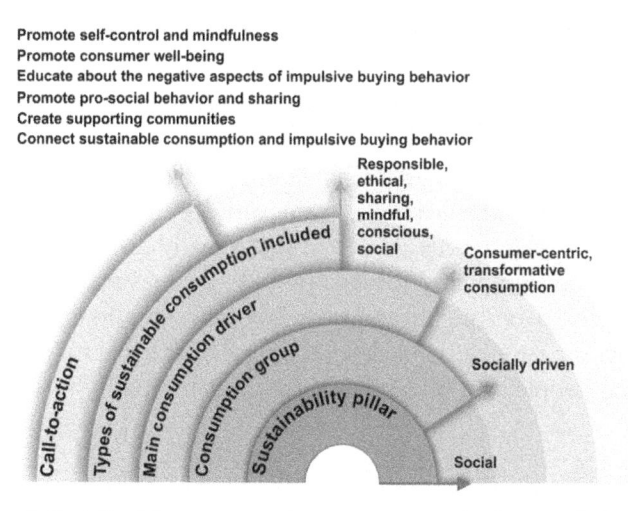

Figure 8. Socially driven consumption group summarised as per Amber at al.[13]

Sustainable consumption isn't just good for our health and happiness, it's also about being socially responsible, helping the environment, and making us feel safer and more secure. This means choosing to buy things that match your values and focus on doing good, not just personal gain. It's about considering things like human rights, fair trade, and fairness overall. Hüttel and Balderjahn[82] believe that cutting back on our consumption can boost our *well-being*. They explain that when we reduce work and travel demands, we get to spend more quality time with our families and enjoy the great outdoors. This shift helps us appreciate the environment more and leads us to a lifestyle that embraces simplicity and modest living.

There is also an emphasis on *pro-social actions*, encouraged by the sharing economy, which can lead to *self-transformation* and help restore social connections lost to materialism, as reflected by Shaikh et al.[83] This helps bring back some of the *social bonds* that materialism tends to weaken, showing how the sharing economy can bring big environmental and economic benefits. During times of change, we need each other more than ever, and social bonding serves as a foundation for navigating multiple crises. Our times are particularly difficult because, in the era of the Internet, we are dealing with misleading information. Therefore, Wei Jie et al.[61] suggest businesses should leverage community influence, contribute to building *knowledge communities*, and take advantage of *socially driven innovations*. Others suggest activating consumer *self-awareness* while presenting brands as environmentally responsible. To summarize, the emerging trend of consumers modifying habits toward sustainable consumption is a powerful catalyst for change. As shown in Chapter 3, more than 60% of articles considered consumers to alter private habits, whereas the emerging *socially driven consumption group*, already comprising about a quarter of consumption types in research, inspires the rise of *new consumers*. By advocating for transformative consumption, the *triple-win sustainable consumption model* encourages us to achieve a balance: benefitting people, the planet, and universal prosperity. Where do we start?

Triple win: sustainable consumption strategy: key takeaways

- There is no perfect solution—finding the best approach involves multiple solutions in unity.
- What is sustainable consumption, anyway? The history and development of its meaning provide background and insights.
- There is multiverse types of sustainable consumption pointing in different directions.
- The triple-win sustainable consumption model identifies three directions that need to be balanced.
- Economically driven consumption group: general sustainable, green, and healthy food consumption revealed.
- Environmentally driven consumption group: voluntary simplicity, sufficiency, frugality, minimalism, and anti-consumption explained.
- Socially driven consumption group: ethical, responsible, sharing, mindful, social, and conscious consumption summarized.

5

Creating conditions where others can thrive

This chapter looks at a new socially driven approach focused on well-being instead of welfare, examines the factors behind impulsive buying, and proposes ways from academic discussions on how to navigate it.

Purpose over profit: the rise of well-being and happiness

My background is in business, where I worked on startups and nationwide projects with requirements for each initiative to outline its exit strategy and end goal at the start of planning. We must apply the same approach when planning practical interventions for sustainable consumption and clearly define our objectives. Otherwise, the approach may become as polarized as the one focused solely on economic aspects of human life. As suggested, we aim for a triple win: benefiting people, the planet, and prosperity for all. But why would people support such a win?

While the first post-growth response was a critique of the idea of unlimited economic growth, the next strong sustainability advocates started questioning the welfare goal of economics based on "insatiable human needs," as put by the pioneer of ecological economics, Herman Daly.[43] The multi-level assessment published by Yehuala[84] reported that though there are differences in the size and generosity of the welfare state, such differences do not generate considerable effects on *individuals' subjective well-being*. The belief that the level of well-being is higher in welfare states and that its distribution is more equitable was tested in another comparative study by Veenhoven[85] of 41 nations from 1980 to 1990. Contrary to expectation, there appears to be no link between the size of the welfare state and the level of well-being within it. The emerging sustainable degrowth concept escalated doubts about the reasoning behind the economic growth strategy and its consequences, such as climate change, pollution, loss of biodiversity, and resource depletion.

These concerns were encapsulated in the concept of "*well-being,*" which incorporates a broader family of variables such as job circumstances, meaningful social relationships, work–life balance, personal development, and many more in contrast to welfare, although as per Maximo,[86] this distinction is not always well recognized. In some countries, like Bhutan, prosperity is measured by Gross National Happiness (GNH) instead of traditional economic indicators. This country is already assessing the overall *emotional and physical well-being* of the nation's population. Additional factors for index calculations include cultural aspects, health, relationships, education, cultural diversity and resilience, community vitality, the standard of living, and so on. The World Happiness Report,[87] a similar initiative, collaborates with Gallup, the Oxford Wellbeing Research Center, and the United Nations Sustainable Development Solutions Network. Dermody et al.[88] suggest that *well-being* and a mindset focused on empathy and community collaboration should be prioritized over the individualistic attitudes typical of contemporary consumerism, where *human capital* and *environmental capital* are valued together more than power elites' dominant ideation of economic capital. Simply put, the notion that money cannot buy happiness has gained popularity, sparking an argument that questions individual prosperity at the expense of others, and the pursuit of personal benefits through sustainable consumption has begun.

Positive influence of sustainable consumption on well-being

The initial set of assumptions suggests that sustainable consumption behavior leads to *positive outcomes for well-being*. As discussed in Chapter 1, multiple academic studies underline *positive well-being outcomes following sustainable consumption patterns*. To Brandão and Cupertino de Miranda,[89] sustainable consumption intends to *reduce environmental concerns, increase security*, achieve a reasonable natural resource distribution, *increase well-being*, create a *healthy life*, and adopt social responsibility. Reflect on the question, "Does sustainable consumption make consumers happy?" Ramos-Hidalgo et al.[90] conclude that sustainable consumption positively related to consumer *well-being, life satisfaction*, and *happiness*, through *encouraging positive emotions*, reinforcing consumer moral identity, creating a *positive self-image*, increasing consumer *happiness*, and satisfying the need for *connectedness* with others.

Shaikh et al.[83] revealed that when consumers engage in the sharing economy, they not only meet others but also *exhibit pro-social behavior*. Even amidst commercialization, they promote *social belonging*, enhance consumer *well-being*, and reduce wasteful consumption. Thus, sharing economic experiences can help restore *social connectedness* lost to materialism. Another study by Nepomuceno and Laroche[91] suggest reducing current consumption levels, promoting anti-materialistic values, and convincing consumers to break away from mainstream materialistic culture to achieve *well-being*. They warn that this may be challenging due to materialism's enduring and resistant nature of value. Investigating general personal well-being (also called psychosocial well-being) as people's ability to lead a *self-determined* and *meaningful life* (different from the concept of happiness), Hüttel and Balderjahn[82] conclude that cutting back on consumption has led some individuals to realize that well-being can be achieved through *reduced consumption, work*, and *travel*, prompting a shift toward leisurely pursuits at home, with family, and in nature, fostering a deeper appreciation for nature and a more straightforward way of living characterized by voluntary simplicity, frugality, and modesty. Geiger and Keller[92] emphasize concern for others' well-being and highlight how evoking *compassion* may enhance pro-environmental intentions by triggering general moral considerations rooted in core values. They acknowledge the necessity for additional research, pointing out that previous studies overlooked the connection between compassion for individuals and sustainable behavior.

Acknowledge the invisible force of impulsive buying behavior

The second set of assumptions is that excessive consumption requires a nuanced, individual-level understanding, focusing on its adverse effects rather than viewing it merely as a broader issue contributing to unchecked economic growth, significant waste, resource depletion, climate change, and other social and environmental consequences. A solid volume of research has stated that impulsive buying can lead to feelings of *guilt, shame, regret*, and *strain on personal relationships*. Daly[43] pointed out that even when used strategically to cope with negative emotions, impulsive buying can backfire and lead to a greater number of *ruminating and negative thoughts*. Vohs and Faber[93] linked impulsive buying behavior to adverse personal outcomes, such as *high consumer debt levels* and *post-purchase dissatisfaction*. Podoshen and Andrzejewski[5] pointed out *low self-esteem* and immaturity. Silvera et al.[94] directly emphasized consequences such as *negative well-being*. Burroughs and Rindfleisch[95] pointed out that a materialistic lifestyle negatively influences long-term implications for the individual consumer and society. Lekavičienė et al.[96] confirm that materialistic consumers face maladies that cause *stress* and *lower subjective well-being*.

Czarnecka et al.[97] conclude that impulsive buying is encouraged by the Western emphasis on individualistic values and hedonistic pleasure, the international spread of e-commerce, and the consumer orientation in *consumption-based economies*, leading individuals to buy impulsively due to the significance of material objects as *social signals* in their culture, simply to obtain artificially proposed "social status." Lu et al.[98] agree, adding that consumers with high impulsive buying levels are *more sensitive to the financial risk* caused by greenwashing behavior. Gawior et al.[99] highlighted a concern that the rising popularity of cashless payment methods and impulsive buying should be considered a crucial issue for the fast fashion industry's influence on individual, social, and environmental well-being through overconsumption.

As highlighted by Shahpasandi et al.,[100] negative consequences of unplanned impulsiveness also include unfavorable conditions for retailers, such as *low customer satisfaction, reduced brand loyalty*, and *high return rates*. Upadhye et al.[101] note the increase in "empty" shopping behavior, often studied within the theory of planned behavior, which explains an individual's *attitudes, subjective norms*, and *perceived behavioral control*. Academic suggestions, such as from Haider et al.,[7] include connecting individualism to *collective well-being*, replacing material goods with *human connections*, and converting mindlessness to mindfulness for *qualitative consumption growth*.

While the research trajectory on sustainable consumption's influence on consumer well-being seems established and valuable, the consequences of impulsive buying behavior need further and more detailed research, especially in the area where impulsive buying behavior is named as *compensatory for psychological well-being*.

Dangerous friendship: psychological well-being and impulsive buying behavior

Lekavičienė et al.[96] highlighted that the coping role of impulsive buying behavior is evident in research on well-being, materialism, and impulsive buying tendencies, suggesting that materialism itself acts as a *coping mechanism for undesirable psychological states*. Another study by Princes[102] emphasizes that impulsive buying behavior is more like a *coping stress* or *adaptive mechanism*. He et al.[103] ensure that the purchasing process triggers positive emotions linked to impulsive buying, enhancing consumers' recovery by *facilitating psychological relaxation*. Cho et al.[65] agree that individuals usually engage in compensatory behavior to *restore their positive emotional state and remove negative emotions*.

COVID-19 studies investigate the impact of external stimuli, like temporary supply shortages during lockdowns, on emotional arousal. Gupta and Mukherjee[104] found that panic led to impulsive and obsessive-compulsive buying during the pandemic, suggesting that impulsive panic buying served as a *short-term restoration phenomenon*. Another study by Phang et al.[105] also pointed to the sense of uncertainty brought on by the COVID-19 pandemic that affected average consumers, who started *panicking, which led to impulsive purchasing*. Chiu et al.[67] found that *negative mood is positively related to impulsive behaviors*, as people seek distractions to *reduce aversive emotions*, sometimes resulting in *impulsive buying to alleviate fear*. Researching motivation for dining out during the pandemic, Jiang and Lau[106] found that while *social values* were crucial in motivating, they were driven by consumers' intense need to *emotionally and socially relieve pressure and loneliness*, transforming their mood. Wang et al.[50] found that both positive and negative emotions influence impulsive buying behavior. They name them typical predecessors for shopping practices with potential hedonic outcomes, where negative emotions hold more influence. Since emotions mediate between impulsive buying tendencies and behavior, researchers conclude it restores our *psychological well-being*.

We have a strong need to satisfy our psychological needs, especially during times of crisis, but relying on impulsive buying is like befriending a dangerous ally. It's similar to alleviating symptoms without addressing the root cause, which not only fails to provide a long-term solution but also intensifies the negative consequences of the current situation. Therefore, multiple studies have suggested practical actions to support psychological well-being and mitigate impulsive buying. Wang et al.[107] emphasize *guiding individuals' awareness* to intervene effectively in reducing their lack of control and anxiety, thereby preventing negative consumer psychology and behavior. Ah Fook and McNeill[108] highlight the importance of recognizing *antecedents to overconsumption* linked to individual impulsivity. Phang et al.[105] advocate for creating *constant reminders*, while Iyer and Muncy[109] propose that if personal reasons for consumption reduction or redirection enhance an *individual's well-being* and life assessment, these should be more welcomed and better received. Lekavičienė et al.[96] confirm that *emotional intelligence* lowers *materialism* and *compulsive buying levels*. In another study by Shams et al.,[110] the mitigation role of emotional intelligence was identified for workplace stressors that lead to *impulsive buying disorder*.

What is the academic stance on factors influencing impulsive buying?

Does impulsive buying behavior relate more to external factors, like *marketing activities stimulating demand*, or internal ones that trigger sudden impulsive urges to *restore psychological well-being*? Through traditional scientific understanding, both.

Marketing *stimuli* are a sample of *external factors* meticulously designed to create retail environments and interactions that enhance shoppers' motivation to purchase. They could relate to factors such as store layout and atmosphere, skills of sales personnel, and the art of pricing and promotions. Indeed, in the era of the Internet and technological development, this list is incomplete on what can influence customers within online shopping, where impulsive buying has only increased. Crawford and Melewar[111] pointed out that browsers usually make more unplanned purchases than non-browsers.

There are also *internal factors* such as *time* (the more time an individual has, the longer time they browse the shopping environment), *gender, good mood, self-esteem, age, culture, hedonic motives, presence of others* (the presence of others increases the likelihood of impulse purchases, for example, when individuals are in a group, they tend to eat more), *money availability*, or *Internet usage*. To update the influencing consumer behavior factors concentrating on the intersection that has a particular interest for our research, I outlined *over 300 influencing factors*. Simplified results are shown in the graphical representation in Figure 9.

As you can see, impulsive buying behavior is a complex topic influenced by many factors. I have categorized them to identify clusters of influences.

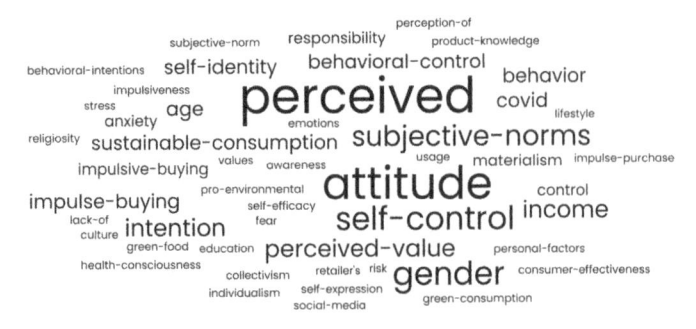

Figure 9. Behavioral factors influencing sustainable consumption at the nexus with impulsive buying behavior

The majority of factors influencing impulsive buying behavior are internal

Prior research tackled myriad factors influencing sustainable consumption at the nexus with impulsive buying behavior. For example, in their article, "The Past, Present, and Future of Consumer Research," published by *Marketing Letters*, Malter et al.[112] pointed out that many concepts—such as identity, beliefs/lay theories, affect as information, self-control, time, psychological ownership, search for meaning and happiness, social belonging, creativity, and status—have emerged as integral factors that influence and are influenced by consumption. Namazkhan et al.[113] examine various factors influencing total (actual) household gas consumption, including *egoistic and hedonic values, environmental self-identity, perceived corporate environmental responsibility* of the energy provider, and *social norms*.

Psychological factors are often mentioned altogether as being interdependent. For example, Dennison et al.[114] noted that psychological factors in their study were viewed as potentially changeable aspects connected to an *individual's attitudes, thoughts, feelings*, and behaviors. These elements were chosen as they could be pertinent and feasible to tackle in psychological intervention. Piligrimienė et al.[115] considered psychological individual factors such as *values, personal norms, beliefs*, and *attitudes*. Dimitrova et al.[71] pointed out that various models have been proposed to explain sustainable consumption behavior, with pre-behavioral determinants like *val-*

ues, *attitudes, norms*, and environmental factors playing significant roles. Liao and Chung[116] discussed psychological factors related to online shopping and consumer behavior, such as *attitude* and *perceived behavioral control*, as well as others: *subjective norm, risk aversion, intention to use* the Internet for information search, and site commitment.

In their study, Di Crosta et al.[117] focused on the psychological factors influencing shifts in consumer behavior toward target products during COVID-19. Drawing from existing literature, they anticipated a surge in purchases, particularly of essential items. The research delved into the drivers of consumer behavior by analyzing *mood states, emotional reactions to the crisis, perceived financial security*, reasons for purchases, and individual characteristics.

For categorization, most influencing factors were grouped by similar meanings. For example, the *self-control category* unites references such as self-control, locus control, perceived behavioral control, consciousness, awareness, mindfulness, responsibility, decisions, self-regulation, or financial self-control. These definitions all have a common core focused on the ability to recognize one's impulses and guide them toward desired actions based on *cognitive abilities*. Although they could be separate categories deserving of individual study, emotions, feelings, and moods were consolidated under one category, "emotions," which refers to *affective/emotional influences*. All five categories are shown as depicted in Figure 10.

1	2	3	4	5
Subjective Values & Norms	Attitude	Self-Control	Perception	Emotions

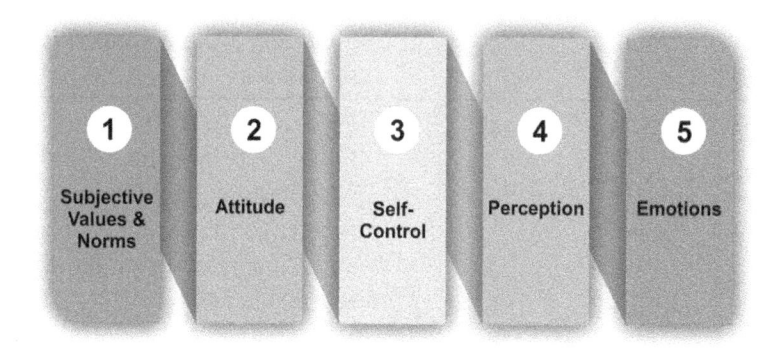

Figure 10. Key psychological factors influencing sustainable consumption at the nexus with impulsive buying behavior

Values, norms, attitudes, and perceptions all have cognitive and emotional components, as well as behavioral ones. Nordlund[118] summarized that values, attitudes, and norms are forces behind intentions and behavior. I broadly *categorized and analyzed key factors* influencing consumer behavior to gain a more straightforward overview rather than achieve theoretical excellence. Four key influencing groups were identified in the academic discourse: socio-cultural aspects, marketing stimuli, personal factors, and psychological factors, as shown in Table 6.

Table 6. Key behavioral factors influencing sustainable consumption at the nexus with impulsive buying behavior

Key factors	Level	%	Research definition
Socio-cultural	External	10	Key social and cultural factors that influence sustainable consumption patterns and sustainable practices
Marketing stimuli	External	15	Marketing practices influencing sustainable consumption within considered academic papers
Personal	Internal	35	Consumer factors that serve as examples for developing sustainable practices, including pro-environmental self-identity
Psychological	Internal	40	Psychological factors that influence sustainable consumption, including subjective values and norms, and a separate section on self-regulation

I collected enough data to identify dynamics within influences. *External factors accounted for only a quarter* of the considered articles. Without any doubt, *internal factors form a leading trend* influencing consumer behavior, a subject of study under impulsive buying. Within articles focused on *internal factors*, a bit less than half related to *personal factors*, categorized into three sectors: personal traits, reported behavior, and *self-identity*. The biggest section pertained to *psychological factors*, including emotions, perception, attitudes, values, and norms.

It is necessary to know that values are an integral part of self-identity, and we will protect them by any means and very emotionally, which forms the most significant challenge for change. These set the stage for a deep investigation of *psychological aspects*, assuming necessary *lifestyle changes* for *long-term personal well-being*. The results align with the earlier findings by Newman et al.,[119] which provide a brief review of factors influencing impulsive buying behavior, highlighting the significance of *individual* and *psychological* factors. Indeed, further investigations should involve a deep comprehension within a few levels, such as understanding individual *consumer needs*, *societal well-being*, and *environmental impact*. Addressing this challenge requires interdisciplinary collaboration, aligning with established suggestions, such as from Dholakia et al.[120] on a *comprehensive exploration of self-regulation desires* or Wang et al.[107] for cross-disciplinary studies backed by *neurophysiological data* targeting the attitude-behavior gap.

Self-control: the key to curbing impulsive buying behavior

Mandolfo and Lamberti[121] pointed out that among the most scrutinized and impactful research is the analysis of impulsive buying as a *self-control failure*. According to Fitness and Curtis,[122] self-control strategies demonstrate an *individual's adaptive ability to understand and regulate emotional and cognitive responses*. Sharma et al.[123] emphasized that a lack of self-control is linked to *consumer impulsiveness*, with studies indicating the moderating effect of self-monitoring. In my research, one out of two papers consider emotion-related behavioral factors, with self-control accounting for nearly half of the critical determinants influencing purchasing behavior, with a separate section within *psychological factors*. It is discussed as the ability to assist people in *overriding their immediate impulses*, *resisting temptation*, and *achieving their long-term goals*. Nguyen et al.[124] identified strong evidence linking self-control with *sustainable consumption*. Their framework positions *self-control* as a determinant of global outcomes, namely the purchase of *environmentally friendly products, spending control, healthy eating*, and *waste control*. In consumption, according to Zhang and Shrum,[125] when *self-control resources are depleted*, people experience stronger impulsive buying urges, which can lead to *increased impulsive buying behavior*. They emphasize that consumers should understand how effective planned problem-solving can help reduce impulsive buying, and prevent using denial or justification to cope with post-purchase regret. Spiteri Cornish[53] warns that in choosing immediate gratification, consumers need to be *aware that using impulsive purchases to feel better is not practical*, as that feeling dissipates rapidly. However, impulsive spending may not be reversible.

Inzlicht et al.[126] defined self-control as *resolving conflict between competing goals*. For instance, choosing between a poutine and a salad for lunch involves balancing short-term enjoyment with long-term health goals or the ability to *delay immediate gratification*. A related concept of *cognitive control* or *executive function* stems from neuroscience. *Cognitive control* and *self-control* are sometimes interchanged. They both involve working toward *long-term goals*, yet the *behaviors* linked to these concepts vary. Whereas *cognitive control* relies on at least three executive functions—task switching, working memory updates, and avoidance—at its heart, *self-control* is most clearly associated with *inhibition*. According to Scherbaum et al.,[127] *cognitive control* is evident in breaking habitual responses. *Attention management* has become common for people who want to take charge of their lives and maintain *cognitive control over their state and thoughts*. In March 2018, Harvard Business Review published Maura Thomas's article, "To Control Your Life, Control What You Pay Attention To,"[128] emphasizing the *importance of attention* in shaping life experiences. The article advises *managing distractions* by *focusing attention* according to one's priorities and goals, controlling external factors like technology and the environment, and mastering internal factors like behavior and thoughts. Practicing attention management *enhances control* over time and life despite inevitable distractions.

However, *attention does not produce action* on its own. Attention opens the door to action, but *emotional engagement* causes people to act. Neuroscientist Paul Zak eloquently summarized his point on values in one of his LinkedIn interviews with Deiric McCann from Genos International: "You might catch my attention momentarily, but if I don't give a heck, I'll revert to what truly matters to me."[129] This is an emotion that causes people to act. Dr. Zak[130] describes "top-down control" as the brain's executive center allocating additional processing power when encountering something *relevant* or *important to an individual*. For instance, he explains that when a smoker sees a pack of cigarettes, neural activation is greater, prompting the attached brain to devote more resources to processing information about cigarettes. His research discovered that the brain first shifts attention and then seeks a *reason to care* about our experiences. Using the measurement of oxytocin, which is a key hormone in emotions such as attraction, trust, care, and bonding, his lab shows that immersion is a neurological state in which one is *attentive to an experience* and *resonates with it emotionally*.

Whether we use *cognitive control* or *self-control*, it seems evident that we need to understand our *emotional attachments* better *to resist* immediate impulses and *impulsive buying temptations* because overconsumption creates an unnecessary threat to the balance of life. Furthermore, researching the mechanism of self-control, Baumeister[131] identifies that self-control could serve only as a short-term defense mechanism. He defines *self-control* as the deliberate *inhibition of impulses*, encompassing the *conscious suppression* of unwanted thoughts, emotions, and actions. His psychological research explores *self-control* or *willpower*, following the *theory of ego depletion*. Through numerous tests dedicated to this theory, Baumeister and his followers found that when we use self-control, it depletes as a finite resource. Moreover, depleting self-control reduces the capacity to suppress disruptive thoughts, increasing the likelihood of negative thinking and heightened vulnerability to negative emotions. Their theory of depleted self-control highlighted consequences that individuals may experience, including:

- Feeling stuck with routines and cannot think outside the box.

- Working without a sense of joy, avoiding deep conversations.
- Seeing others as "interrupting and toxic."
- Refraining from asserting themselves.
- Polarizing their worldview by a simplified "black and white" paradigm.
- Facing a decreased ability to make complex decisions.
- Halting their learning and inclusiveness of others' opinions.
- Stifling their creativity and other human abilities.

Depleted individuals experience stronger impulsive buying urges and are more likely to abandon challenging tasks, lose courage, and struggle with complex decisions, leading to diminished performance in activities requiring them to step out of their comfort zone.

Even though *self-control* is proposed to play a vital role in sustainable consumption and is suggested to be strengthened by many researchers, such as Wang et al.,[50] it appears to be a finite resource that needs to be maintained attentionally. While we may encourage customers to invest in self-control, depletion backfires with significant consequences, which is insufficient for long-term solutions curbing impulsive buying behavior. Exploring alternatives, such as emotional regulation and other psychological well-being factors, seems more beneficial. *Emotional regulation* has much more potential than any control could achieve via instruments such as suppression, task switching, working memory updates, and even avoidance. The core of the *control function* lies in the *presence of conflict*, which could be resolved differently if we allow ourselves to *understand our emotions and impulses better*.

Emotional intelligence: raising evidence for new mitigator of impulsive buying behavior

Investigating *alternative concepts related to emotional regulation*, I revealed a cluster of studies on *emotional intelligence* as a *mitigator of impulsive buying behavior*.

Wei Jie et al.[61] argue that, from a marketing perspective, emotions serve as a crucial tool for prompting customers to *satisfy their immediate desires*. They suggest *emotional intelligence* could be vital to managing the current link between *online activities and consumer impulse purchases* and see it as a new element that aids in controlling consumption. Sharma et al.[123] conducted research linking impulsive buying with consumer impulsiveness and underscored the moderating effect of *self-monitoring*. *Self-monitoring* is a facet of *emotional intelligence* that reflects an individual's ability to observe, evaluate, and manage their moods and can be measured through *self-regulation* or *self-control* assessments. Lekavičienė et al.[96] indicate that creating training programs focused on *emotional intelligence* skills can lead to more sustainable consumer behavior. Their research revealed that the development of emotional intelligence skills-based training programs contributes to more sustainable consumer behavior, mitigating the vulnerability to materialism and related addictive behavioral consequences.

The term *"emotional intelligence"* was introduced to psychology in a series of papers by Mayer and Salovey and popularized by Goleman.[132] According to Mayer et al.,[133] emotional intelligence comprises *skills* such as being able not only to direct one's emotions but also to understand and influence other people's emotional responses. They believed it was developed through a long process of environmental adaptation. Therefore, *emotionally intelligent* behavior is supposed to showcase an individual's skill in monitoring, assessing, and modifying *moods*. In her work "Why Emotional Capital Matters in Education and in Labor?", Gendron[134] highlights that Goleman and Mayer, Salovey, and Caruso have also argued that *emotional intelligence is probably not a strong predictor* of performance. Instead, *it provides the bedrock for competencies* that could be increased.

Shams et al.[110] identified the *mitigation role of emotional intelligence* for workplace stressors that lead to impulsive buying disorder. Wei Jie et al.[61] emphasized *emotional intelligence* as a new element that aids in controlling consumption. According to Mayer et al.,[133] emotional intelligence comprises skills thought to enhance the accurate understanding and communication of emotions, effective emotional management in oneself and others, and leveraging emotions for motivation, planning, and success in life. Therefore, *emotionally intelligent* behavior should showcase an individual's skill in monitoring, assessing, and modifying *moods*.

Sharma et al.[123] conducted research linking impulsive buying with consumer *impulsiveness* and underscored the moderating effect of *self-monitoring*. *Self-monitoring* is a facet of *emotional intelligence*,[133] which reflects an individual's ability to observe, evaluate, and manage their moods and can be measured through *self-regulation* or *self-control* assessments. Multiple studies indicate that *emotional intelligence* influences impulsive buying behavior and serves as a mitigating factor.[135–137] Lekavičienė et al.[96] indicated that training programs focused on *emotional intelligence* skills can lead to more sustainable consumer behavior, reducing *susceptibility to materialism* and associated *addiction*. Their research revealed that developing emotional intelligence skills-based training programs contributes to more sustainable consumer behavior, *mitigating the vulnerability to materialism* and related *addictive behavioral consequences*. It has been suggested that training programs can help consumers improve their *emotional intelligence* while also lowering their levels of *materialism* and *compulsive buying*, where specific *emotional ability*-based training can diminish materialistic and excessive buying inclinations.

Matthews et al.[138] highlighted that being psychologically healthy under stress requires *emotionally intelligent persons*; if not, the disorders will act at their peak. They emphasized that selecting coping mechanisms is highly dependent on *emotional intelligence*. This book synthesizes various academic perspectives highlighting that internal factors significantly impact impulsive buying, often serving as a coping mechanism for *psychological well-being*. It shown that academic research recognize that businesses can exploit *consumer vulnerabilities* to trigger impulsive purchases. While this highlights our deep involvement in compensatory behavior, multiple studies suggest using self-control as a mitigation strategy. However, my investigations found that self-control is only effective in the short term and that emotional intelligence could be helpful.

Creating conditions where others can thrive: key takeaways

- Purpose over profit: the rise of well-being and happiness as key priorities in a new world emphasizing a holistic approach over welfare and financial gains.
- Sustainable consumption has positive influence on well-being, supported by research and real-life examples.
- The invisible force of impulsive buying with hidden effects on personal lives and the harm it can cause should be acknowledged in full.
- We have a strong need to satisfy our psychological needs, especially during times of crisis, but relying on impulsive buying is like befriending a dangerous ally.
- What is the academic stance on factors influencing impulsive buying? Insights from research on what drives impulsive buying and the importance of addressing these factors to promote sustainable consumption provided.
- The majority of references behind impulsive buying point to internal and psychological factors closely tied to emotional well-being and requiring urgent attention.
- One of two papers consider emotion-related behavioral factors, with self-control accounting for nearly half of them, but self-control is a depleting resource.
- Emotional intelligence is a promising avenue that can help manage impulsive buying, though it might not offer quick or widespread results.

6

Emotional Capital for the Triple-Win framework

Building on psychological factors and the need for well-being, this chapter demonstrates how empowering others and fostering social cohesion can drive positive change, further developing the concept of emotional intelligence. It highlights how integrating business strategies with social empowerment can initiate a consumption revolution, paving the way for a sustainable and secure future for all. You will explore the concept of the unique type of capital required for such change, known as emotional capital, and examine 50 business strategies used for this purpose, culminating in the emotional capital for triple-win framework.

Emotional competencies

There is a buzz in the modern world about *emotional intelligence*, and despite some critique, there is a set of publications on social and emotional competencies that state that emotional intelligence plays a key role in determining success in both personal and professional life. Several researchers developed the concept of emotional intelligence toward *emotional competencies*, and you could find works with over 70 of them.

The latest developments include refinements from Goleman, which you can find in the collaborative book, "The Emotionally Intelligent Workplace,"[139] Chapter 3. The initial Goleman 1998 model identified five dimensions of emotional intelligence represented by 25 competencies. Three of those dimensions—self-awareness, self-regulation, and motivation—described personal competencies, that is, knowing and managing emotions in oneself. Two dimensions—empathy and social skills—described social competencies, that is, knowing and managing emotions in others. The new model reflects the development of the concept, including works of Goleman's colleague Boyatzis, collapsing the 25 *competencies into 20*, and the five domains into the four. This model represents *self-awareness, self-management, social awareness,* and *relationship management.* The empathy domain, initially a distinct aspect of emotional intelligence, lost its unique significance and became part of the broader social awareness domain, which also includes service orientation and organizational awareness. Goleman's refined model excludes qualities like *developing others* and *leveraging diversity.* In my view, this decision removed the potential for emotional intelligence to expand beyond individual competencies to abilities that provide direct social benefits. As a result, we lost a critical force that fostered social cohesion and served the common good. Nevertheless, Gendron[134] was the first to propose that if emotional competencies are vital for improved social, economic, and personal performance, they should be regarded as *capital.*

Development of the emotional capital concept

Emotional capital is a relatively new concept that, nevertheless, is already deeply connected with other aspects of human life, including those that are central to this book: behavioral psychology and economics. Eyel and Durmaz[140] note that the effects of *individuals' emotions on individual behaviors* were not extensively investigated until recent years. They define emotional capital as *abilities or habits* that *transform the management of emotions into various social benefits.* Zembylas[141] pointed out that unrecognized mechanisms and emotional norms often serve "affective economies." He refers to Sara Ahmed's work, "Affective Economies,"[142] where she highlights that *emotions are active in affective economies*, aligning individuals with communities through the intensity of their *attachments.*

Emotional capital is traditionally attributed to a "first mention" of Jackson[143] who examined grief and religion in "The Meaning of Death" work. Marci Cottingham[144] pointed out Jackson's argument that religion enables individuals to confront death with a firm sense of reality, a *healthy expression of emotions*, and the ability to *reinvest emotional capital* where it will yield the best results in life. Thus, emotions were attributed to *healthy expressions* and *connected with the quality of capital*, which could be reinvested elsewhere. The concept was developed further by Helga Nowotny in her work, "Women in Public Life in Austria."[145] Working on emotional capital conceptualizations, Madhavan et al.[146] highlighted that Nowotny defines emotional capital as *knowledge*, *contacts*, *relations*, and access to *emotionally valued skills and assets*, which hold within any social network characterized at least partly by *affective ties*. The critical moment here is understanding that emotional capital, *ultimately linked to relationships*, arises and thrives *within social environments and not as an individual asset*. Simply put, you cannot demonstrate the value of emotional capital unless you invest it in others, transmitting your psychological resources. This approach highlights the importance of applying this resource rather than just achieving high scores on emotional intelligence's individualistic assessments. Reay[147] emphasized that endorsing Bourdieu's analysis of women as responsible for maintaining social relationships, Nowotny saw emotional capital as a *resource women have in greater abundance than men*. She stated that emotional capital is a "heuristic device" that denotes *emotional resources passed on from mother to child*. Froyum[148] agrees that emotional capital suggests that *adults transfer emotion management skills to children*, where *emotion management* is the power-infused way individuals *cultivate particular feelings* among others or themselves. Gillies[149] defines emotional capital as *emotional investments* made by parents as part of their desire *to promote their children's well-being and prospects*. Feeney and Lemay[150] agree and define emotional capital as a *positive emotional investment* into one's relationship. They name it an accumulated stock of "*relationship wealth*" made up of a set of *positive, shared emotional experiences* that constitute a resource inherent to a particular relationship. To them, this resource is presumed to promote positive relationship development and relationship success.

Froyum[148] emphasizes that emotional capital treats emotions and their management as skills or habits that translate into *social advantages*. Lively and Weed[151] examined emotional management and found that recent research on social movements indicates it can be used to *drive social change*. Thus, social studies on *emotion management* reveal its functionality across various levels: interpersonal interactions, meso-level structures (like communities), and macro-level organizations (such as nations, religions, or cultures). This aligns closely with the academic perspective on *consumption levels* presented in Chapter 2, which includes micro- (individual), meso- (groups), and macro- (systems) levels, suggesting that *emotional capital* can be implemented universally across all levels. Lively and Weed concluded that through adept emotion management, individuals receive *interpersonal* and *material benefits*, existing status hierarchies and structural arrangements are maintained, and *group cohesion* is fostered through sympathy and gratitude exchange.

This underlines that emotional capital benefits all level of relationship environments: *personal, professional*, and *social*. I assert that it is indeed feasible to convert existing emotional resources by enhancing the liquidity of emotional capital—a fundamental quality and characteristic of any form of capital, as emphasized in Jackson's works.[143]

Emotional capital as a tripartite concept: from individualistic emotional competencies to social cohesion

Developing the line with social environments, Cottingham[152] suggests that emotional capital is more than just a set of individual resources, such as emotional intelligence and emotional competencies. *Emotional capital* posits a *direct relationship between macro-structures and micro-resources*. Macro-structures representing the social aspect utilize emotional capital to support and develop social groups. This perspective is supported by the work "Development and Assessment of the Personal Emotional Capital Questionnaire for Adults" by Khazaei et al.[153] who define emotional capital as consisting of (1) *emotion-based knowledge*, (2) *managerial skills*, and (3) *abilities* that aid in personal development and *group membership*. Again, they pointed out three levels of emotional capital such as *personal*, *group*, and *organizational*.

Emotional capital offers numerous advantages during challenging times, transformations, and both external and internal changes. Khazaei et al.[153] highlight that situations like downsizing, reduced funding, and restructuring allow employees with high emotional capital to effectively engage with clients and the public. Maintaining competitive advantages is a struggle, and emotional capital helps in fostering positive attitudes toward anxiety and stress. They revealed that for sustainability and success, organizations must effectively develop and maintain their employees' emotional capital, while also enhancing managers' emotional capital, which increases social performance and boosts employee performance. High emotional capital benefits both business owners and job applicants, allowing companies to remain sustainable during external changes and provide customers with specific values. However, this book is not solely focused on developing leadership theory or mere investing in personal development but focuses on *social transformations*.

Gendron[134] observed that modern industrial societies and powerful nations increasingly emphasize *competition*, *individualism*, *liberalism*, and *performance*—enhancing *individualistic emotional competencies*—but she defines emotional capital as a *set of resources that support* not only personal and professional development but also organizational growth and *social cohesion*. In its narrower perspective, *social cohesion* revolves mainly around three core aspects: a *sense of belonging*, *social relations*, and an orientation toward the *common good*.[154] In the conceptual article, Chan et al.[155] define *social cohesion* as a set of attitudes and norms that includes trust, a sense of belonging, and the willingness to help, as well as their *behavioral manifestations*. Gendron's work also found that *emotional capital* directly contributes not only personal and social, but *economic success*. She concluded that if emotional or compassionate behavior can be explained through an *economic approach*, conversely, emotional behavior must be considered in economic theory as it *can have significant returns and impacts on economics*. This is important in a view of this book where emotion-based psychological characteristics named key influences for impulsive buying behavior fueling over-consumption.

The concept of emotional capital embodies qualities widely recognized by researchers, highlighting how personal emotional competencies can be *actively applied for others*. Emphasizing this active intention, I build on the definition of Cottingham's emotional capital as a tripartite concept, which is composed of (1) emotion-based knowledge, (2) emotional management skills or competencies, and (3) *capacities to feel* that link self-processes and resources to group membership and social location. This definition clearly explains that emotional capital consists of knowledge and personal skills that can be shared with others if the *capacity to feel* is present. In my view, this does not refer to the capacity to feel emotions of self or others or the ability to experience emotions healthily, as in the concept of emotional intelligence. Instead, it is the *active ability* to transform emotions into "something beneficial for society."

To illustrate, the 2024 *Humans@Centre report*, "Transformation leadership: navigating turning points," highlights the ability to *empathize and actively engage with others* at the heart of modern leadership.[156] The report concludes that new leaders must "sense others" by detecting early warnings about necessary interventions, *listening* to emotional signals, *making sense* of what they hear, and *taking actions* that rejuvenate energy levels, rebuild trust, and foster new ways of working on performance. This goes beyond mere social awareness or communication skills. It exemplifies social cohesion at its best, where people connect through emotional bonds and actively care for, help, develop, and *invest their personal emotional capital in empowering others*. As such, I suggest that these active abilities form *active emotional practices*, which could serve as *behavioral manifestations* of the emotion capital.

Based on the explanations provided, I define *emotional capital as a concept composed of (1) emotion-based knowledge, (2) emotional management skills or competencies, and (3) social investments: active emotional practices for social cohesion*. My proposition introduces emotional capital as a unique type of capital for social transformations and a new asset for business impact. It shifts the focus from solely addressing individual needs of employees or leadership to fostering social cohesion through much broader application and *consumer empowerment*. I assert that by applying emotional capital, professionals across industries can create environments that promote innovation and resilience, ensuring their organizations remain profitable and *constructive forces within their communities*. To achieve this, I propose *a new business narrative: stop selling and start building the future with customers.*

Five dimensions of emotional capital for business impact and social cohesion

How can businesses address active emotional practices for social cohesion? Which capital investments would yield greater impact beyond taxes and philanthropy? My proposal is not new: it's more effective to teach people how to catch a fish rather than simply giving it away. This approach empowers them and prevents dependency. With this in mind, I present the Five Dimensions of Emotional Capital model, which incorporates five dimensions from previous theories on emotional knowledge, intelligence, competencies, and practices. As previously suggested, these dimensions are intended for active social investments.

I integrate five dimensions with active business goals and 50 aggregated business applications from research studies to develop the Emotional Capital for the Triple-Win framework. Exploring over 300 practical propositions, I address the question: "If emotional capital is a new resource that businesses can invest in for a triple win—reducing impulsive buying in favor of psychological well-being and sustainable consumption—what could be invested for social good?" This framework addresses overconsumption, which we use as a coping mechanism for enhancing psychological well-being.

The idea is simple: overconsumption drives multiple global crises, and cutting back on impulsive buying—responsible for up to 90% of purchases—can make a big difference. How do we do this? By tapping into personal tools like self-control and emotional intelligence. But real change requires a bigger shift. We need both sides—businesses with their powerful marketing strategies and customers prioritizing their well-being—to work together. Instead of seeing sales growth and sustainable lifestyles like sufficiency or voluntary simplicity as opposites, why not aim for a triple win? I propose to create a future where people, the planet, and prosperity all thrive by addressing emotional capital to meet consumers' psychological needs and well-being, decoupling it from impulsive buying behavior. This offer ventures into uncharted territory, where challenges may arise, potentially limiting us or rendering this proposal ineffective. However, I am eager to explore this powerful possibility that could contribute to a better life without overconsumption and its consequences.

Let's consider five emotional capital dimensions for social investments and business impact: creating sustainable awareness, fostering a new mindset, standing with people, empowering through transferring knowledge/skills/practices, and leading by example.

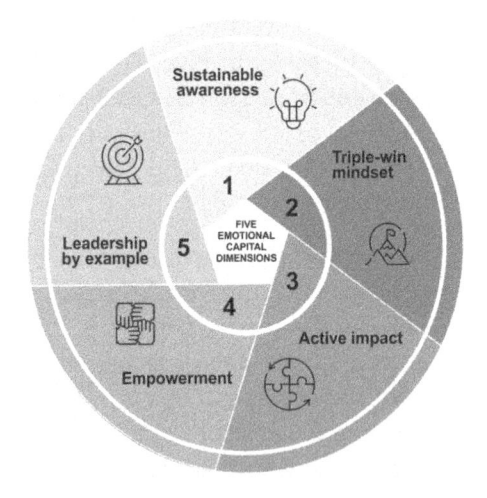

Figure 11. Five Emotional Capital Dimensions for Business Impact

Dimension 1: Sustainable awareness

Awareness helps to understand emotions, thoughts, and actions, improving self-management and connection with others. As a sustainable application and in business, it fosters awareness among employees and consumers regarding environmental and social issues, aligning shared values to benefit people, the planet, and prosperity for all. In a view of sustainable consumption, awareness involves recognizing impulsive buying dynamics and allocating resources for their transformations supporting people: employees and customers.

Active business goal: create sustainable awareness

Leadership skills: awareness, shared triple-win values

Dimension 2: Triple-win mindset

Traditionally, a new-goals-related mindset encompasses emotional engagement, personal responsibility, inner motivation, and a long-term approach to achieving goals. Sustainable consumption motivation balances personal, social, and environmental aspects, affecting thoughts and actions. For businesses, this involves fostering a sustainable mindset, applying critical thinking, educating on opportunities, and using emotions to motivate us to work through the hard times. It helps decouple psychological well-being from impulsive buying behavior and rejects business and marketing practices based on people's vulnerabilities.

Active business goal: foster a triple-win mindset

Leadership skills: active responsibility, critical thinking, and long-term approach

Dimension 3: Active impact

Social and problem-solving skills encompass abilities to excel in social systems through adaptability, communication, conflict management, and collaboration. Key competencies include connecting with others, innovating for them, managing change and conflict, building bonds, and fostering teamwork. These skills facilitate positive interpersonal relationships and enable businesses to connect with and positively impact communities, standing for people.

Active business goal: create impact, becoming a positive force for people& the planet

Leadership skills: social and problem-solving skills

Dimension 4: Empowerment

Businesses should empower customers, not make them dependent on their needs. Emotional engagement, fostered by empathy, facilitates the sharing of knowledge, skills, and practices. By cultivating practical empathy, businesses identify consumers' developmental needs, enhance abilities, uncover potential, and provide encouragement and support through collaborative activities that benefit people, the community, and the environment.

Active business goal: empower by transferring knowledge, skills, and practices

Leadership skills: engagement and development of others

Dimension 5: Leadership by example

Business advocacy for a triple-win strategy involves aligning internal strategies, actions, and resources without causing harm to themselves or others. Business self-regulation and management encompass controlling insatiable shareholders' demands and impulses, trustworthiness, and taking responsibility for business outcomes and consequences. Leading sustainable practices, businesses promote triple-win for long-term success through everyday actions, not patronizing messages or false promises.

Active business goal: advocate for a triple win

Leadership skills: "Walk your talk" approach

Practical applications for consumption revolution

Designing Emotional Capital for the Triple-Win Framework, I allocated all 300+ practical propositions from more than 200 researchers with proposed emotional capital dimensions.

First, it has been found that nearly half of the propositions are associated with *cultural change*, *education*, and *consumer transformation*. It happens so because *sustainable consumption* is a powerful and long-term-oriented paradigm, enabling us to increase the quality of life for future generations mitigating overconsumption, but it requires change. Applying systems thinking from Meadows,[157] we know there are system properties where interventions can transform entire systems, resulting in incremental change, known as *leverage points*. The *leading paradigm* or mindset is the strongest among them.

We need to *decouple psychological well-being* from impulsive buying behavior, which we use as a coping instrument. Therefore, promoting personal benefits and "even more sustainable" products is impossible without addressing *self-transformation* and *inner development*. Consumers are deemed to take their part in that process. Annika Nordlund[118] emphasizes that discussions on *personal values* should have a strategic focus. She refers to *openness to change* versus *conservation* and *self-transcendence* versus *self-enhancement*. *Self-transcendence* prioritizes collective interests, encompassing values like universalism and benevolence while self-enhancement prioritizes individual interests, incorporating values like power and achievement. "Transcendence" is a valid and longstanding term in personal development. Still, excessive focus on the "self" doesn't help, even through the lens of emotional intelligence: decades of investment in leadership emotional quotient haven't led to any significant social shift. The speed of social transformation appears to rely on social values and instruments, not individualistic ones.

This situation creates a unique opportunity for businesses to step in. While businesses may pose risks, they also play a vital role in organizing society through efficient structures, contributing to *social value* creation, and enhancing *social safety* and *well-being*. This leads us to infer that the primary actions suggested by academia for businesses revolve around *education, communication*, and *establishing individual connections with sustainable consumption practices*.

The next quarter of practical applications focuses on traditional growth and marketing strategies, offering direct suggestions to boost impulsive buying behavior by fostering emotional attachments to products or encouraging parasocial relationships between customers and business owners. This may sound alarming in the context of overconsumption, and understandably so. However, instead of demonizing these concepts, we can broaden our perspective by recognizing that resource scarcity drives the need for degrowth. This approach becomes more sensible if we shift away from material purchases, as seen in the experience economy, for example, toward educational products. The statista.com[158] published a revenue forecast for the online education market, projected to reach US$203.80bn in 2025. Revenue is expected to show an annual growth rate of 8.20%, resulting in a projected market volume of US$279.30bn by 2029. The online university education market has a projected market volume of US$136.80bn in 2025. Education is a sample of traditionally known economic products from the range of transformative experiences heavily decoupled from material resources (although not 100%).

Similarly, considering the *sharing economy*, where resources are reused, and sales are multiplied by companies like Airbnb and Uber, we can better understand how to derive more value from the same resources. Next, numerous examples and tools are available to learn from the abundance that *regeneration and the multiplication of natural capital* can create. Let's remain aware rather than fearful, avoiding polarized opinions that cater to short-term solutions. A long-term perspective should not view growth as a threat, as not all growth is detrimental.

The next slice is calling to *advocate for sustainability via governance and policy proposals implementations*. As concerns about global challenges—like income inequality or climate refugee migration—grow, the call for businesses to drive *positive social change* is spreading from academia to the practitioner community. Maltz and Pierson[159] point out that leaders of major companies, including investment firms like BlackRock and JPMorgan, have already taken this call. Yet, there is a massive request for social support, as progress is impossible without societal transformation for systemic change. This demands inner motivation and a shift in mindset to be integrated into governance and policies. Lastly, only about 10% of actionable recommendations pertain to *innovation*, despite Anand et al.[160] identifying it as a critical driver for practical forces like international businesses, which are crucial for sustained growth and competitive advantage, especially in emerging economies. Amber et al.[1] point to the fact, that traditionally, companies are renowned for identifying new products, leveraging emerging technologies, and fostering innovation, however, they refer to interesting details from two publications. The first one, van der Waal et al.'s[161] research, indicates that while multinational enterprises significantly drive innovation related to the Sustainable Development Goals—accounting for 34% of all patent applications—only 12.2% of these patents are explicitly linked to the SDGs. In the second paper, Dörrenbächer et al.[162] conclude that while papers highlight multinational corporations as solutions to grand challenges, yet these entities also face complications in addressing such issues.

Next Amber et al.[1] performed an analysis for example instruments that influence each actionable proposition used by researchers from the considered literature scope. A graphical representation and the Iceberg model were used, presenting actionable propositions in top-descending order to quickly grasp the idea of how well they backed-up by instruments, as presented in Figure 12. The adopted top-down approach prioritizes actionable propositions, which emerged as the most developed. There is a thickness utilized to emphasize propositions associated with more examples of instruments offered.

The leading choice does not indicate the number of citations but is based on the quantity of example instruments assessed. For example, the marketing objective "stimulate impulsive buying" encompasses 19 example instruments yet constitutes only 8% of all references, likely due to extensive prior research.

The number of instruments is essential for understanding how effectively actionable propositions are comprehended and prepared for practical application. As a result, other objectives present significant opportunities for developing practical instruments.

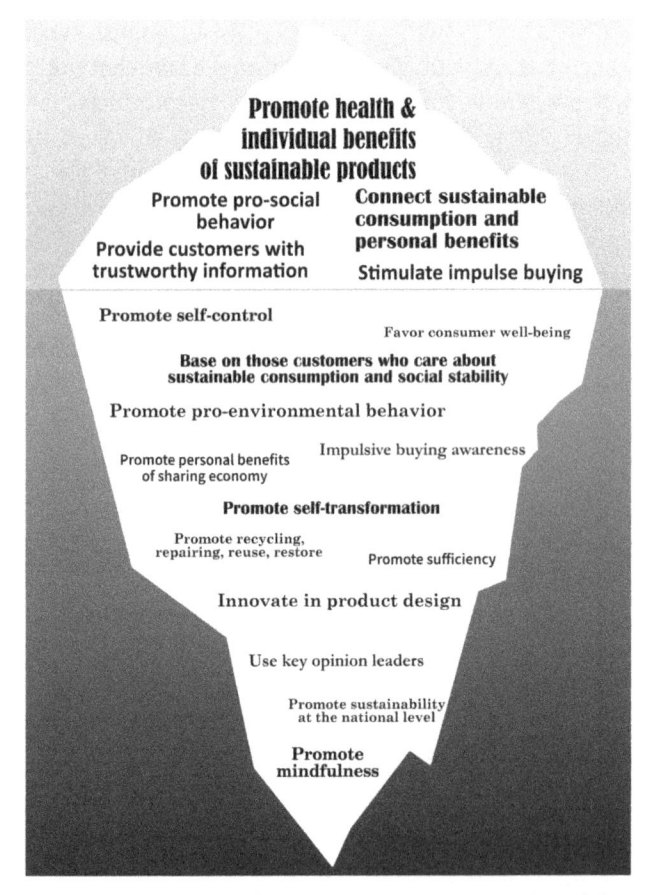

Figure 12. The Iceberg model of sustainable consumption, adapted from Amber et al.[1]

The five most developed actionable propositions are presented in Table 7.

These objectives along with all other practical instruments proposed serve as an inspiration for the development of the framework with 50 innovative ways aim to revolutionize consumer behavior to achieve suggested triple win in consumption.

Table 7. *Five actionable propositions most backed up with practical instruments*

Theme	Goal	Actionable propositions
Growth & Business	Increase green consumption	1. Promote health and individual benefits of sustainable products
		2. Stimulate impulsive buying
Culture & Education	Connect, inform, educate	3. Connect sustainable consumption and personal benefits
		4. Promote pro-social behavior
Governance & Policy	Advocate for sustainability	5. Provide customers with reliable information

Emotional Capital for the Triple Win: 50 innovative business strategies

My research highlights a direct contradiction between traditional understanding of marketing's role in stimulating demand, and acquiring goods or services to satisfy consumer needs with the growing advocacy for new consumption types, such as anti-consumption, sufficiency, minimalism, or voluntary simplicity. As discussed, the global population consumes 70% more resources than the planet can naturally regenerate, with private consumption being a major contributor to this overconsumption. Additionally, most consumers distance themselves from those who buy excessively when questioned about their own behavior.

The "attitude-behavior gap," where individuals who view themselves as sustainable consumers continue to make unsustainable choices, continues to impact consumer behavior. Significant lifestyle changes should involve a deep understanding of consumer needs, societal well-being, and environmental impact. While there is no universally agreed-upon definition of sufficiency, I tend to agree with Gossen et al.[73]

that it could be understood as avoiding both overconsumption and underconsumption, suggesting a reduction of material consumption levels in affluent societies. Despite considerable attention to improving sustainable consumption by mitigating impulsive buying, I found only initial evidence or concrete steps toward achieving this goal.

While technical solutions and public policy are crucial, they are *insufficient when isolated* from human interaction. In tackling overconsumption, *shared responsibility of businesses and consumers* in mitigating impulsive buying influences, rooted in personal and psychological factors, must be acknowledged. I foresee *businesses become leading forces* in this transformation by adopting a new understanding and practices of *emotional capital*. The traditional view of businesses *exploiting resources and their customers* is shifting toward *mutual development*. Academic discussions refer to a trend when people want to connect with people and not with brands anymore. Brands used to serve individualistic values and *social status*, which are increasingly vanishing as a part of the financial welfare concept, making a way of increasing popularity for collective values and *well-being*.

Consumers are part of a *socio-environmental system* embedded in the nature and cultural fabric, not just a profit source. When consumers trust sellers, they believe these sellers will act ethically and not exploit their vulnerabilities. For businesses to thrive, collaboration with customers to create a better future is crucial. Gossen et al.[73] emphasize that although marketing strategies are often accused of stimulating overconsumption, businesses increasingly show potential as enablers of sufficiency. The emphasis on resource allocation solely for profit is moving toward a balanced *regenerative cooperation* that benefits everyone. Therefore, prioritizing *social cohesion* and *genuine relationships* over simple sales transactions with people is vital. To finalize, 50 outlined business tools that influence consumption transformation were aligned by the Emotional Capital for the Triple-Win framework as shown in Figure 13.

Drawing on a decade of publications in the growing research field at the intersection of sustainable consumption and impulsive buying behavior, this book underscores the importance of *cultural and educational changes* as crucial factors for achieving sustainable consumption. This entails significant *lifestyle changes*, process adjustments, and *time* to cultivate *new values*, prioritizing discussions on transforming consumption.

1 Sustainable Awareness	2 Triple Win Mindset	3 Active Impact	4 Empowerment	5 Leadership by Example
Create impulsive buying awareness	Share ultimate responsibility	Base on those customers who care about sustainable consumption and social stability	Warn about role of the survival mode in overconsumption	Mind consumer engagement paradox
Educate about the consequences of impulsive buying	Employ values of impact and activism	Support unique way values and beliefs are behaviorally expressed – a sustainable lifestyle	Educate about "green consumerism"	Evolve business strategy for a triple win
Educate about emotional reasons for overconsumption	Deal with uncertainty with straightforwardness	Support local communities	Help to build long-term emotional regulation	Provide customers with trustworthy information
Educate about value of well-being over welfare	Understand sustainable degrowth	Build knowledge communities	Link sustainable consumption with positive emotions	Embrace the role of marketing communication in promoting sustainable consumption
Embrace personal values and true meaning of self-care	Support sufficiency	Cultivate "being more human" approach	Foster mindfulness	Use a post-growth marketing mix
Promote health benefits related to sustainable consumption	Educate about voluntary simplicity	Mind social consciousness phenomenon	Suggest taking a pause	Don't use patronizing messaging, but suggest practices and direct benefits
Leverage diverse personal values for sustainable consumption	Showcase anti-consumption effects	Understand the influencing direction of social networks	Take an active part in finance planning and education	Don't build on vulnerabilities
Embrace individual actions and help to make informed choices	Promote minimalism	Invite key opinion leaders, not merely influencers	Enhance consumers' sustainable consumption attitudes	Blacklist sales based on stress, fear, or negative emotions
Don't be trapped by cultural polarization of individualism and collectivism	Actively support zero waste movement	Promote pro-social behavior	Embrace customers with pro-environmental self-identity	Promote sales but don't stimulate impulsive buying related to material purchases
Create better stories for the collective compass	Promote sharing economy	Promote pro-environmental behavior	Promote consumer self-efficacy	Innovate as a crazy and search for new opportunities

Figure 13. Emotional Capital for the Triple-Win: 50 innovative business strategies

The Emotional Capital for the Triple-Win framework targets the next generation of business leaders, founders, and innovators with 50 science-backed strategies to revolutionize consumer behavior. It lays the groundwork for change, addressing inner development promptly, leading to improved finances, relationships, and, most importantly, psychological well-being. This endeavor represents both an *opportunity* and a *responsibility*, where each individual contributes to a *collective goal*, allowing businesses to take an exciting turn. Instead of maintaining the status quo, *business corporations* could become a powerful force driving the *consumption revolution*.

In the upcoming chapters, each of these 50 strategies will be explained in detail, often with examples, to enhance understanding of their value and potential impact.

Emotional Capital for the Triple-Win framework: key takeaways

- Conceptual development from emotional intelligence to emotional competencies, or skills used to empower individuals, but this is no longer enough.

- The concept of emotional capital has emerged, showing how empathy was once limited to social awareness and communication skills but has now expanded toward active social investments.

- Five dimensions of emotional capital for business impact model suggest leadership development should shift its focus from individual empowerment to fostering social cohesion.

- Practical applications for the consumption revolution are presented, based on a decade of academic research, offering actionable insights for changemakers and business innovators.

- The Iceberg Model of sustainable consumption identifies the most effective tools available today while also addressing the rapid pace of development in the field.

- The Emotional Capital for the Triple-Win framework brings together 50 innovative business strategies within a comprehensive framework of five emotional capital dimensions. These strategies are crucial for social transformation, fostering change by social empowerment. Collectively, this supports the consumption revolution for a more sustainable future.

PART 2

50 INNOVATIVE WAYS TO LEAD THE CONSUMPTION REVOLUTION

7

Create sustainable awareness

Sustainable awareness involves recognizing impulsive buying dynamics and psychological resources in oneself, others, and complex systems. It helps individuals understand emotions, thoughts, and actions, improving self-management and connection with others. It fosters awareness among employees and consumers regarding environmental and social issues, aligning shared values to benefit people, the planet, and universal prosperity. What can businesses do about awareness with sustainable consumption as a goal? Let's explore the first ten business strategies and scientific arguments behind them.

1. Create impulsive buying awareness

Sermboonsang et al.[163] highlighted that *cutting down on impulse purchases* and promoting sustainable consumption is vital. Yet many individuals fail to grasp the environmental consequences of their consumption habits—a brief review of impulsive buying behavior by Newman et al.[119] shows the importance of individual factors and how *negative feelings* could lead individuals to buy functional necessities for daily survival. This result is consistent with previous literature showing that during a health crisis, people tend to focus on aspects and behaviors that can help them regain control and certainty, such as impulsive buying.

A study by Armstrong Soule and Reich[164] delved into consumer views on a novel sustainable approach called *green demarketing*. Can a profit-driven company champion ecological sustainability by promoting reduced consumption? They concluded that the impact of *environmental reputation* was quite significant. However, Kuanr et al.[165] found demarketing campaigns like Patagonia's "Don't Buy This Jacket" *don't decrease impulsive buying behavior*. Chang and Watchravesringkan[166] emphasize that to mitigate the impact of "environmentally friendly consumerism" and remain within planetary boundaries, it is crucial to focus on enhancing sustainable consumption by curbing impulsive buying behavior. Upadhye et al.[101] suggested that ethical firms and retailers may strive to reduce uninhibited impulse purchases that may lead to later regret and dissatisfaction by educating customers about the negative aspects of impulsive buying and spreading awareness about reducing impulsive buying through *planning interventions*.

Burroughs and Rindfleisch[95] pointed out that consumption, especially of hedonic consumer products, is essential for happiness among modern consumers—however, Mogilner et al.[167] suggested that while consumers seek happiness and marketers are increasingly aiming to tap into consumers' pursuit of happiness, the definition of happiness may vary. Spiteri Cornish[53] stated that consumers should be *more conscious of their spending patterns* and try to contain their impulsive buying, create awareness of their emotions, and add reflection (think of recent use of their possessions once they experience marketing stimuli). Dholakia et al.[120] suggested using self-control mechanisms toward rejection, reclaim, and restriction. Nguyen et al.[124] offered the practice of *mindful consumption*.

2. Educate about the consequences of impulsive buying

Impulsive buying has been associated with negative traits such as *low self-esteem, immaturity,* and *financial issues*. Vohs and Faber[93] stated that impulsive buying behavior is linked to *high consumer debt* levels and leads to *post-purchase dissatisfaction*. Podoshen and Andrzejewski[5] noted that a materialistic lifestyle has negative long-term consequences for both individual consumers and society. Research conducted in Lithuania by Lekavičienė et al.[96] indicates that materialistic consumers *suffer from stress* and *decreased well-being and cannot control their buying behavior, which leads to social and financial problems*. Ortiz Alvarado et al.[168] argue that people feel an impulse to *alleviate negative states*, which is only a short-term solution. Moser et al.[169] state that impulsive buying causes *financial strain*, following feelings of *guilt*, *shame*, and *regret*, and strains *family relationships*. Even when used strategically to cope with negative emotions, impulsive buying can backfire, leading to more *ruminating* and *negative thoughts*. Silvera et al.[94] point to a low level of consumer *self-care*, referring to consequences of buying urges such as *negative well-being* and multiple others. Sharma et al.[123] provided the first evidence of the moderating role of *self-monitoring* on impulsiveness.

3. Educate about emotional reasons for overconsumption

Impulsive buying behavior has been associated with consumer *impulsiveness*. Wang et al.[170] suggested using adaptive selling performance to handle an encounter with similar traits and non-similar traits buyers more attractively. *Trait models of impulsivity* focus on differences between people. Following the traits models, researchers assumed that some people tend to buy impulsively—studies, for example, by Iyer et al.,[135] suggested that individuals scoring high on *impulsivity traits* are more prone to engaging in impulsive purchases.

Yet, dynamics went beyond trait models because of mass influence. Spiteri Cornish[53] observes that any of our impulsive choices are well-known to businesses and intricately woven into the fabric of retail success. Encouraging spur-of-the-moment purchases becomes a symphony of urgency,[62] social influence,[63] and retail design.[61] Malter et al.[112] emphasized the emerging *experiential perspective* foreshadowed by Alderson, Levy, and others, advanced by Holbrook and Batra[171] and Hirschman, and elaborated by Pine and Gilmore,[172] Schmitt, and countless followers who regarded consumers as *flesh-and-blood human beings* rather than information-processing computer-like machines. This initiated a massive trend for *emotion-related studies* regarding consumer behavior beyond impulsivity traits. An academic consensus recognizes that individuals are not purely rational beings. *Contextual factors* and *psychological processes* influence consumer decisions. Impulsive buying involves sudden, intense urges to make immediate purchases.

Taking into account the information and observations provided, it is evident that we are contending with a relatively *global phenomenon of overconsumption*.[45] Common characteristics obscure personal differences, resulting in impulsive purchasing behaviors and *consumerist lifestyles* encouraged by business influencers and supported by legal and government structures for tax revenue. This economic strategy aims to improve livelihoods and reduce poverty, but it carries colossal damage as the planet cannot sustain continuous overconsumption.[173] The suggestion is to be aware of this and be open about impulsive buying behavior and its connection with material purchases. Unless we achieve de-materialized economic growth, as suggested by the SDG 2022 report,[174] we must *be aware of resource limitations, overconsumption, circularity necessity*, and *supply and demand dynamics*.

4. Educate about the value of well-being over welfare

As discussed in Chapter 1, advocates of *strong sustainability* began to challenge the *economic welfare* objective, centered on insatiable human needs, as the sole focus of human life. The new concept of "well-being" captured a broader range of variables. In contrast to welfare—though this distinction is not always clearly recognized—*well-being* is a *multidimensional concept* that encompasses financial gain and various aspects of life, including *job circumstances*, meaningful *social relationships, work–life balance, personal development*, and many more.

Well-being is frequently linked to sustainable consumption practices. Being mindful of environmental and social considerations during consumption is associated with *heightened well-being, life satisfaction*, and *overall happiness*. Embracing sustainable consumption can *foster positive emotions, improve self-image, enhance happiness*, and fulfill the need for *social connections*. Reducing consumption, work, and travel can *deepen one's relationship* with the environment and prioritize *family time*. This approach alleviates environmental concerns, *enhances security*, ensures equitable resource allocation, promotes social responsibility, and *supports well-being through a healthier lifestyle*. There are separate categories in well-being which are directly involved in sustainable consumption such as self-care, healthy food consumption, work–family time, and many more. Promoting these directions, businesses can create social benefit and act as a positive force in their communities.

5. Embrace personal values and the true meaning of self-care

Multiple sustainable consumption research projects agree that customers are not sufficiently motivated by *environmental values*, and more emphasis on *personal benefits* is necessary for sustainable consumption. Values belong to the *internal factors* within our research on impulsive buying behavior influences. They are the *leverage point where businesses could step in*, changing their goals and orientation for a long-term sustainable consumption perspective.

Rana and Paul[175] emphasized that customers' decisions on organic foods are shaped by more than just *altruistic factors* such as environmental protection and animal welfare; *egoistic factors* like *health* and *food safety* also play a significant role. *Health for self* and *loved ones* is one of the highest social priorities, as we learned during COVID-19. An interesting example was developed in China, which began using *health streaming apps* like "Haodf" and "Guahao" during pandemic, creating a new business model for mobile health, known as mHealth. It provides health information or healthcare through mobile devices or tablets. An app is a program enabling user interaction through a touch-based interface. Rodríguez et al.[176] emphasize that the app aims to streamline specific tasks or aid in daily activities. These apps aimed to encourage *healthy habits, provide health knowledge* promptly, and enhance public health literacy through free consultations and tailored services.

According to Lu et al.[177] a 2022 industry report by iResearch, explains that 27.5% of life streamers in China were from the medical or medical aesthetic field, ranking first among all application scenarios, underscoring the significance of the health service industry. These apps *enhance self-efficacy* (related to individualism) by monitoring individuals' *physical and mental states*, aiding in setting achievable goals and making modifications. Researchers examined willingness to pay for mHealth services within that category. They found that the factors linked to consumer spending include *health attitude, self-efficacy* and *preferred lifestyle*, expressing focus on "self."

Some scholars argue that *true altruism* may not even exist because every action involves some degree of *self-interest*. This raises questions about whether pure altruism is possible and how to define it. For example, Kago and Venkataraman[178] conclude that the *gap between altruism and egoism* is not as broad as we make it out to be. Traditionally, altruistic actions aim to *benefit others*, while egoistic actions are *self-serving*. The dichotomy doesn't imply the separate existence of egoism and altruism. Researchers argued that both actions may stem from a common motivational source, suggesting that one doesn't negate the other. If *selfless actions result in personal loss*, it can be seen as a *motivational extreme*, theoretically unjustifiable, and practically challenging.

Another study by Mazhar et al.[76] confirmed that *both personal orientations*, such as *egoistic* and *altruistic* (along with *biospheric* and *hedonic*), are linked to pro-environmental behavior. However, in *egoistic cases*, individuals often opt for environmentally friendly behaviors after *weighing costs against benefits*. If they perceive the financial cost to be lower than the expected *social status*, they are more likely to adopt eco-friendly practices. These findings confirmed an earlier study by Steg et al.[179] which found that people are more likely to engage in sustainable energy behavior when they believe such behavior has relatively *low individual costs and high individual benefits*, resulting in overall positive evaluations of the relevant actions. To summarize, businesses are advised to be ready for sustainable consumption strategy adjustments based on different consumers' values. Still, it is a must to connect the true meaning of self-care for a long-term sustainable consumption perspective.

6. Promote health benefits related to sustainable consumption

Researchers recommend businesses support customers by highlighting the *personal advantages of sustainable products* like eco-friendly food[180] or minimalist wardrobes[181] promoting a *healthier lifestyle*. In their study on meat anti-consumption, Ling Xie et al.[182] found that *animal welfare* was not very encouraging, and Phang et al.[105] emphasized that *concern for future generations* did not necessarily decrease consumer purchases during the pandemic. This contradicts the foundational idea that consumers with sustainable consumption behaviors tend to have a more profound holistic outlook and concern about moderation in consumption.

However, the study by Nguyen et al.[183] found that focusing on *health-related attributes* of products as *personal benefits* is an effective driver for sustainable consumption. Tariq et al.[184] emphasized that the slogan, "you are what you eat," resonates with many consumers, resulting in a heightened demand for organic products and a growing awareness of *health* and environmental protection. This awareness influences consumer behavior regarding food and health choices, with organic food being viewed as healthier due to its descriptors such as "local," "fresh," "natural," and "pure," compared to conventional options. Jakubowska and Sadilek[75] explained that *sustainable food* is linked to using sustainable ingredients and production processes, providing adequate product quality and sensory attributes. Consumer *health attitudes* greatly influence their inclination to purchase environmentally friendly food. When consumers view green food positively, their desire to buy it grows. This finding aligns with multiple prior research on eco-friendly products. Therefore, researchers advised green food businesses to enhance consumers' *positive perceptions* and *attitudes* toward green food by emphasizing its *health-related benefits* and *boosting consumer beliefs and knowledge*. Another study found a strong connection between *health, life routines* (considered via religiosity), and *well-being*.[182]

Health consciousness represents a significant opportunity to promote sustainable consumption in health-related areas. This includes behaviors like *intermittent fasting, regular exercise*, using *bicycles* and other *sport-related products* for their health benefits, and incorporating the latest *health-related technology* and *green luxury items* into everyday life. Shahzad et al.[185] showed that *health-conscious attitudes* rather than other factors influence consumer anti-consumption behavior toward soft drinks. They indicate that attitudes toward soft drink anti-consumption result in intentions to avoid consuming them. Their study confirmed that one's attitude toward anti-consumption significantly predicts actual behavior, highlighting *health attitude* as a strong predictor of anti-consumption behavior.

7. Leverage diverse personal values for sustainable consumption

Researching "Why we buy what we buy?", Sheth et al. stated that *subjective values*, once considered significant predictors of consumer decision-making,[186] have become *the most relevant* research area in the age of globalization. This emphasizes the significance of *individual consumption patterns*. For example, Liu et al.[187] found that in the context of COVID-19, *functional value*, *health value*, and *environmental value* all play an essential role in organic purchases, which implies that consumers are more inclined to buy *environmental and healthy organic food*. The results indicated the significant association of *sustainable consumption attitude* with *perceived values*.

A study by Ladhari et al.[188] found that the impacts of *personal values* (micro-level variables) and *culture* (macro-level variables) on perceived service quality are distinct. For instance, this study discovered that individuals who *value accomplishment* prioritize *achievement* and *societal recognition*. Being goal-oriented and efficient, they have little tolerance for *inefficiency in service providers*.

Gawior et al.[99] observed that *hedonic motivations*—such as *gratification shopping, value shopping, novelty-seeking shopping*, and *adventure-seeking shopping*—are related to impulsive buying behavior. They observed that spending time with close friends and family during shopping (*social value*) is associated with *hedonic values* and a *sense of belonging*, both of which support the finding of the positive impact of social bonding on experience satisfaction. The results of this study confirm that *positive emotional* and arousal compensations such as fun, pleasure, love, friendship, and acceptance are outcomes of social bonding behaviors. They concluded that this evidences unsustainable overconsumption, which has a higher negative environmental and social impact. Zhang et al.'s[189] empirical findings showed that consumers' perceived *utilitarian* and *hedonic values* positively affect their urge to buy impulsively and *impulsive buying behavior*.

The theory of consumption values states that five of them, *functional, emotional, social, conditional,* and *epistemic*, are effective in behavioral choice. Cao et al.'s[190] research findings revealed that functional (*price*), emotional, social, and epistemic values strongly impacted purchasing decisions. However, the study indicated that functional (*quality*) and conditional values did not significantly affect buying behavior in the organic food sector. This could be due to the *trust-based dynamic* between organic food buyers and sellers. Frequent conditional promotions might lead to consumer skepticism toward organic products, resulting in the overlooked importance of functional value (quality) and conditional values. This serves as an example where businesses need to understand diversity of subjective values and be prepared to navigate them effectively.

8. Embrace individual actions and help to make informed choices

Hüttel and Balderjahn[191] direct making people aware that they have to contribute to environmental and climate protection. Consumers may *doubt their ability* to effect change, struggle to identify *necessary actions*, or engage in power struggles to *evade responsibility*. Changing lifestyle habits proves difficult, yet they *don't even know what exactly needs to be changed*, so practical support of businesses could be inevitable. A study by Shobeiri et al.[192] suggests that companies should include a *thought-provoking approach* to environmental protection's benefits in packaging green products.

Let's use an example to understand it better—State of the Planet is the resource of the Columbia Climate School, which Columbia University established to support groundbreaking research, deliver innovative education, and foster essential solutions from the community to the planetary scale (www.climate.columbia.edu/). On April 30, 2020, an article titled "Plastic, Paper, or Cotton: Which Shopping Bag is Best?" was shared by this website, featuring insights from regular contributor Renée Cho.[193] With reference to a 2014 study by the Progressive Bag Alliance, a *comparison of grocery bags was made* from high-density polyethylene, compostable plastic, and paper. The findings showed that high-density polyethylene bags had lower fuel and water usage, greenhouse gas emissions, and waste production. While paper bags are renewable and biodegradable, they contribute to tree consumption, with over 10 billion paper bags used annually in the U.S., leading to the felling of 14 million trees. On the other hand, cotton totes have the highest environmental impact due to land use, water consumption, and chemical usage. Fertilizer use significantly contributes to eutrophication. Harvesting, processing, and transporting cotton to market require substantial energy, and their bulkiness increases shipping costs. Cotton totes are challenging to recycle, given the limited textile recycling in the U.S., where only 15.2% of textiles were recycled in 2017. Consequently, a cotton bag must be used 7,100 times to match the environmental footprint of a plastic bag. Although the article by Cho concludes that prioritizing bag reuse over single-use options is crucial to reducing ecological impact, how significantly does this article affect *pro-environmental consumption* and sustainable consumer choices by offering high-density polyethylene bags? The accurate answer is *yet to be discovered* because the options provided do not include natural, biodegradable, cost-efficient, and positively waste-related choice.

This example provokes thoughts about what qualifies as environmentally friendly, what information can be deemed trustworthy, and what actions to take. That was precisely Patagonia's choice (regarding packaging), demonstrating its commitment to introducing a ban for paper packaging as part of the tree conservation movement. Patagonia's partnership with Canopy's Pack4Good initiative focuses on sustainable alternative packaging, aiming to decrease Patagonia's tree dependence by using *agricultural waste*. Another innovative option is the Frayme Mylo™, the world's first luxury bag made from *mycelium*—the root-like structures of fungi. Other alternatives could involve materials like *biodegradable plastic (bioplastic) made from fish scales*, pioneered by Lucy Hughes, a product design student at the University of Sussex. Her material, MarinaTex, earned her the 2024 James Dyson Award.

Balderjahn and Appenfeller[4] point out that individual consumption reportedly contributes around 70% of total consumption, highlighting the substantial impact of *small steps and choices at the personal level* are essential. White et al.[194] aim for consumers to recognize, embrace, and reward sustainable values and actions in ways that promote sustainable consumption and maximize the firm's sustainability and strategic business benefits by highlighting how sustainable behaviors can generate positive outcomes. By helping people navigate product-related uncertainties, businesses build long-lasting relationships, ensuring customers don't feel like mere targets of sales tactics.

9. Don't be trapped by cultural polarization of individualism and collectivism

Horcea-Milcu[195] highlights that *values* are theoretically connected *to deep leverage points* in the same way as worldviews and paradigms. Wang et al.[50] highlighted that *individualism-collectivism* depicts the difference between the common cultural orientations that emphasize the significance of an individual versus those that underscore the group's harmony. The self-construal theory discusses how individuals define themselves as *independent* from others or *interdependent* with others. In consumer behavior, self-construal influences impulsive or symbolic behavior, with *independent individuals* tending toward *impulsive consumption* and interdependent individuals leaning toward *symbolic consumption*. Consequently, *collectivist cultures* prioritize communal well-being and cooperation and have long been seen as *champions of sustainable consumption*. Their consideration of the broader impact of consumption decisions on the community and natural environment is considered as an inspiring model for all.

A study by Sirgy et al.[196] dedicated to the quality of life revealed a significant difference in *self-concept between Westerners and Asians*. Westerners often focus on the personal self, defining themselves by unique traits (independent/individualists), while Asians prioritize the social self and interpersonal relationships (interdependent/collectivists).

Their research argues that consumers with *individualists* may exhibit higher *materialistic tendencies*, valuing material possessions and their acquisition. Asuamah Yeboah[197] points out that values prioritizing environmental protection and social responsibility promote *pro-sustainability attitudes and behaviors*, while values focused on *materialism* and short-term gains impede sustainable consumption. Consequently, *individualists* might be more actively involved in shopping and could potentially overspend, attaching importance to the social status and image portrayed by possessions. Academics agree that values such as collectivism and social support help promote a *self-sufficient lifestyle*.

A multi-country survey of consumers in Australia, the U.S., Hong Kong, Singapore, and Malaysia conducted by Kacen and Lee[198] confirmed the significant influence of regional factors (individualism-collectivism) and individual cultural differences (independent-interdependent self-concept) in shaping impulsive purchasing behavior. *Unexpectedly, affective feelings* played a more substantial role in the impulsive buying behavior of Asians compared to Caucasians. Researchers conclude that, while collectivists possess the *same impulsiveness trait* as individualists, they restrain this impulse and align their actions with cultural norms. This alignment, driven by *cultural norms*, reduces impulsive buying behavior, underscoring the intricate dynamics of consumer behavior.

Kuanr et al.[165] also suggested that when *environmental concern* and sustainability drive *voluntary simplicity*, *collectivism* encourages it positively, as opposed to *individualism*, which hampers such behaviors. They discovered that collectivist values support anti-consumption practices like voluntary simplicity and brand avoidance, which aligned with their expectations. However, surprisingly, their research found that individuals with individualistic values exhibited higher *self-efficacy*, which led to an *indirect positive link with anti-consumption behaviors*.

Czarnecka et al.[97] agree that values such as collectivism and social support are viewed as helping to promote a self-sufficient lifestyle. Yet, their study found that *vertical individualists* (prioritizing personal needs over others and valuing competition) and *vertical collectivists* (supporting group supremacy over individuals) were more prone to acculturation in global consumer culture, leading to impulsive consumption behaviors influenced by this culture. As such, impulsive buying behavior could be promoted via community, like a sufficiency lifestyle, depending on current cultural values. The concept of an emerging global consumer culture maintains that individuals share similar personal values across different cultures.[188]

Another study by Hofmann et al.[199] revealed that consumers with strong *interdependent self-construal* have more positive attitudes toward social media posts, and smiling endorsers boost attitudes, sharing, word of mouth, and purchase intention. This confirmed a stronger community influence on consumer behavior, including impulsive purchases resulting from social relations and social media influence. Following this way of thinking, Wang et al.[50] included only *collectivism* in their theoretical model as a potential *cultural driver of impulsive buying behavior*, with evidence that collectivism is more powerful than individualism in spurring impulsive buying behavior. They pointed out that individuals from collectivistic societies are more prone to impulsive buying behavior compared to those from individualistic societies, with collectivistic consumers finding contentment in purchases made with important individuals like friends or family, referring to a report which shows that 68% of online purchases in China are impulsive. Businesses should be prepared to navigate this complex landscape and avoid oversimplifying sustainable consumption. Once again, the modern demand for sustainable consumption challenges many contemporary concepts.

10. Create better stories for the collective compass

Dermody et al.[88] point out that *materialism*, regarded as a dominant value embedded within Western culture, now has a growing influence in Eastern emerging economies, particularly China and India. As such, materialism drives economic growth as a *global phenomenon*,[5] where cultural values such as individualism or collectivism no longer make sense. Numerous previous studies have identified a negative correlation between the *value of materialism* and *sustainability*. Kilbourne et al.[200] demonstrated that materialism impedes sustainable consumption. They emphasized that materialism is deeply embedded in American society and continuously reinforced through social interactions. Lee[201] described *materialism* as a consumption orientation that seeks success and happiness by acquiring and possessing material goods. Conversely, a *voluntary simplicity* lifestyle describes a nonmaterialistic way of living that seeks mental and spiritual well-being through low consumption, material simplicity, and ecological awareness. Thus, they conclude that *voluntary simplicity* should be considered the opposite of materialism. Kasser[202] agreed that the interplay of cultural values focusing on consumption, materialism, and short-term gains can hinder sustainable consumption practices. Lee[201] underlined that *materialism* is classified as an extrinsic value that *decreases pro-ecological behaviors*.

Materialists often carry *more debt* and *lower well-being*, which is known within the research community as the high price of materialism.[202] Nepomuceno and Laroche[91] explored the factors influencing materialists' inclination to resist consumption. They discovered that *improving self-control* and *fostering long-term orientation* increase the intention to resist consumption and frugality scores. Materialism can be divided into three dimensions: *centrality*, *happiness*, and *success*. Resistance to consumption was stronger for those who believed possessions were a *source of happiness* but not for those who believed that possessions *signal success* or for those who believed that acquiring possessions is a *central goal* in their daily lives. Consequently, it makes sense to show that materialism does not lead to long-term happiness and life satisfaction,[203] promoting *self-control* and *long-term orientation*. However, a change to *cultural values* is needed to change dimensions of materialism connected to *life goals* or *status/success*, signaling pitfalls of materialism and offering other goals embedded in the social fabric.

As a collective compass, *cultural and social values* provide shared meanings that guide behavior, shaping how we perceive and interact with the world. They are a crucial factor in understanding sustainable consumption, often discussed in two aspects: enhancing or hindering sustainable consumption. Illustrating individualism, collectivism, and materialism, we delve into cultural narratives, highlighting the uniqueness of the place and people's perspectives on potential actions.

Businesses and policymakers, as an essential part of the overall societal structure, can intervene in terms of *cultural values shift* to achieve consumer self-regulation.[204] Entrepreneurs and CEOs are welcome to the open stage for *new narratives* on cultural values. Let's create something that celebrates our differences and teaches younger generations how individualists and collectivists came together and shared their gifts. Collectivists guide individualists on communal living, showing the value of well-being and the role of loved ones besides material possessions. Individualists impart *self-reliance* and *self-efficacy*, strengthening each community member. These two factors are solid mitigators for materialists who rely on external signaling to determine their *status/success* or *life centrality*. This shift moves away from materialism associated with possessions or seeking satisfaction in purchases made for or with loved ones, signaling success to peers or family, toward embracing well-being and fostering *individual freedom* and *true power* in *connection with others and the planet*. It promotes valuing our common human home and striving to become responsible Earth resource caretakers for future generations.

Create sustainable awareness: key takeaways

1. Create impulsive buying awareness
2. Educate about the consequences of impulsive buying
3. Educate about emotional reasons for overconsumption
4. Educate about the value of well-being over welfare
5. Embrace personal values and the true meaning of self-care
6. Promote health benefits related to sustainable consumption
7. Leverage diverse personal values for sustainable consumption
8. Embrace individual actions and help to make informed choices
9. Don't be trapped by cultural polarization of individualism and collectivism
10. Create better stories for the collective compass

8

Foster triple-win mindset

Developing a *sustainable mindset* helps individuals recognize the opportunities within sustainability, apply *critical thinking, and use long-term approach*. By educating ourselves and others about new opportunities, such as degrowth, sufficiency, anti-consumption effects, minimalism, and sharing economy of waste circularity, we can stay motivated and committed, even when facing challenges. Channeling our emotions toward our goals drives us to push through obstacles and make a real impact. Sustainable motivation helps individuals and supports the collective effort to build a more secure and sustainable future for everyone, starting with *shared responsibility*.

11. Stand with people: share ultimate responsibility

There is an increasing frequency of publications post-2012, indicating a *burgeoning field at the intersection* of sustainable consumption and impulsive buying behavior. A distinct academic discourse is evident, easily traceable in social media and public talks, relating to shifts in responsibility and corrective actions regarding sustainable consumption. This is a long-standing situation, which I traced back to the beginning with the first two publications appearing in the *International Journal of Consumer Studies*. In 2012, this journal dedicated its March issue to exploring sustainable consumption. The issue, curated by Carola Grebitus, opened with the crucial question "What is sustainable consumption?"—a reflection of academic focus at the time. This edition featured a variety of perspectives on eco-friendly practices in fashion, agriculture, waste control, and food. Verain et al.'s[205] research from this pool on sustainable food consumer segments ranked among the top 40 most popular articles out of 2,088 published from 1977 to 2020. Responsibility discussion initiated by Süle's article[206] focused on whether consumers can develop a conscious approach to sustainability, challenging *oppressive marketing techniques*.

A few months later, Pereira Heath and Chatzidakis[47] responded with their work, "Blame it on Marketing': Consumers' Views on Unsustainable Consumption," calling attention to consumers' roles in promoting sustainability, arguing that consumers must take *sustainable responsibility*. The authors delve into consumer attitudes toward excessive consumption and their perception of it being an environmental problem, marketing's role, and *personal responsibility*. The study highlights the unawareness of ecological consequences, attributing responsibility to marketing, potentially *hindering consumers' part in consumption*. They concluded that surveyed consumers often do not accept *personal responsibility* for excessive consumption or acknowledge their impact on the environment, raising concerns given the high educational level of their research sample.

Dermody et al.[88] highlighted that in certain countries like Sweden, 81% of the population views climate change as a significant global issue, with *personal responsibility* at 57% (the highest in Europe), positively impacting ecological and human well-being. Kalaniemi et al.[14] asserted that achieving environmental sustainability requires *reducing consumption, significant lifestyle changes,* and *technological innovations*. An increasing number of researchers are concentrating on a particular intersection that investigates customers' responsibility for impulsive behavior within sustainable consumption studies. Spiteri Cornish[53] believe companies should be held accountable for influencing a buying behavior that can be detrimental to consumer well-being.

Unlimited economic development involves addressing social concerns, while sustainable development requires fundamental changes in the behavior of governments, private institutions, and individuals. Lorek and Fuchs[58] emphasized that sustainable consumption involves consumption patterns relevant to industries, governments, and households. According to Liu et al.,[48] changing household consumption patterns is widely recognized as essential for achieving sustainable consumption. Nguyen et al.[124] stress that consumers are active participants and must take responsibility for a sustainable planet. Prior academic research supports the view that most individuals in the developed world consume beyond sustainable levels. However, Pereira Heath and Chatzidakis[47] found that many consumers do not perceive their actions as significantly impacting the environment.

The objective is not to examine power dynamics but to understand how to facilitate change. This book outlines steps businesses can take to encourage responsible consumer choices. It emphasizes taking ultimate responsibility for their part of the equation by considering consumer behavior as a crucial aspect *heavily influenced by commercial and marketing activities* and re-organizing them accordingly.

12. Employ values of impact and activism

The analysis of the *voluntary simplicity lifestyle* using interviews based on the Schwartz Model by Osikominu and Bocken[207] uncovered four *core values* in charge: *stimulation, self-direction, universalism,* and *benevolence*.

- *Stimulation* highlights the importance of excitement, novelty, and life challenges.
- *Self-direction* signifies independent thinking and action, involving making choices, creating, and exploring purposes such as building community connections, resilience, balancing impact and well-being, and contributing to systemic change for the sake of humanity.
- *Universalism* involves appreciating, understanding, tolerating, and protecting all people's and nature's welfare.
- At the same time, *benevolence* focuses on nurturing meaningful relationships, spending quality time, deepening understanding of family and friends, and fostering mutual reliance.

These results align with a key idea of this book: we need active practices, such as self-direction or stimulation, alongside qualities that help us appreciate and aim for the greater good, like universalism or benevolence. Compassion is also gaining popularity, as it is linked to social cohesion. In a comprehensive survey study of 981 participants, Geiger and Keller's[92] findings revealed that *compassion*, the sensitivity to the suffering of other individuals, is also relevant for pro-environmental intentions. Areias et al.[69] confirmed a positive association between *compassion* and *sustainable purchase criteria*. They highlighted that those guiding principles—like *altruism*, willingness to *help*, *activism*, or concern for the *wellness of others and society*—play an essential part in establishing a contrast with the *self-centered (egoistic) principles*, such as guilt-driven, pro-environmental consumption observed in Chatzidakis's[208] research.

13. Deal with uncertainty with straightforwardness

Businesses can assist customers in *navigating uncertainty* by offering essential information influencing personal consumption decisions. For instance, they can encourage the use of reusable products or suggest alternatives, promote reducing meat consumption, suggest local markets instead of supermarkets, and advocate waste sorting with clarity, supported by scientific evidence. There are a bunch of examples from COVID-19 studies showing how people and businesses can establish trust or lose a reputation in a very short time. To illustrate, impulse buying was traditionally associated solely with hedonic motives or positive emotions, or the phenomenon of escapism, where individuals strive to break free from their mundane life situations due to boredom. However, businesses should be informed about the connection between *negative emotions* and *uncertainty* with *impulsive purchases* when dealing with *panic buying*. The COVID-19 lockdown created an uncertain situation that even affected ordinary consumers, who started *panic purchasing*.[209]

Sajid et al.[66] highlighted the impact of *fear of coronavirus* on increased eco-friendly product buying behavior. It is deemed appropriate for business actions to be aligned with *ethical business practices*, prioritizing *consumer support* rather than solely *economic targets* to sell as much as possible. This necessitates *straightforwardness* from business owners and marketers aligning with *responsibility for demand direction* and *care*. Consider embracing *straightforwardness* to foster *trust*. It could be beneficial to be transparent, acknowledging that your solutions are based on available information and not using uncertainty as a push for sales.

14. Understand sustainable degrowth

To Benton,[210] *sustainable degrowth* is both a concept and a social-grassroots movement originating in ecological economics, social ecology, economic anthropology, and environmental and social activist groups. The paradigmatic propositions of degrowth are that unlimited economic growth is not sustainable and that human progress without economic growth is possible. He points to the historical pedigree of degrowth connected to anti-industrialists' views of John Ruskin, William Morris, Henry David Thoreau, and Leo Tolstoy, as well as Edward Goldsmith, E.J. Mishan, Leopold Kohr, E.F. Schumacher, Erich Fromm, Paul Goodman, and Ivan Illich. Georgescu-Roegen, the author of "The Entropy Law and the Economic Process,"[211] challenged what he called the "growth mania" of mainstream economists, and this is where the fount of degrowth intellect lies. Influential works of Georgescu-Roegen led him to be considered "the father of degrowth." Kallis[212] formulated sustainable degrowth as a *downscaling of society's metabolism*, i.e., a degrowth of material production and consumption.

Sekulova et al.[23] found degrowth is generally defined as a collective and deliberative process aimed at the equitable downscaling of the overall capacity to produce and consume. Cosme et al.[213] point out that degrowth is increasingly viewed as a solution to achieving sustainability. Defined by participants of the First International Conference on Economic De-Growth for Ecological Sustainability and Social Equity (Paris, 2008) as a "voluntary transition towards a just, participatory, and ecologically sustainable society," the target of degrowth is creating a new "post-development" pattern that is socially just and within ecological limits.

15. Support sufficiency

Degrowth advocates for *sufficiency lifestyles*, promoting *voluntary simplicity* and *reducing consumption* to meet planetary boundaries. Sufficiency represents a shift toward challenging the dominant social paradigm at individual, community, and societal levels. Lorek and Fuchs[58] described sufficiency as changes in consumption patterns and reductions in consumption levels. Sufficiency involves reshaping consumption practices by using material goods for *extended periods*, *reducing demand*, *minimizing impulsive consumption*, embracing *nonmaterial experiences*, and fostering an *"enoughness" mindset* and behavioral change. Haider et al.[7] highlighted that the "sufficiency turn" of social corporate responsibility can be viewed as the third evolutionary phase at the individual level while also shifting sustainability toward the societal level to challenge the prevailing social paradigm. Sufficiency can manifest on personal, community, or societal scales.

Suggestions focus on *sufficiency lifestyle behaviors* like *brand avoidance* from Kuanr et al.,[165] moderate thinking from Wang et al.,[107] reflection from Dholakia et al.,[120] or self-monitoring suggested by Nguyen et al.[214] Living simpler, less materialistic lives through voluntary simplicity can positively impact individuals, society, and the planet by focusing on *minimal consumption, sustainable choices*, and pursuing *non-materialistic sources of satisfaction*. To Iwata,[215] self-sufficiency, combined with anti-materialism, mindful shopping behaviors, and purchasing durable goods, can curb excessive consumption. This lifestyle shift involves prioritizing time and energy over consumer goods, potentially leading to lower income and consumption levels in exchange for increased free time.

Similar sustainable lifestyles include "eco-villages" and "transition towns." For example, the Global Ecovillage Network[216] brings communities together for a regenerative world through five regional networks and the youth arm, NextGEN, worldwide. With around 10,000 communities and projects promoting ecological harmony, the network connects policymakers, governments, NGOs, academics, entrepreneurs, activists, and individuals worldwide to develop strategies for resilient communities and cultures. Eco-villages promote *belonging through community* ties, shared objectives, and social processes, aiming to establish economic practices that support *resource sharing, mutual aid,* and robust *local economies*. They actively seek *sustainable alternatives* to the mainstream economy and *monetary systems*, redefining wealth and progress *holistically*. Key features include *local currencies, sharing, social entrepreneurship, circular economy,* and *collaborative ownership*.

16. Promote voluntary simplicity

The concept of *voluntary simplicity*, rooted in historical and philosophical origins, evolved from ideas like Thoreau's transcendentalism centered on the value of embracing a *simple life,* the *beauty of nature,* and the *interconnectedness* that ideally should unite all living beings, emphasizing living with *minimal possessions* for deliberate life organization. It advocates for a *simple outward life* and *rich inward experience* as an alternative to modern stressful and consumption-driven lifestyles. Our research-related types of sustainable consumption in the voluntary simplicity driven group also encompass *anti-consumption, frugality,* and *minimalism*. Minimalism is often associated with *slow consumption* and *zero-waste living*.

Osikominu and Bocken researched the *values, practices, and impacts* of the *voluntary simplicity lifestyle*. Their article, "A Voluntary Simplicity Lifestyle: Values, Adoption, Practices, and Effects,"[207] explores the various values of this lifestyle choice:

1. "*Self-direction*" underscores the importance of independent thought and action, encouraging a life characterized by choice, creativity, and exploration.

2. The value of "*stimulation*" emphasizes the significance of excitement, novelty, and confronting life's challenges. Numerous interviewees expressed dissatisfaction with work-centric and consumption-driven lifestyles, leading them to favor voluntary simplicity.

3. "*Benevolence*" highlights enhancing well-being in close relationships, fostering *meaningful connections,* and deepening *familial and friendly ties.*

4. The value of *"universalism"* advocates for tolerance, understanding, and protection for all beings and the environment.

Participants in their study embraced *diversity*, sought *equality and justice*, and aimed to *minimize harm* through their actions, reflecting a strong *spiritual connection to nature*. They named external triggers people pointed to as *factors that switch them for voluntary simplicity*: dissatisfaction, stress, negative materialistic experiences, and personal traumas. These situations prompted them to engage in introspection and *self-identity reevaluation*, leading to their adopting the *voluntary simplicity lifestyle*.

17. Showcase anti-consumption effects

A study by Hobson[36] calls for "stronger" interventions such as those expounded by the degrowth movement, where change is needed in consumer behavior because "weak sustainable consumption" governance cannot address the challenges of sustainable development. Lorek and Fuchs[57] suggest the linkages between consumption and sustainable development can be more effectively explored by adopting a "strong sustainable consumption" perspective. *Strong sustainable consumption* calls for decreased consumption levels, where anti-consumption is one of the instruments available.

Anti-consumption involves two types of action: (1) intentionally *rejecting* or (2) *reusing items* to *avoid acquiring material goods*. It promotes frugality and voluntary simplicity to *save resources* and *reduce waste*, but may *conflict with green consumption* due to its materialistic footprint. Research has suggested promoting anti-consumption by highlighting the advantages of reduced consumption for *human well-being*, aiming to *reduce impulsive buying* and encourage sustainable consumption. Ling Xie et al.[182] found that anti-consumption results from three factors: *animal welfare, environmental sustainability attitudes*, and *consumers' lifestyles*. For *lifestyles*, it will be helpful to focus on the *personal benefits of anti-consumption*, which may be more effective than emphasizing larger *societal concerns*. Kuanr et al.[165] revealed that individualistic values influence anti-consumption behaviors through *self-efficacy*. Businesses could use promotion efforts to strengthen *consumer self-belief* and *behavior empowerment*, showcasing the advantages of anti-consumption and embracing a simplistic way of life. It could involve the benefits of *balanced healthy food habits* or maintaining a *healthy level of savings free of impulsive purchases*. Shahpasandi et al.[100] suggest consumers may be reminded that when they impulsively buy items they do not need they later *regret their purchases*, or the fact that they are not required to follow the *mainstream materialistic culture*. Dholakia et al.[217] suggest that promotion of anti-consumption could be based on such practices as *boycotting brands* or *intermittent fasting*. *Religion and spirituality* have been found to significantly influence believers' lives for millennia by offering direction on consumption and guiding daily *anti-materialistic behaviors*. For instance, Muslim consumers avoid pork, while Indians refrain from beef. Religious dietary practices are famous for their norms for *fasting periods*, both short and extended—the study by Ling Xie et al.[182] revealed a moderating effect of religiosity between *meat anti-consumption* and *human well-being*, confirming that meat anti-consumption for consumer well-being can be enhanced through *religiosity*. Azazz and Elshaer[218] agreed that religiosity could significantly influence and shape moral behavior, overcoming the consumerism ideology. Nepomuceno and Laroche[91] remind us that religious and spiritual practices hold a longstanding promotion of *anti-materialistic values*.

For *environmental concerns*, education plays a crucial role in promoting sustainable consumption. Educating individuals on their *consumption habits' environmental impact* and providing them with the knowledge and *skills to make more informed choices* can empower them to become responsible consumers. Besides personal efforts, *institutional changes* are vital for promoting sustainable consumption. This involves enacting policies that *support reduced resource utilization* and *waste reduction* and offering *incentives for embracing sustainable practices*. Iyer and Muncy[109] suggest that creating incentives to reduce consumption or establishing consequences for overconsumption would probably resonate better with consumers than mandates that enforce reduced consumption.

18. Promote minimalism

Understanding the *development path for minimalists*, de Mendonça et al.[219] proposed a visual representation of a *non-linear minimalist "becoming" as a process* composed of overlapped stages such as *awakening, learning, adaptation,* and *transformation*. They referred to the movement's *beginners* and *veterans* by showing the developmental parts of minimalism. Through becoming minimalists, the participants constructed identity narratives around personal projects, using *coping strategies* and *compensatory mechanisms* to achieve "a better life." For example, they agreed that "less is more" in consumption, but there was no consensus on what that statement meant, so they adapted *consumption practices on their path* toward "happiness." Their research offers to support customers by developing suitable offers that help consumers in their *minimalism journey*. I am a long-time advocate for minimalism, and my personal factor was the beauty of simplicity. Bardey et al.[181] acknowledge that originally related to *music, art,* and *architecture*, minimalism is now associated with *interiors* or *beauty*. Best known for having *clean, contemporary lines, monochromatic color palettes, architectural flare,* and *timeless nature*, minimalism represents its own category in fashion. Inspired by fashion brands and designers such as Issey Miyake, Yohjii Yamamoto, and Acne Studios, the minimalist style stems from two leading cultures: Scandinavian and Japanese. Leo Babauta's take on minimalism (as detailed on https://mnmlist.com/minimalist-faqs/) involves *shedding unused or unnecessary items* to create a clean, *uncomplicated environment* and *lifestyle*. It means living without fixating on possessions or *overwhelming oneself with tasks*, opting for *minimal possessions*, a *simple wardrobe, light belongings*, and a *carefree approach to life*. However, if you have less stuff, this alone will not make you minimalist. Minimalism is a way of living, characterized by an *orientation of valuing fewer goods*, achieved through consumption restriction as well as minimizing possessions. The "feature-frugal approach" guides individuals to *concentrate on the essentials*. In "Minimalism Explained," by Colin Wright,[220] minimalism is illuminated as a *reevaluation of priorities* to discard *unnecessary possessions, ideas, relationships,* and *activities*. The primary goal is to embrace life to the fullest rather than amass possessions for the sake of it.

Kakkar et al.[221] explained that minimalism as a practice is now increasingly inculcated in the *product design* process, wherein any additional features that may distract users are taken away while keeping the bare essentials. This *"feature-frugal approach"* helps individuals to maintain focus and not indulge in unnecessary consumption attitudes. We may refer to the *no-frills business model* seen in *budget airlines*, *discount retailers*, *vacations*, and *used vehicles*, which aligns with minimalism.

Bardey et al.[181] discussed the impact of fashion overconsumerism and overproduction, which have led to the fashion industry becoming one of the most polluting industries globally, introducing the *capsule wardrobe trend*. While the study's participants initially associated sustainability with using sustainable materials in fashion, they later recognized the influence of their actions on overconsumption. The study highlights that the three-week minimalist closet experience has helped them detach from fashion trends' pressure and allowed them to find joy in their *personal style*.

19. Actively support zero-waste movement

The zero-waste initiative strives to *reduce waste* by advocating practices prioritizing recycling, reusing, recovering, and repairing. For individuals, adopting a zero-waste lifestyle may involve *buying second-hand items*, using *reusable bags and containers*, *composting food scraps*, and *avoiding single-use products*. This movement encourages consumers to *rethink their consumption habits* and *minimize their environmental impact*. Bardey et al.[181] suggest expanding interest in the zero-waste movement, focusing on *sustainable alternatives* and *resource efficiency*; the zero-waste initiative seeks to create a circular economy where *materials are used for as long as possible*, ultimately leading to a cleaner and healthier planet for future generations.

The press release titled "Right to Repair: Making Repair Easier and More Appealing to Consumers"[222] highlights the reinforcement of repair rights. The directive—supported by 584 votes in favor, 3 against, and 14 abstentions—aims to boost the repair sector, reduce waste, and make repairing goods more accessible and cost-effective.

It clarifies manufacturers' *repair obligations*, promotes *extending product lifecycles* through repairs, and ensures *timely and economical repair services*. Additionally, consumers are informed about their repair rights, with goods repaired under warranty receiving a one-year extension of the legal guarantee to encourage repair over replacement. Consumers will have rights to repair technically repairable products under ecodesign measures, with manufacturers offering repair services and spare parts. A European platform will connect consumers with repairers, refurbished goods sellers, and local repair initiatives. The European Commission has introduced a proposal for a directive on the right to repair, effective from July 31, 2026.

Customers do not need to wait for a specified date, as they can choose companies that already offer repair and parts sales services. For example, Brabantia is committed to achieving 100% circular design, known as cradle-to-cradle, where materials and components can be repurposed or recycled indefinitely (yes, including compostable waste bags). They started by addressing a minor issue with the touch-lock mechanism of their waste bins. By focusing on this issue, they provided a spare part at a nominal fee, allowing all customers to replace it with ease. Additionally, since 2014, Brabantia has formed a partnership with WeForest, allowing customers to support tree planting initiatives with each purchase of a dryer or drying rack. As a result, over 2.8 million trees have been planted in areas such as Amhara, Desa'a in Ethiopia, and Burkina Faso. In 2023, Brabantia received its official B Corp certification, acknowledging its positive impact on both people and the environment.

I was fascinated with the consumer engagement level in the Brabantia manifesto, which the company placed on their website (www.brabantia.com/):

> Call it a purpose, a mission or even a compulsion. Whatever words you choose, it's a real thing. Caring for others and the environment, caring for the earth that nurtures us, the air we breathe and the water that helps us flourish. We're not perfect, but we're all responsible and we all have a part to play. Some small, some big. It's in everything we do and always has been. We create products where beauty meets sustainability. And right

now, it's more important than ever. Why? Because there's no longer a choice between profit or planet. We're entering a period in time where all of us have the chance to make a difference. With every action we take, with every decision we make. That's why we're choosing to leave the next generation a legacy, not a mess. We're making the move to 100% circular design by 2035. How about you?

Another example is ePowerFun, a German company founded by a passionate entrepreneur. After completing a banking apprenticeship, studying business administration with a marketing focus, and gaining experience in various advertising agencies, Stefan Köhler successfully transitioned his hobby into a career. Since 1998, he has overseen the marketing and sales of RC cars for the renowned brand "HPI Racing" in Germany and Austria. Since 2017, Köhler has been avidly using electric skateboards and e-scooters, including at iconic locations like the Hockenheimring and the legendary Nordschleife of the Nürburgring. This passion led to the creation of ePowerFun.de GmbH. The company offers a wide range of spare parts at affordable prices on its website (https://epowerfun.de). Moreover, the scooters are conveniently packaged in cardboard boxes available for separate purchase, providing a practical solution for relocations.

The next resource sample addresses the realm of *second-hand clothing*, which once dominated a significant market share in the previous century owing to economic constraints. However, its prevalence waned as the economy progressed. It is *reemerging in light of environmental concerns* stemming from resource wastage despite the products being more cost-effective nowadays. *Second-hand clothing is a movement* that is no longer limited to small corners of the world. An article titled "Why eBay is Showing Secondhand Fashion on the Runway," by Webb,[223] highlights eBay's efforts to elevate pre-loved fashion by participating in the New York and London fashion schedules. How does this contribute to the broader goal of establishing a circular economy for all? This initiative aims to *raise awareness* and *elevate pre-loved fashion*, with significant success shown in increased searches for sustainable fashion after similar previous campaigns. eBay's strategy is integrating second-hand fashion into mainstream culture through high-profile events like the Endless Runway shows. According to a study by Lang and Zhang,[224] more than half of the users with no experience trading idle items will consider trading second-hand items online or offline in the following year.

Recycling and upcycling are vital practices in sustainability, repurposing old materials into new ones. They help in reducing waste and carbon footprint. Recycling takes old materials and breaks them down into new materials that can be used for other products. Upcycling involves creatively *reusing old materials to give them new value*. These practices can range from transforming old textiles into a new jacket to repurposing various items like wine corks, plates, magazines, and more into functional or decorative pieces. The idea of upcycling envisions transforming old goods into new treasures, potentially supported by businesses providing platforms for creating, showcasing, and selling upcycled items.

Freecycling is at the heart of a nonprofit effort where people freely exchange items within their communities. For instance, the nonprofit organization Freecycle (www.freecycle.org/) has local groups worldwide where members can post items they want to give away or request items they need. Everything is free, intending to *keep usable items out of landfills*. Dholakia et al.[217] discussed *dumpster living*, which involves salvaging valuable items from containers discarded by their owners. Individuals may find themselves searching for discarded items, but *society can elevate this by offering assistance and boosting self-esteem* for those seeking help. For example, the website www.interregeurope.eu/ promotes details about projects like the *Social Refrigerator* best practices. The foundation wezpomoz.pl, meaning "lend a hand," actively supports individuals by providing food assistance. Its efforts involve distributing food to needy people, setting up social refrigerators, stocking them, and collaborating with food banks. A social refrigerator in Wrocław allows residents to deposit and retrieve food, irrespective of their financial situation, following specified guidelines. This food-sharing concept originated from students in Germany who noticed the benefit of sharing surplus food in dorms. The initiative has distributed around 21,000 kg of food packages to those in need, equating to 470 packages per week, across the 16 social refrigerators in Wrocław. Restaurants, bars, bakeries, and grocery stores frequently contribute to the social refrigerator. Volunteers, donors, or recipients can post details and images on a dedicated Facebook group to publicize a sudden influx of donations.

We can do numerous things as creative beings, and innovative practices emerge when we redirect our focus from ourselves to the community and society.

20. Promote sharing economy

White et al.[194] highlighted that a sharing economy demonstrates a substantial case where joint environmental and economic gains are possible. Haider et al.[7] emphasize the social gain of the *non-reciprocal aspect of sharing* as it fosters *joint ownership*, creating an extended connection to those we share with. He illustrates the benefits of sharing through examples like mothering and "share-consuming" resources within a household, behaviors that *build bonds*, *break relationship barriers*, and *enhance well-being*. Dermody et al.[225] concluded that this helps to encourage alternate economic perspectives that are not Western masculinist but related to the *community*.

However, an article by Eckhardt and Bardhi[226] examined the disruption caused by the sharing economy with convenient and cost-effective access to resources without the burdens of ownership. Using the example of Zipcar, the authors illustrate that users who engage with Zipcar experience a *lack of reciprocal obligations*, resulting in an anonymous experience akin to staying at a hotel, where interactions among users are minimal despite sharing vehicles. The authors conclude that this evolving perspective signifies a transition from the sharing economy to an *access economy*. Airbnb and Uber offer individuals the chance to earn income by sharing their space and providing transportation services through a platform that, in turn, also offers various other services like payment systems, security, guarantees, communication norms, and more. Another example of sharing is given through the lens of the gig economy. It involved cases when individuals provide their services part-time or casually to companies, regardless of size.

From a sustainable consumption perspective, sharing helps *reduce resource consumption* and *waste*. Like the sufficiency economy, the sharing economy has gained considerable attention, with examples like shared access to *public infrastructure*, including public transport and streetlights. Sharing a car or communal laundry experience offers different benefits than sharing a meal experience, enhancing psychological well-being. Yet, Shaikh et al.[83] emphasize that advantages of the sharing economy remain beneficial for everyone. For example, *longevity* is a crucial aspect of overconsumption, with second-hand clothing being viewed as an ethical and sustainable choice, underscored by retailers specializing in second-hand items. Chakraborty and Sadachar[227] believe such information helps to increase purchase intentions for used/rented apparel. This is in line with the offer from Lee[201] to inform customers that commercial sharing systems assist materially simple and sustainable lifestyles. Utilizing commercial sharing systems, whether public, commercial, or personal, promotes social engagement with underutilized resources and decreases waste disposal. Szmigin et al.[228] assure that *marketing strategies that resonate with consumers' emphasis* on thrift, value, and sustainability—within the context of a leaner sharing economy—are crucial.

Foster triple-win mindset: key takeaways

1. Stand with people: share ultimate responsibility
2. Employ values of impact and activism
3. Deal with uncertainty with straightforwardness
4. Understand sustainable degrowth
5. Support sufficiency
6. Promote voluntary simplicity
7. Showcase anti-consumption effects
8. Promote minimalism
9. Actively support zero-waste movement
10. Promote sharing economy

9

Create impact, becoming a positive force for people and the planet

Social and problem-solving skills encompass the ability to excel in social systems through adaptability, communication, conflict management, and collaboration. Key competencies for businesses to create impact are involving people, getting support, and helping to transform. This includes connecting with others, being a team player within the community, managing change and conflict, building bonds, and fostering teamwork. These skills facilitate positive interpersonal relationships and enable businesses to connect with and positively impact communities, standing with people.

21. Base on those customers who care about sustainable consumption and social stability

Do you know who *superfans* are and what their role is? Neuroeconomist and Professor Paul Zak discuss the role of "superfans"[130] using the term for those customers whose immersion in the brand is very high. These people spend time and money promoting brands and easily share information on social media. To illustrate, he pointed out that all major studios have departments that create opportunities for superfans to continuously engage with content from their favorite TV shows and movie franchises, where identifying attributes of superfans enables entertainment distributors to engage them almost immediately. Superfans are a segment of customers who believe in the brand, and they serve as a solid base for further development, advocating for products and services. Ramos-Hidalgo et al.[90] pointed out that managers should target a group of customers who *already emphasize* the importance of sustainable practices. How could such customers be identified?

Demographic criteria could be used, such as *age*—research by Shaikh et al.[83] suggested companies must target young consumers since they generally try to align their consumption habits to ensure *minimum harm to societies* and the *larger environment* (ages 18–25). Next, we already discussed that consumers' values should be at a center. For example, Ahmed et al.[229] investigated how *green customer value* (e.g., *environmental image* and *perceived value*), *green attitude*, and the *green marketing mix* (product, packaging, price, promotion, place) influence green purchasing intentions. Their study revealed a significant positive relationship between all these influences and *green purchasing intentions*.

Oh and Chul[230] suggest since *ethics* is one of the main drivers for sustainable consumption, target consumer groups would be *receptive to ethical appeals*. *Ethical obligation* is a *consumer's perception* or behavior that shifts consumption from a personal concern to a societal one and impacts ethical consumption intentions positively. Interestingly, *environmentally responsible consumption* may stem from moral emotions, such as *guilt*. For example, Areias et al.[69] *point out that studies* both on connectedness to nature and guilt have consistently shown linkages with *pro-environmental behavior*. However, it has been discovered that although guilt can enhance pro-environmental actions and consumption, it only does so under reparatory circumstances or up to a specific fear threshold. Additionally, guilt may lead to hazardous and norm-violating behavior. Hence, it is advisable to refrain from using negative emotions as catalysts for sustainable consumption in business marketing campaigns. Instead of relying on negative emotions, businesses should focus on positive messaging and solutions-oriented approaches associated with sustainable consumption.

According to a study by Ling Xie et al.,[182] *consumer social responsibility* is pivotal in influencing anti-consumption practices. Their study also found that sustainable consumption is associated with *religiosity*, moderating the relationship between meat anti-consumption and human well-being. Azazz and Elshaer[218] agreed that religiosity could significantly influence and shape moral behavior, deterring religious individuals from participating in socially unethical activities and showcasing its significant impact. Thus, their research aligns with a prior study by Rayner and Easthope,[231] which concluded that the religious world might support overcoming the consumption ideology where different factors are associated with consumption, such as social, economic, or lifestyle. Spinelli et al.[232] highlighted that understanding how people with religious, *spiritual*, or secular values behave in the marketplace could be strategically important.

22. Be aware of lifestyle, the unique way values and beliefs are behaviorally expressed

Lifestyle represents the distinctive characteristics that aid in identifying people, who already support ideas of sustainable consumption. Horleys[233] explains that *lifestyle* is the unique way values and beliefs are behaviorally expressed and operationalized through personal construct ratings of daily activities. Lu et al.[177] define it as a psychological concept that encompasses how individuals behave in their daily routines. Pícha and Navrátil[234] point out that one of the recent trends in consumer markets is the Lifestyle of Health and Sustainability, commonly known as LOHAS. Höfer[235] explains that these consumers are seen as environmentally aware, socially attuned, and with a view of the world that considers personal, community, and planetary outcomes. It can be challenging to identify socio-demographic groups that are LOHAS consumers. However, they have *behavioral similarities*. They tend to favor local producers, seek high-quality and effective *natural products*, and can be seen as "*early adopters*" who look for the latest recipes, formulas, and *technologies*, investing in *personal development*. Urh[236] add that these consumers invest in mind–body–spirit connections, *self-help*, *leadership*, and spirituality connected with *ecological lifestyles*.

Ramos-Hidalgo et al.[237] emphasized the importance of sustainable *customers with an active position*. For instance, Market Forces activists discovered that investment choices marked as "sustainable" or "socially responsible" in super funds were still fossil fuel firms, such as coal producer Whitehaven and prominent oil and gas companies. This revelation sparked heated debates on social media platforms and led to conversations advocating for increased socially responsible fund alternatives as a choice for individual investors. Consumers appreciate bank services that endorse climate change initiatives, following the same principle.

Enthusiastic advocates of sustainable consumption could also be explored among those customers who *prioritize well-being*. They are transitioning toward leisurely activities at home and with family, cultivating a profound reverence for nature and an uncomplicated lifestyle marked by intentional *simplicity*, *thriftiness*, *humility*, and *modesty*.

23. Support local communities

Stronger connections among people lead to mutual support and thriving local businesses; people love supporting others. For example, in Cyprus, the Cypriot and English communities showcased this bond through shopping preferences. While Cypriots frequented local brand Kokkinos supermarkets, the English opted for Metro or Lidl. Amidst the pandemic, Alion emerged as a successful organic and plant-based delivery service, uniting individuals from diverse backgrounds under a shared passion for a healthy lifestyle. Alion's reputation soared as a delivery platform that ensured fresh produce from local farms reached consumers within 24 hours. Its success story is a testament to the power of local businesses in promoting sustainable living, inspiring others to follow suit.

According to Chang and Watchravesringkan,[166] collaboration with local communities is not only beneficial but crucial for promoting local services. Customers now actively seek businesses connected closely with local communities to offer sustainable products, transcending beyond just food—for example, Bardey et al.[181] emphasized that consumers look toward fashion brands to champion local businesses and communities, echoing this sentiment. Lee and Wan[62] suggest not forgetting about informative content for the local community, focusing on socially responsible food products, fair-trade items, and goods from rural farmers. Shobeiri et al.[192] suggest that it is also possible to organize new connections based on sub-segmentation, such as the connection of like-minded responsible consumers through supporting online and new offline communities.

24. Build knowledge communities

Another way to overcome vulnerability and grow stronger together is by *creating communities*. Ahmed et al.[229] suggest there is a growing demand for *knowledge communities*. Wei Jie et al.[61] proposed that establishing knowledge communities could be an innovative strategy to encourage knowledge-sharing and learning from one another and provide a platform for skills development and continuous improvement. Sajid et al.[66] suggest such communities can exist in physical, virtual, or hybrid forms and act as a central hub connecting different players such as producers, retailers, manufacturers, and consumers while also being the focal point of knowledge. For instance, Kakkar et al.[221] refer to the app "Headspace," which allows users to form meditation groups, exchange experiences, and engage in diverse mindfulness practices. "Headspace" operates on a subscription model, but businesses may opt for different networking approaches. Next, the TV channel "Gaia" offers free subscriptions with mindfulness-related content and organizes offline events. The "Gaia" audience is international, with the company event center situated in Boulder, Colorado. Rather than selling tickets for online participation in separate events, the TV channel provides a paid subscription that includes all on-demand recordings of events.

Emphasizing knowledge sharing within communities, Kuanr et al.[165] recommend embracing *experiential testimonies*. This entails shifting the focus from simply rating brands or product characteristics to the genuine experiences of actual buyers whose consumption behaviors benefit the environment or the development of mental health. Ahmed et al.[229] pointed out that sharing experiences enhances *green word-of-mouth strategies*. During his TEDx talk in Busan, South Korea, activist Daniel Hires stressed, "When we get together today, we usually get together to consume."[238]

He emphasized the shift needed from consuming to creating when we gather. He highlighted the profound connection formed through collaborative creation, enabling insight into others' passions, origins, and aspirations for the future. Daniel suggests that *shared experiences create deep, meaningful connections*. Therefore, he suggests we better cook together rather than get food at the restaurant; play together instead of sitting individually with a computer; or create something together rather than order a service from somebody else. Significant others' influence can inspire and encourage people to make thoughtful, sustainable choices. By *socially adopting practices* supporting sustainable consumption, we cultivate a deeper connection with each other and our environment and lay the foundation for more sustainable social and cultural values.

25. Cultivate a "being more human" approach

During COVID-19, business and customer relationships were shaken, and some enterprises capitalized on FOMO and fear of the virus. Cho et al.[65] showed the significance of *emotions* in determining individuals' behavioral impulses. Instead, Trzebiński et al.[239] found that higher *hope levels*, *life meaning*, and *satisfaction* correlated with reduced anxiety and COVID-19 stress. These findings suggest that *emotional factors may buffer against anxiety* and unproductive thoughts during *uncertainty*. Yanmei Jiang[240] opted for a *more humane approach*, emphasizing the importance of understanding consumer cognition during outbreaks such as COVID. Areias et al.[69] point to raising awareness of emotional responses among consumers and enhancing emotional stability. White et al.[194] propose cultivating emotions such as awe, empathy, and moral elevation, which provide promising avenues. They argue that anti-consumption does not necessarily lead to deprivation or reduced quality of life. Instead, Markauskaitė and Rūtelionė[203] suggest it can enhance happiness.

White et al.[194] explain that *to stay on one side with a customer means "being more human,"* providing a positive effect, sometimes termed the "warm glow." It is vital in how individuals, companies, and brands are judged, as warm individuals tend to foster cooperative relationships. This perception of warmth, linked to sincerity, correlates with brand loyalty, affection, and positive word-of-mouth. Tang et al.[241] conducted eight studies showing that even indulgent consumption can signal interpersonal warmth, leading to positive effects. The study revealed that healthy eating is often perceived as lacking the warmth associated with indulgent consumption, which is frequently regarded as more expensive and linked to higher social status. Essentially, healthy eating may be viewed as psychologically "colder." Marketers can aim to convey warmth to enhance the appeal of healthy products. By promoting a "more human" approach to sustainable consumption through a friendly image, businesses can counteract the products' perceived lack of emotional appeal and guide consumers toward healthier choices. Cultivating a *warm image* is vital for nurturing strong customer relationships and fostering *consumer trust*.

Khalil and Khalil[77] found that social and *environmental sustainability awareness practices* positively influence green *consumer trust*. Under the adverse greenwashing business effect, *consumers' trust* is gaining intense importance. Thus, Lu et al.[180] found that *greenwashing* influences consumer *attitudes*, fostering suspicion and distrust toward corporate green advertising tactics and diminishing consumers' buying power. When companies engage in greenwashing to deceive consumers, it hinders the development of trust and long-term relationships, ultimately lowering purchase intentions. Ramadan et al.[242] state *consumers' trust* is considered a critical factor that governs relationships in a typical retailer–consumer relationship. However, their study is the first to demonstrate that retailers' membership programs, such as Amazon Prime, may come at *the expense of consumers*. These programs reinforce impulsive behavior while giving the shopper a *false sense of self-control* and *affective attachments*, which paradoxically enhances shoppers' ties to retailers, leading to *increased impulsive purchases*. When those actions are understood, consumer trust in a business can erode rapidly, posing a challenge to regain.

26. Mind social consciousness phenomenon

Ling Xie et al.[182] have shown a positive impact of consumer *social responsibility* toward anti-consumption due to moral avoidance for humans and the environment. Tariq et al.[184] referred to the phenomenon of *social consciousness*, which was identified as a new factor that aids in controlling consumption. There is an emphasis on *health consciousness* influencing overconsumption; for example, the idea that excess meat leads to elevated blood cholesterol levels, disrupting consumer attitudes and fostering disillusionment and detachment from consumption. Gupta and Mukherjee[104] noted that consumers are increasingly aware of human vulnerabilities, showing concern for pollution and climate change *impacts on health* and *the environment*, and acknowledging the drawbacks of excessive consumption and binge shopping—a separate study by Peluso et al.[243] corroborated these findings, exploring pro-environmental and *sustainable expenditure*, which surged by 10% amid the pandemic.

This illustrates how *shared negative emotions* like fear can drive impulsive consumer behavior. The pandemic has dramatically increased an individual's safety and health concerns, and people are increasingly focused on health benefits. Using China as a sample, Qi and Ploeger[244] emphasized that health consciousness emerges as one significant driver of green food purchase intention. This correlates with previous findings that consumers' health concerns are one of the primary determinants influencing their environmentally friendly food behavior intentions.

27. Understand the influencing direction of social networks

Individuals are influenced by their *social networks*, such as *peers*, *family*, and *friends*, which shape their choices based on their surroundings. Observing others embrace sustainable practices can

Create impact, becoming a positive force for people & the planet   141

inspire individuals to do the same, with *peer influence* and the need for *social belonging* playing a pivotal role in promoting sustainable consumption, as per Asuamah Yeboah.[197] Salazar et al.[245] found evidence that specific social groups influence the buying behavior of sustainable products, with information from *family and friends* being more consistent and impactful. Hence, Wei Jie et al.[61] suggest marketing managers may rely on significant others to impact sustainable consumers' purchasing decisions.

Consumer social groups such as family, friends, and other reference groups were found to play a vital role in *avoidance behavior*. Shahzad et al.[246] demonstrated the importance of *social influence* in the context of Chinese consumers, with *health consciousness* being the most prominent factor of soft drink anti-consumption. Their study highlighted that consumers believe their actions help reduce obesity, with previous studies providing supporting evidence for obesity reduction and health consciousness. Their results clearly demonstrate the positive impact of social influence on anti-consumption behavior. However, they emphasized that these results may not be suitable across all collective societies, such as in Pakistan, *where socialization influences soft drink consumption positively*.

In this context, understanding the dynamics of social influence, including *marketing communication* and the impact of *social media*, is crucial for developing strategies that encourage sustainable behaviors. A prior review of *social media influence* revealed an emphasis on persuading customers to care more about environmental issues and decrease their consumption. Ling Xie et al.[182] highlighted *social marketing* as a strategy for targeted social transformation linking consumer habits to public health, and may emphasize reducing consumption of specific products. Zafar et al.[63] noted that *social influences* affecting consumption are increasingly gaining traction, including *trust, social interactions*, and *parasocial relationships* with *key opinion leaders*.

Chiu et al.[64] advised that managers actively engage in social networks and create more opportunities for social interactions online. Ghaffar et al.[247] highlighted the pivotal role of social media in *content development, idea exchange*, and *opinion sharing*, significantly enhancing *communication between consumers and companies*—and greatly improving communication between consumers and businesses, particularly those promoting eco-friendly products—by offering customers a more engaging shopping experience. Ling Xie et al.[182] summarized that an essential role of social marketing has emerged in the current era that suggests favorable social activities can enhance sustainable consumption.

28. Invite key opinion leaders, not merely influencers

Hamdan and Abdullah[248] point out that *key opinion leaders* traditionally emerge from fields of expertise and are recognized for their knowledge and authority, while *influencers* often gain popularity through relatable content and engagement. There is a growing demand for key opinion leaders' influence to encourage a *sufficiency lifestyle*. Wang et al.[50] propose that key opinion leaders play a crucial role in knowledge communities and engage in public service ads. Wei Jie et al.[61] *revealed that* community influence, in return, fosters collaboration with entrepreneurs. White et al.[194] suggest that linking sustainable options to aspirational *role models*, like celebrities and athletes known for *their healthy lifestyles* and *mental well-being*, can enhance the social desirability of such behaviors.

However, *social climate* can also stimulate *impulsive buying*. Analyzing the enduring impact of social influences is essential for achieving long-term change—the study's results by Tariq et al.[184] revealed that Chinese online *organic food consumerism* is transferring from e-commerce to *social commerce*. Pellegrino et al.[80] discovered that *the link between the intensity of social media* and impulsive consumption behavior strongly and significantly influences *materialism* and *consumption*. Exploring socially mediated interactive patterns, Zafar et al.[63] examine actual purchasing behaviors like online *shopping frequency*, *hedonic browsing*, and *flow experience*. They indicate that deriving pleasure from engaging with content fosters parasocial connections between users and digital celebrities. Fashion companies capitalize on this by utilizing digital celebrities' influence in marketing to steer potential consumers toward impulsive buying. This impact is utilized by creating initiatives that transform digital celebrities into brand evangelists and building customer communities around parasocial interactions. Lu et al.[180] discussed impulsive buying in the fast-fashion industry as irrational consumer behavior manifested by buying more than needed, instinctively and impulsively, exceeding the purchase plan, and generating waste.

Another study by Lee and Wan[62] assessed how the *perceived value* of mukbang watching mediates the relationship between *stimuli*, *impulse food purchase*, and consumption *intention*. Mukbang is a Korean term that means "eating broadcast." It refers to a video in which the host eats large amounts of food while interacting with viewers on social media. All three studies in this research demonstrated that components of perceived value—*utilitarian, hedonic*, and *social value*—influence consumers' willingness to eat and buy food while watching mukbang live streaming shopping. Thus, watching such live streaming results in *overconsumption behaviors*. Brandão and Cupertino de Miranda[89] suggest that utilizing influencers who share their experiences is acceptable; however, they emphasize the critical need to expand the understanding of influencers and their consumption behavior.

29. Promote pro-social behavior

According to Geiger and Keller[92] *compassion*, as a moral emotion, significantly complements abstract *altruistic values* (e.g., helpfulness or social justice) as guiding moral principles in life. They suggest that the *pro-social behaviors* associated with *compassion* (such as alleviating others' potential pain) promote increased sustainable practices. A strong trend is calling for pro-social behaviors, where the "sharing economy" showcases significant environmental and economic benefits.[194]

Shaikh et al.[83] determined that when consumers engage in the sharing economy, they not only meet others but also exhibit pro-social behavior, even amid commercialization. This fosters *social belonging*, consumer *well-being*, and *reduces wasteful consumption* for materialistic consumers. Wei Jie et al.[61] *emphasize that* sharing economic experiences can help restore social connectedness previously lost to *materialism*. Suggestions such as these propose creating knowledge *communities* where entrepreneurs may use community influence. Shaikh et al.[83] invite promoting "*self-transformation*" through *pro-social behaviors*.

Dermody et al.[225] suggest encompassing the *commons-orientated people power* advocated by the United Nations. Liegey and Nelson discuss commons and communing in their insightful guide, "Exploring Degrowth."[249] They highlight co-created, co-governed, and co-accessed cultural and natural resources and related activities, emphasizing that this is a critical question in degrowth. Activists suggest creating and experimenting with new types of co-governance that are notably more equal, transparent, democratic, and sustainable than those influenced by market logic. Kuanr et al.[165] suggested that companies involved in *collectivistic appeals* may use social marketing campaigns to highlight the impact of their anti-consumption practices on the broader community.

30. Promote pro-environmental behavior

Initially, customers must learn about environmental issues to encourage pro-environmental purchasing behavior. Disseminating knowledge about environmental issues, especially their consequences in our daily lives, remains crucial. Our disconnection from nature has led to children fearing animals and insects, with little awareness of plant names, let alone their culinary or medicinal uses. For that reason, Areias et al.[250] offered to enhance human relationships with nature and the environment and use *connectedness* to enhance pro-environmental consumption. Their study found that *environmental altruism* is *connectedness*, an internal value that leads to behavior that benefits the natural environment without expecting anything in return. They considered *consumerism a symptom of separation*, consisting of constantly pursuing ethereal moments of excitement under promises of self-esteem and belonging through fashion advertisements and social media. This leads to an underlying insight that reconnection can positively impact fashion consumption. Their study confirmed that measuring connectedness and relating connectedness to pro-environmental consumption are positive and present solid levels of reliability. The concept of connectedness underscores the importance of cultivating care for others and the environment, reducing social and environmental burdens.

The principles, such as *recycling*, *reusing*, and *repairing*, are favored among environmental advocates, including proponents of the circular economy, voluntary simplicity practitioners, and degrowth movement supporters. It can be effectively integrated into production through the extension of warranty periods. For example, this summer, I noted that BOSH is now offering a ten-year warranty on their air conditioners, a significant improvement from the previous standard of approximately five years. To extend warranty periods, manufacturers must possess confidence in the long-term quality of their products, which aligns with sustainable production principles. This can also be accomplished by providing affordable, modular upgrades to minimize waste. For instance, Fairphone, a Dutch electronics manufacturer, designs and produces smartphones and headphones that are committed to reducing their products' ethical and environmental impact. Fairphone ensures fair labor practices for its workforce and suppliers using recycled, fair trade, and conflict-free materials. Furthermore, the company facilitates user repairs through modular design and access to replacement parts, encouraging device longevity and contributing to sustainability initiatives.

It became habitual to have your nearest recycling point in the EU where organizations place educational information about them and their work, such as this:

> The company is a non-profit organization which will distribute the reusable clothes to not so well-off families either within Cyprus or abroad. Other textiles, including clothes, handicrafts, and works of art made from recycled materials, are also available to the public at low prices to cover the cost of recycling. Sorting and distribution also operate abroad, where textiles are exported, and the textiles that cannot be reused are recycled to produce wiping cloths, fibers for new clothes, insulation, and other useful materials.[251]

Cho et al.[65] *point out that* practices like recycling paper, plastic, and glass, using toners, recycling baskets, energy-efficient showers, and refillable hygiene product dispensers are all aimed at decreasing material, energy, and water consumption. Chang and Chen[252] assure this approach influences consumer behaviors, as research highlights that engaging in pro-environmental actions can lead to "self-transformation." To encourage recycling, reusing, and repairing, Areias et al.[69] *offer* showcasing or actively engaging in processing recycled goods, such as clothing, through *experiential learning*.

The *exchange of goods* served as the foundation of ancient economic systems long before the advent of money. *Freecycling* has been deeply rooted in our culture for generations, allowing individuals to pass items from one household to another. During my visit to Bali, I encountered a more sophisticated interpretation: women gathered for a social event, each bringing clothes to exchange. This experience was enjoyable and mutually beneficial, occurring without monetary transactions, yet it gave us a delightful evening and positive energy. At its core, freecycling emphasizes giving away items rather than discarding or selling them. Dermody et al.[225] indicate that this practice could improve opportunities for reusing and repairing products, thereby enhancing our understanding of *alternative consumption methods*. This approach may include creating and exchanging upcycled goods, enriching consumers' experiential knowledge as both producers and consumers, and providing workshops focused on product repair.

Another idea that targets pro-environmental behavior is known as *"less is more."* The concept of embracing *minimalism* to enhance happiness has gained significant traction in Western society. One notable trend is the capsule wardrobe, characterized by its selection of limited, high-quality clothing pieces designed with timeless aesthetics. By steering clear of seasonal trends, these wardrobes strive for a sophisticated, minimalist appearance. Bardey et al.[181] note that detoxifying the wardrobe enables individuals to eliminate unnecessary items, empowering them to prioritize quality over quantity and achieve a more organized life. This could be useful for mental health because we minimize the negative consequences of our choice process. For those interested, exploring the research conducted by Professor Roy Baumeister[131] and his colleagues provides insight into why successful people, like Mark Zuckerberg or Barack Obama, opt for a consistent daily wardrobe—an intentional simplification of complexity. After conducting myriad tests with his colleagues, they concluded that many choice options led to the depletion of self-control and weakened the ability to block out disruptive thoughts, leading to a tendency toward negative thinking and heightened susceptibility to negative emotions. Depleted individuals are more inclined to give up on challenging tasks, lose courage, and make complex decisions, resulting in diminished performance in activities requiring stepping out of their comfort zone. This example shows how endorsing anti-consumption, as suggested by Shen et al.,[253] underlines the importance of conveying the environmental advantages of personal buying habits. Emphasizing the positive effects of decreased consumption on human well-being could have a substantial influence, which finally will make a real change.

> **Create impact, becoming a positive force for people & the planet: key takeaways**
>
> 1. Base on those customers who care about sustainable consumption and social stability
> 2. Be aware of lifestyle, the unique way values and beliefs are behaviorally expressed
> 3. Support local communities
> 4. Build knowledge communities
> 5. Cultivate a "being more human" approach
> 6. Mind social consciousness phenomenon
> 7. Understand the influencing direction of social networks
> 8. Invite key opinion leaders, not merely influencers
> 9. Promote pro-social behavior
> 10. Promote pro-environmental behavior

10

Empower by transferring knowledge, skills, and practices

We have already discussed the dangerous relationship between psychological well-being and impulsive buying behavior in Chapter 4. Now, it's time to explore more details. When business practices are genuinely organized around consumers rather than solely catering to insatiable human needs, they can empower consumers and foster collaboration for a better future. This vision inspires a shift away from short-term fixes, such as profiting from fluctuating moods and investing in impulsive behaviors that backfire. Instead, create a space where your customers can thrive.

31. Warn about the role of the survival mode in overconsumption

Researchers intensively discuss that emotions play a vital role in shaping decision-making processes where *managing*, *regulating*, and even *perceiving emotions* are crucial aspects influencing purchasing choices. Ladhari et al.[254] pointed out that the role of emotions in *hedonic service* settings is well established, but their role in *utilitarian service* settings has received scant attention. *Utilitarian motives* refer to efficiency, effectiveness, accomplishment, rational behavior, and *goal-seeking*. However, COVID-19 made its adjustments into research on consumer behavior when people were caught by one goal: to survive.

Before the pandemic, authors rarely relied on *practical reasons* or *negative emotions* to drive impulsive purchases—however, Newman et al.[119] emphasized how psychological factors influence consumer behavior, showing how *negative emotions* can drive people to purchase essential items for *daily survival*. Cao et al.[190] delved into the correlation between *anxiety* and organic purchasing habits, exploring why consumers opt for specific product categories over others and choose one brand over another. Billore and Anisimova[255] identified a surge in fear-driven and panic-buying publications that have gained global traction since the pandemic, encompassing both scientific and non-scientific works on impulsive purchasing.

Yanmei Jiang[240] found that individuals weigh the emotional outcomes of their actions before deciding. They seek pleasure (positive emotions) and avoid pain (negative emotions). In making purchase decisions, people may sidestep unpleasant feelings related to not buying or delaying a purchase. In the dining context, they aim to avoid the negative emotions linked to missing out on dining out. Gupta and Mukherjee[104] advocated utilizing the *fear of missing out*, rumination, and loss aversion to boost retail sales.

Cho et al.[65] recommended encouraging compensatory consumption to address emotions like *nostalgia* or *boredom*. Sajid et al.[66] highlighted the impact of *fear of coronavirus* on increased eco-friendly product buying behavior. Chiu et al.[67] found that negative mood is positively related to impulsive buying behavior of fitness products because people seek distractions to reduce aversive emotions, sometimes resulting in impulsive buying to alleviate fear. Phang et al.[105] found a link between *intolerance of uncertainty* and panic buying, driven by the anticipation of negative outcomes, despite their low probability.

To Wang et al.,[50] impulsive buying behavior is a typical shopping practice with the potential for hedonic outcomes, which are influenced by *positive* and *negative emotions*. However, researchers highlighted that *negative emotions* hold more significant influence, leading to possible negative consequences such as financial problems and post-purchase regret, where emotions mediate between impulsive buying tendencies and behavior. As a result, they solely incorporate *negative emotions* in their theoretical framework as a potential emotional motivator for impulsive buying behavior.

32. Educate about "green consumerism"

Sometimes negative feelings lead to positive outcomes. For example, Ling Xie et al.[182] researched excessive meat consumption, which can lead to high blood cholesterol levels. They found that awareness of such effects caused *negative feelings* that disrupt consumer attitudes, resulting in disappointment, disconnection from consumption, reduced intake, and fostering *anti-consumption tendencies* and behaviors toward *specific products*. However, researchers discuss evidence that *negative emotions* can lead to *increased consumption* of healthier lifestyle products. Cao et al.[190] agree and confirm that anxiety prompts people to reflect on their consumption behavior, promoting the development of healthy eating habits and lifestyles, which can *increase organic purchases*. Marketing managers are encouraged to develop strategies using persuasive content from "important ones," whose opinions can influence consumer choices. In social commerce, *health communities aim to positively shape consumer attitudes toward organic products*. Multiple studies on COVID-19 *panic buying* behavior confirm that *negative feelings led consumers to make excessive purchases*.

While organic food benefits human health, issues like overconsumption and waste management are influenced more by *quantity than quality*. Emotional triggers should not be deemed healthy if they are *impulsive and lack rational analysis*. Often, impulsive purchases become waste or unnecessary items, turning fitness devices into mere clothes hangers. Verplanken and Herabadi suggest[256] impulse purchases could be a way to *manage emotions*, whether during *positive moments* as a self-reward or in *negative times* as self-comfort, and while impulsive buying may seem irrational, *it can serve a purpose*. He et al.[103] use an example, where unnecessary consumption behavior can assist consumers in *conserving their psychological resources* by freeing them from situations that require controlling and suppressing impulses. I already discussed in Chapter 4 that impulsive buying could serve as a *psychological well-being mechanism*. The question is whether these practices lead to *green consumerism*, when individuals continue to overconsume but with more sustainable products.

Pereira Heath and Chatzidakis[257] highlight there is a link between impulsive buying, *overconsumption*, and *environmental harm*, even though excessive consumption is not the main concern for consumers. It is imperative to employ strategies that enhance motivation for reducing consumption. Purchasing a 10th hat, 15th dress from organic cotton, or 50th recycled plastic bag are all examples of a misunderstanding of sustainable consumption. It is difficult to imagine how they empower customers. Nonetheless, they contribute to the climate crisis, resource limitations, and environmental degradation. As consumers, we need businesses to invest time, money, and efforts in alternatives, and genuinely transition from a product-based economy to triple-win options, helping us live meaningful lives.

33. Help to build long-term emotional regulation

Steg et al.[179] suggest that strategies to target and strengthen individuals' *intrinsic motivation* to engage in sustainable behavior may be promising, as such strategies are more likely to result in durable behavior changes. Articles have discussed tools that can assist with emotional management, specifically *emotional intelligence*, *self-control*, and *psychological safety*. Nepomuceno and Laroche[91] suggested that resistance to consumption may be increased by enhancing one's perception of *self-control* and *long-term orientation*.

Impulsive buying behavior contradicts *long-term customers' well-being*, adding to multiple crises and overshooting natural resources and planetary boundaries by fueling *unlimited consumerism and production*. It creates complications in implementing the social concept of *sufficiency*, a lifestyle advocated by sustainability. Voluntary simplicity, popularized by the degrowth movement, aims to establish a new "post-development" model that is socially equitable and ecologically sustainable, offering a path to achieving sustainability. Sufficiency involves adopting a lifestyle that balances resource use within the planet's limits, which, as Alcott[258] notes, requires reducing consumption.

Awais et al.[259] suggest that comprehending insights of the frugal consumer can help understand and drive sustainable consumption. Nepomuceno and Laroche[91] agree that researchers, public governance, and policymakers should recognize the drivers behind voluntary resistance to consumption. Hüttel and Balderjahn[191] offer to promote mindfulness, *empowerment*, and *self-efficacy*. Frank et al.[260] found that increased *self-awareness* often appeared to be accompanied by an improved ability to deal with unpleasant experiences, resulting in increased well-being. They underline that *dealing with unpleasant experiences* and *caring for oneself* has been repeatedly suggested as an essential competency for sustainable consumption and sustainability-oriented behavior. Markauskaitė and Rūtelionė[203] suggest activating consumers' *self-consciousness* while promoting brands as environmentally responsible.

Understanding the impulsive buying motives of customers concerning emotional regulation is crucial for business strategies. What if businesses choose not to capitalize on vulnerabilities but instead focus on helping customers regulate their emotions effectively, making responsible choices that nurture enduring healthy relationships for both parties?

34. Link sustainable consumption with positive emotions

In order to manage anxiety and panic in a healthier way, Oh and Chul[230] suggest companies evoke *positive emotions* linked to sustainable consumption. They suggest incorporating emotional elements in modeling ethical consumption behavior and utilizing diverse marketing techniques to promote positive emotions. It provides a theoretical implication about the usefulness of employing *affection* variables in ethical consumption studies. Researchers concluded that on the practical side, firms marketing ethical products may find it helpful to use ads that invoke *positive feelings* associated with ethical consumption, such as *self-gratification*, *happiness*, and *subjective well-being*, which is a comprehensive concept encompassing personal health and *emotions*, *social interactions*, and *intellectual aspects* of an individual's life. A study by Ares et al.[261] demonstrated that *well-being* was predominantly linked to calmness, health, happiness, *positive emotions*, satisfaction with specific aspects of life, and food products across the five countries. Brandão and Cupertino de Miranda[89] found that sustainable consumption intends to reduce environmental concerns, increase security, achieve a reasonable natural resource distribution, increase *well-being*, create a *healthy life*, and adopt social responsibility. Ramos-Hidalgo et al.[237] underline that *evoking positive feelings* such as hope, humor, empathy, and other practices *enhance consumer happiness and well-being*.

Waters et al.[262] noted that perceiving circumstances negatively triggers unpleasant affective states while *viewing situations positively leads to pleasant experiences*. Diener et al.[263] *point to* growing evidence that *positive emotions* influence variables vital for workplace success, such as positive beliefs, creativity, work engagement, positive coping, health, teamwork and collaboration, customer satisfaction, leadership, and performance.

The study conducted by Ismael and Ploeger[46] linked organic food with *well-being*, highlighting *positive emotions* like *happiness, satisfaction*, and a *sense of responsibility*. Participants perceived organic food as more influential on their *physical health* and *emotions* than on their social life. An important implication of their research is promoting organic food consumption by emphasizing its beneficial effects on *subjective well-being*. Ramos-Hidalgo et al.[98] emphasized that consumption that incorporates environmental and social concerns positively relates to *consumer well-being, life satisfaction*, and *happiness*. They revealed that sustainable consumer behavior may create *positive emotions*, reinforce consumer moral identity, create a *positive self-image*, and satisfy the need for *connectedness* with others.

35. Foster mindfulness

In the article "Why did I buy this?" Spiteri Cornish[53] emphasized that consumers *should be more conscious of their spending patterns* and try to control impulsive buying. Practicing *mindfulness* aids in reflecting with increased levels of *awareness*[69] and focuses on daily experiences, fostering *eco-friendly actions* and *personal well-being*, and *connecting mindset* and behavior. Mindfulness helps reduce *perceived stress*[264] and promotes responsible initiatives. By converting *intentions into actions*, it can help cultivate ecological well-being on *individual and societal levels*.

Mindful consumption is a crucial link between mindset and behavior, aiming for a customer-centric, holistic approach to sustainability. By encouraging *temperance in consumption* and *altering impulsive behaviors*, mindfulness can lead to more sustainable lifestyles. A recent study by Schomburgk and Hoffmann[265] explored self-control and provided empirical evidence supporting *mindfulness* to curb buy-now-pay-later practices by enhancing consumers' financial self-discipline and *reducing impulsive purchasing behavior*. They explained that *mindfulness is an inner capacity to lessen financial desires*, leading to fewer wants and thus increasing well-being.[266]

Sermboonsang et al.[163] validated that *learning mindfulness* can impact consumption behaviors. Their study applied mindfulness-related concepts to business education by relying on transformational learning techniques for reducing impulsive buying in a six-week Smart Consumer University class. The initial test from the pilot program shows *changes in awareness* and some consumption behaviors toward less impulsive buying. By *shifting mindset*, individuals moved toward sustainable consumption by *understanding the impact of their choices*. This led to more mindful behavior, curbing overconsumption. They conclude that positive behavioral changes will likely be more prominent with a longer time frame in future educational programs. This study encourages *self-regulation* and its development as a crucial aspect of *breaking old habits*.

Wang et al.[107] examined the impact of *moderate thinking* (Zhong-Yong thinking) on individuals during the COVID-19 pandemic. East Asian cultures prioritize this *intuitive* and *intricate thinking*, meticulously considering the distinctive challenges within their environment. This focus is demonstrated in Confucian philosophies, precisely the Chinese concept of Zhong-Yong thinking, which revolves around attaining equilibrium and fostering *mindfulness* of one's surroundings. This study found that those with moderate thinking show *better emotional regulation* and *less impulsive buying*. Low moderate thinking linked to stronger impulsive buying effects, while high moderate thinking associated with weaker impulsive buying effects. Researchers concluded that encouraging moderate thinking can aid in *holistic and balanced perspectives* to stand against overconsumption.

A comprehensive experiment was done by Frank et al.[260] where short-course participants experienced mindfulness-related benefits such as increased *self-awareness*, development of *ethical virtues*, and *improved well-being*. These effects suggest that mindfulness can enhance personal competencies crucial for sustainable consumption. While some participants *applied their learning to sustainability topics*, overall consumption-related effects varied. Mindfulness interventions may serve as self-confirmatory processes, enhancing awareness and *coping abilities*. However, the application of these skills *depends on individuals' mental models*. Participants can use mindfulness to support sustainable consumption but may also apply it in other areas of life or to accept unsustainable behaviors. Findings from this study confirm a certain potential of mindfulness practices for developing personal sustainability competencies. However, researchers do not justify the current hype on *mindfulness* and its enthusiastic advocacy in sustainability research. Overall, researchers concluded that consumption-related learning activities might benefit from embedding mindfulness practices, primarily targeting individuals (1) *willing to establish more sustainable consumption patterns* or consumers (2) *already practicing mindful consumption*. It has been suggested that *mindfulness practice* might be a *promising complement* to environmental and sustainable education, but with further research and development needed.

36. Suggest taking a pause

Dholakia[217] suggested that *the desire to consume* may function as a *limited motivational resource*. They found that purchase impulse becomes depleted upon *reflecting* on favored personal possessions, leaving less desire for subsequent shopping urges. Across four studies in their research, consumers who reflected on their recently used personal possessions experienced less desire for an *unexpectedly encountered product*, were *less likely to buy impulsively*, and expressed a *lower willingness to pay for new products*. Consequently, a suggestion is

Empower by transferring knowledge, skills, and practices 157

to add a step of *reflection* (thinking of recent use of their possessions once they experience marketing stimuli) as a self-control-related mechanism toward *rejection, reclaim,* and *restriction.* This is a promising direction in line with the primary emotional regulation mechanism known simply as "take a pause."

When considering a pause, most might envision a day or few hours for reflection. However, it may surprise you that it doesn't take that long. The best clue about the *length of the pause* I came across was in the mission of the nonprofit company Six Seconds, which offers tools and methods to help individuals put emotional intelligence theory into practice. In one of their articles, they recounted a discussion back in 1997 when the team gathered around a kitchen table to plan the launch of the new nonprofit organization. They emphasized the importance of demonstrating how emotional intelligence can be simple and practical—something anyone can develop without complicated procedures. Anabel "research says" Jensen, the company's President, shared insights from recent research on emotional responses. She mentioned investigating how long it takes for someone to recognize the feeling of compassion, *which turned out to be around six seconds.* Emotions are neurohormones, chains of amino acids that transmit messages throughout the brain and body. Primarily produced in the hypothalamus, these chemicals impact every living cell in our bodies, playing a crucial role in our overall regulatory function. Each release of these chemicals, from production to breakdown and absorption, lasts four-to-seven seconds. Missing those initial six seconds means forfeiting the wisdom and energy these emotions offer. Additionally, if we experience certain feelings for longer than six seconds, we essentially choose to recreate and refuel those feelings. Hence, the company advocates, "*It takes six seconds to manage anger. It takes six seconds to create compassion. It takes 6 seconds to change the world.*"[267] Shahpasandi et al.[100] emphasized that consumers may impulsively buy items they do not need and regret their purchases later, therefore taking a pause benefits both sellers and buyers. Why not train your frontline staff to suggest to customers that they "*take a moment*" and encourage gratitude for valuable advice?

Another example is *planning prompt,* a simple yet effective method of resisting impulsive buying. Upadhye et al.[101] suggested businesses can encourage customers to plan their shopping before entering the store, including technology like the "Wise Shopping App" mobile application, which could serve consumers as a planning prompt. At the same time, Awais et al.[259] persist in expanding the understanding of sustainable consumption behavioral factors, focusing on *frugal consumers*, *minimalists*, and those embracing a *voluntary simplicity lifestyle* by choice rather than *inhibition or self-control*. These insights can benefit governance, policymakers, and marketing managers striving to enhance consumer well-being via sustainable consumption.

If up to 90% of all purchases are impulsive, it seems most of us need help to build a high shopping–life balance where consumer engagement in the marketplace does not lead to *consumer overspending, excessive debt, financial bankruptcies*, and *family ruin*.[196] We need more time and methods to deal with *dependencies* and *immediate gratification*.

37. Take an active part in finance planning and education

A range of financial instruments, from credit cards to buy-now-pay-later (BNPL) schemes, support impulsive purchasing. These methods rely on one key element: they are used as a "solution" during *orchestrated urgency to buy*. This is because human impulses are short-lived, so if a consumer can remain calm during the moment of impulse, it becomes increasingly difficult to manipulate their behavior. Therefore, while using instruments like creating a pause, it's important to recognize the *artificial sense of urgency* created by unethical practitioners. Advertising messages like "Only two left," "Black Friday starts in one hour," "Two days until the end of special promotion," and others, are designed to create a sense of scarcity and are manipulating consumer choice. Researchers suggest that BNPL providers should be aware of the negative associations of their payment schemes with consumers' overall psychological and financial well-being.

Schomburgk and Hoffmann[265] recommend retailers to make payment processes more "mindful" by increasing the number of clicks or steps and suggest that *BNPL providers*, such as Klarna, should target *heavy users* of their services and integrate a question in their mobile or online app, such as "Can you afford this purchase? Think before you act." Public policymakers may want to encourage the BNPL industry to adopt instant messaging to bring awareness to the consumer and prevent people from becoming "trapped in a debt cycle." This idea is not out of the blue; many online shops send friendly reminders to customers before subscription renewals, showcasing *supportive relationships* rather than just *transactional ones*. Consumers appreciate providers who use their bank card data responsibly and avoid automatic renewals, or at least clearly remind them about them, so as not to exploit consumer vulnerabilities.

Gawior et al.[99] advocate for sustainable education on the rationality of purchasing, complemented by education on credits and loans—and their potential negative side effects—in their study on credit card use, hedonic motivation, and impulsive buying behavior consequences. This could significantly help with the percentage of consumer debt directly resulting from impulsive buying. Wang et al.[170] even suggest that *intensive impulsive buyers*, being different from general buyers, might require different treatment from these sellers and must be *treated separately*. Ah Fook and McNeill[108] suggested stopping *BNPL programs* as a driver of increased impulse purchasing in online retail. Wang et al.[170] pointed to the need for policymakers to introduce plans that may *counsel impulsive buyers* on how to manage their finances and impulses because these buyers may meet untoward outcomes of their *excessive impulsive buying*.

Sirgy et al.[196] recommend implementing programs to enhance consumer literacy, financial planning, and budgeting to help consumers use credit cards responsibly. They also suggest providing financial education to improve money management skills and reduce financial worries. Czarnecka et al.[97] propose targeting consumers with financial instruments that encourage better budgeting and long-term financial planning.

Overall, it is advised to support consumers rather than expecting them to resolve their financial challenges alone. While vulnerability is a personal responsibility, exploiting it is manipulation, which does not absolve the manipulator of responsibility. Offering BNPL schemes as a payment option could pose a reputational risk and harm the brand if consumers feel compelled to purchase products they later realize they cannot afford. Sacrificing short-term sales to consumers who cannot afford it could prevent long-term reputational damage associated with selecting BNPL as a payment option.

38. Enhance consumers' sustainable consumption attitudes

Attitudes represent individuals' mental outlooks and are predominantly shaped by underlying values and beliefs. When individuals strive for a more sustainable lifestyle, they are influenced by a *sustainable consumption attitude*. Attitude reflects an individual's positive or negative beliefs about behavior consequences, influencing subsequent responses. Liu et al.[187] confirmed that *sustainable consumption attitudes* positively influenced purchase behavior. Oh and Chul[230] showed that *consumer attitude* toward ethical consumption is positively related to ethical obligation, self-identity, and altruism. Also, ethical obligation and altruism positively influenced *ethical consumption intention*. Further, *attitude* and positive-anticipated affection positively affected ethical consumption intention. Mazhar et al.[76] revealed that *egoistic* and *hedonic values influence attitudes* toward purchasing green products. However, Nguyen et al.[268] did not find any association between *attitude* and *altruistic values*. It was found that *attitude* stimulates *ecologically conscious consumers' behavior*. Their research has also validated earlier studies that *green purchase intention* positively affects green buying behavior.

The findings by Ahmed et al.[229] have demonstrated a positive and significant impact of green customer value, green marketing mix, and *attitude* on the green purchase intention of U.S. customers. The study has further concluded that the green psychological benefits (mediator) and green advertising (moderator) significantly influence the relationship between *attitude*, green customer value (environmental image and perceived value), green marketing mix, and green purchasing intention. Lu et al.[177] found that a more *positive attitude* toward mobile health services leads to a greater willingness to pay for them. Roşu et al.[264] revealed that *negative attitudes* (perceived barriers) and others' behavior (*descriptive social norms*) were significant predictors of the *intention to over-purchase* and the actual *stockpiling* intention/behavior during the COVID-19 pandemic.

Tariq et al.[184] studied the *factors influencing consumers' attitudes*. They discovered that information cues like nutritional content, production methods, and environmental friendliness play a significant role in influencing attitudes toward organic food purchases. Social media, ratings, and reviews influence *consumer attitudes* and drive online impulsive buying. Researchers emphasize the importance of website features in providing information on organic food. Informative webpages showcasing product quality and certification strongly influence purchasing decisions. Chang and Watchravesringkan[166] identified *general environmental attitudes* that include consumers' evaluations of the environmental attitudes of governments, manufacturers, and commercial advertising. Factors like *concerns* about conserving apparel resources, the influence of subjective norms, and perceived behavioral control play a role in shaping *intentions* to purchase sustainable apparel, like items made from recycled materials or second-hand apparel.

Another study of shock events by Ismael and Ploeger[46] showed that *attitude*, perceived behavioral control, *moral attitude*, health consciousness, and impact of COVID-19 significantly *positively influence intentions to buy green food*. Consumer attitudes greatly influence their inclination to purchase environmentally friendly food. When consumers view green food positively, their desire to buy it grows. This finding aligns with prior research on eco-friendly products. Therefore, researchers advised that green food businesses should work on enhancing consumers' *positive perceptions* and *attitudes* toward green food by emphasizing brand benefits, running promotional campaigns, and boosting consumer beliefs and knowledge.

39. Embrace customers with pro-environmental self-identity

Johnston and Burton[269] revealed that reduced consumption and increased *self-reliance* can be achieved through the *reuse* and *recycling* of products and services. In their study, Dermody et al.[88] observed that those who already display *lower levels of materialism* seamlessly integrate it into their purchasing decisions and other sustainable practices that favor sustainable consumption and promote product longevity through *reusing, repairing,* and *purchasing second-hand* items. Still, Kuanr et al.[165] *points out that voluntary simplicity* practices are also oriented toward low consumption and include material *self-reliance*. Thus, sustainable consumption findings may stem from the strong sense of *personal responsibility* for environmental issues and be related to *pro-environmental self-identity*, a dynamic and environmentally friendly self-concept. Mazhar et al.[76] *emphasize that pro-environmental self-identity* is an individual's self-perception that accepts pro-environmental actions deriving consumption from the desire for *self-expression*. Dermody et al.[225] *noted that* in the context of sustainable consumption, *pro-environmental self-identity* significantly impacts buying behavior related to sustainable consumption. Consumers with this identity make active, sustainable consumption choices akin to Seyfang's[270] notion of *civic consumption activism*. Mazhar et al.[76] found that *pro-environmental self-identity* and *ecology-conscious consumer behavior* affect green purchase intentions. Steg et al.[179] *reveal* that when a person realizes they engaged in sustainable energy behaviors (or, more generally, *pro-environmental behaviors*), they are more likely to see themselves as a *pro-environmental person*, which motivates them to act in line with this identity in subsequent situations.

Dermody et al.[88] highlighted that low *perceived consumer effectiveness* is one of the market-based barriers to sustainable consumption. The stronger this perceived power is, the more it strengthens *pro-environmental self-identity*. A study conducted by He et al.[103] suggests that the *perceived effectiveness* of consumers is a more influential predictor of environmentally sustainable behavior than factors such as environmental concern, attitudes toward green products, or knowledge. *Perceived consumer effectiveness* refers to the belief in one's ability to influence individual consumption behaviors, thereby positively contributing to resource protection. While unnecessary consumption behavior may aid consumer recovery, it can also deplete social resources and challenge the self-belief of those with high *perceived consumer effectiveness*. This challenge may lead to discomfort or increased stress for consumers, undermining their positive self-image as ethical individuals.

40. Promote consumer self-efficacy

Chao et al.[271] highlight that *self-efficacy* reflects the degree to which consumers perceive their ability and motivation to perform the desired behavior. Bandura and Adams introduced the idea of *self-efficacy*,[272] which they defined as an individual's evaluation of their ability to *perform actions* necessary to navigate potential situations. *Self-efficacy* pertains to a person's beliefs about their capacity to execute a plan across various contexts, effectively reflecting their confidence in succeeding in specific scenarios. While Bandura and Adams initially developed this concept, it has since been examined by psychologists from multiple perspectives. Halper and Vancouver[273] found that *self-efficacy* can foster persistence when one is aware of one's current state of performance, while unrelated to persistence when feedback was ambiguous.

Self-efficacy differs from *self-confidence*, which involves trusting in one's abilities, qualities, and decisions. *Self-confidence is deeply intertwined with self-esteem*, which mirrors our self-value. Robust self-esteem establishes the foundation for self-confidence, *empowering individuals to tackle life's hurdles adeptly*. It is crucial to also distinguish between *self-esteem* which relates to self-worth, and *self-confidence* which revolves around faith in one's capabilities and expertise.

Kuanr et al.[165] discovered that *self-efficacy* impacts *voluntary simplicity* because individuals with individualistic values exhibited higher *self-efficacy*, which led to an *indirect positive link with anti-consumption behaviors*. Earlier, Oh and Chul[230] emphasized that companies should not just promote and educate the public about the societal benefits of ethical consumption but also *highlight the significance of individual actions*. Targeted promotion strategies could link purchases to specific environmental impacts. Businesses can seriously gain by promoting *self-efficacy* and educating that material goods do not compensate for the lack of well-being and self-esteem, thus directly empowering their customers. Iwata[215] confirmed that *self-sufficiency* (combined with anti-materialism, mindful shopping behaviors, and purchasing durable goods) can curb *excessive consumption*.

Another factor for sustainable consumption could be derived from *hedonism*. Brandão and Cupertino de Miranda[89] emphasized that consumers may view *sustainability as utilitarian* and *luxury as hedonic*. However, they found the link of hedonism as a part of newly formed "*sustainable luxury*," where sustainability adds significant value. This indicates that *self-expression* (plus hedonism, high quality, perceived social image, and perceived value) can influence sustainable consumption behavior. Respondents in their research expressed positive views on luxury sustainable services, showing intentions to purchase, plan, and engage in sustainable behavior when selecting luxury services. Their research emphasized that *self-expression* is a key factor, possibly linked to showcasing individuality through luxury service usage. They highlighted that such behaviors allow individuals to enjoy activities that reflect their *status, knowledge, preferences,* and *social image*, which they found crucial in promoting sustainable consumption behavior among consumers.

Social image and individualism often face criticism from a sustainable consumption perspective. However, the focus on the individualism–collectivism dichotomy is as unproductive as the growth–degrowth debate. Materialism affects both individualists and collectivists similarly, and without social transformation, addressing unlimited growth is impossible. As discussed in Chapter 6, leveraging diverse personal values is crucial for sustainable consumption, addressing each uniquely. We must capture every consumer's heart by focusing on what matters to them. Iyer and Muncy[109] highlight that customers could choose to be happier micro-anti-consumers rather than be disgruntled macro-anti-consumers by force. This points to the need for businesses to *reshape perceptions* of genuinely sustainable products as proposed by Mazhar et al.,[76] *foster consumer appreciation* for products with sustainable attributes as suggested by Chang and Watchravesringkan,[166] and develop advocacy strategies to *enhance consumers' sustainable consumption attitudes pointed by* Cao et al.[190]

Empower by transferring knowledge, skills, and practices: key takeaways

1. Warn about the role of the survival mode in overconsumption
2. Educate about "green consumerism"
3. Help to build long-term emotional regulation
4. Link sustainable consumption with positive emotions
5. Foster mindfulness
6. Suggest taking a pause
7. Take an active part in finance planning and education
8. Enhance consumers' sustainable consumption attitudes
9. Embrace customers with pro-environmental self-identity
10. Promote consumer self-efficacy

11

Advocate for a triple win (and help others)

Business advocacy for a triple-win strategy involves aligning internal strategies, actions, and resources without causing harm to themselves or others. Business self-regulation and management encompass controlling shareholders' demands and impulses, trustworthiness, and taking responsibility for business outcomes and consequences. Leading by sustainable practices, businesses promote triple win for long-term success through everyday actions, not patronizing messages or false promises.

41. Mind consumer engagement paradox

Vrontis et al.[274] emphasized that *emotions serve as antecedents of impulsive buying behavior* along with other psychological factors such as values and norms, attitudes, or perceptions. Wei Jie et al.[61] pointed out that from a marketing perspective, emotions are a pivotal tool in stimulating customers to fulfill their *immediate desires*. The trend is found among studies focused on *consumer emotions*, *immersive experiences*, and *emotional engagement*. Consumer engagement is explored in various industries, using fashion as an example, as in the study by Gawior et al.,[99] or other sectors directly linked to *emotional responses*, as in the study by Chakraborty and Sadachar,[227] *interactive immersion* by Lu et al.,[177] or *emotional bonds which* Ramadan et al.[242] suggest for retailers are based on moral factors such as *trust*. The study conducted by Chang and Watchravesringkan[166] revealed that consumers' *engagement* with "clean label" products significantly impacts their *intention to purchase*.

Multiple studies support this offer to use *emotional engagement*. Thus, Lu et al.[177] proposed that businesses should strive to facilitate *consumer immersion* and respond quickly to demand. Wei Jie et al.[61] suggested forming an *emotional connection with business owners* to encourage impulsive purchases. Walker et al.[275] called for prioritizing the *emotional experience* of dining at a restaurant: décor, physical environment, service, and food quality. Sajid et al.[66] advised relying on the *fear of coronavirus's effect on green product purchasing behavior*. Jiang and Lau[106] pointed out that hedonic and *social motives* influence the intention to dine out. This is driven by consumers' intense need to *emotionally and socially relieve pressure and loneliness*, transforming their mood post-COVID-19.

Magids et al.[276] point out that when companies connect with customers' *emotions*, the commercial outcome is multiplied. In their article "The New Science of Customer Emotions"[277] by Harward Business Review, they described a business paradise:

> When companies connect with customers' emotions, the payoff can be huge. Consider these examples: After a major bank introduced a credit card for Millennials that was designed to inspire emotional connection, use among the segment increased by 70% and new account growth rose by 40%. Within a year of launching products and messaging to maximize emotional connection, a leading household cleaner turned market share losses into double-digit growth. And when a nationwide apparel retailer reoriented its merchandising and customer experience to its most emotionally connected customer segments, same-store sales growth accelerated more than threefold.

This raises significant social concerns *regarding neuromarketing tools and emotion-based marketing techniques* for boosting sales. Thus, *emotional engagement leading to increased purchases could be seen as manipulative*, resulting in a *loss of consumer trust* and a *defensive attitude*. In our information-saturated world, there is a *constant battle for consumers' attention* with limitless marketing tactics. Customers defend themselves by cultivating *self-control* to remain "in control" during this invisible war. However, attention is not the only factor. We stay focused longer when *emotionally connected*, which has been shown to drive *exponential sales growth*. Nonetheless, every business leader is also a customer, and there should be no divide between them. Businesses must be *genuine in their sales efforts*, clearly *understanding contemporary crises* and their consequences. Founders, entrepreneurs, and business leaders must address a simple question: Do emotionally attached customers feel any better than brainwashed customers?

42. Evolve business strategy for a triple win: for people, the planet, and prosperity for all

It is the right time to change business priorities, as we already know that we don't want financial benefits to be the sole outcome. The triple-win principle suggests entrepreneurs and business owners plan and implement ventures that benefit people, the planet, and prosperity for all. Although it sounds challenging, it could also be an exciting opportunity. This understanding may help businesses, perhaps for the first time in history, create and showcase real samples where businesses are not merely trade entities but socially connected, innovative units that serve as a positive force, empowering people and the environment. Focusing on modern sustainability brings a ton of benefits. It opens the door to new products and markets, takes advantage of emerging technologies, and sparks innovation. It also boosts efficiency and helps build stronger connections with customers, keeping them engaged and loyal in meaningful ways. It's important to identify more sustainable products and implement informative certifications while increasing publicity for environmental protection. It is also important to limit (by zero) misleading marketing messages spurring impulsive purchases and support customers. For such a change, few modifications are needed from traditional businesses and entrepreneurs. Entrepreneurs who are already valuing people and business goals must enhance their environmental education and practice environmental connection. Traditional enterprises need to evolve their business goal from serving customers' needs to empower their customers, connect more with people, implement socially driven innovations and initiatives, and devote their activities for environmental support and development.

Why do I believe such change is possible? This belief is backed by science, which suggests that people care for anything they are emotionally engaged with and pay little long-term attention where no such connection exists. The same science indicates that people value mutual collaboration and appreciate those who help them rather than those who suppress and exploit them. With this understanding, I think many entrepreneurs and business owners may feel encouraged and relieved, as they aren't obligated to serve shareholders who neglect to incorporate people, planet, and prosperity for all into their business plans. Although this may still be the case, once we create small showcases—islands of common sense—it will spread, as small groups of people have already implemented significant changes and transformations throughout our history. Why shouldn't it be for the good in our times?

43. Provide customers with trustworthy information

Chang and Chen[252] raised the question that although consumers are willing to purchase organic products that are more respectful of human health and the environment, messy and fuzzy food information may cause them to make incorrect decisions. Lu et al.[177] paid particular attention to the *information quality*, indicating its importance in shaping consumer behaviors and perceptions regarding sustainable consumption. For instance, Tariq et al.[184] *point out that* overall *product knowledge* plus *quality and safety certification* significantly impact sustainable purchasing decisions. Climate change is a prime example of a situation where the *perceived lack of knowledge* negatively impacts consumer attitudes and willingness to purchase sustainable products.

Researchers noted that *insufficient knowledge* hinders sustainable consumption, while developing a *pro-environmental identity* can help overcome barriers. This research also underscored how knowledge gaps impede sustainable consumption behaviors, even when individuals witness adverse climatic events. Thøgersen[173] discovered that individual consumers struggle to pinpoint behavior changes that truly benefit the climate, with the key implication from behavioral research being that consumers require substantial *support to transition to a climate-friendly lifestyle*. As such, they point out that companies should prioritize *quality information* dissemination. For them, it could be done via carbon footprint representation in prices, offering climate-friendly products that outshine unfriendly alternatives, and *providing reliable and understandable carbon labeling* for easier climate-conscious decisions.

Cao et al.[190] *add that* one of the key aspects of effective packaging is *transparency*, as consumers increasingly demand more details about the products they purchase. Liu et al.[187] suggest it could be enhanced by *utilizing media and social platforms* to showcase production processes, where companies can provide consumers with the transparency they seek. Chang and Chen[252] argue that certification plays a crucial role, particularly in addressing food safety issues and boosting consumer confidence. The application of certifications like the "clean label" can significantly enhance trust and purchase intentions among consumers. Brandão and Cupertino de Miranda[89] explain that this not only assures customers of the product's safety but also aligns with their preferences for eco-friendly and honest marketing. Additionally, Lu et al.[180] suggest use of blockchain technology, which offers innovative solutions for identifying greenwashing and ensuring the authenticity of ecological claims. By incorporating such advanced technologies, companies can further reinforce their transparency commitment.

Finally, Wang et al.[278] remind us that monitoring and restricting fake positive reviews can prevent misleading information and ensure genuine consumer feedback. Knowing that integrating detailed product information and valid certifications in packaging not only meets consumer demands for transparency and safety, but also strengthens long-term brand reputation by nurturing consumer trust, is encouraging. Various researchers have demonstrated that factors such as comprehensive product knowledge, quality certifications, and climate change awareness influence sustainable purchasing decisions.

Chang and Chen[252] emphasize that consumers benefit from basic environmental knowledge and personal nature experiences, while Ahmed et al.[229] recommend enhancing connectedness. However, Areias et al.[250] suggest that *becoming more informed* creates *empowered force and is the most influential approach.*

44. Embrace the role of marketing communication in promoting sustainable consumption

Modern marketing communication specialists face unprecedented challenges. On the one hand, research suggests that communicating messages about sustainability can be difficult due to the lack of an agreed definition or shared understanding of sustainability and potential individual differences in values and attitudes.[279] Another major dilemma of sustainable marketing communication relates to "which dimensions of sustainability should be emphasized" and "what extent the sustainability benefits should be emphasized" Bagdare.[280] On top of all, Nguyen et al.[214] commented that different groups of consumers have different targets. Thus, they pointed that ecologically conscious consumers are concerned with issues relating to the environment. Green consumers are concerned with non-genetically modified organisms (non-GMO), fair trade, or locally produced products. Pro-social behaviors include avoiding child labor and products that are tested on animals while promoting ecologically produced, energy conservative, recyclable disposal, and ozone-friendly products. Socially responsible consumers purchase based on sellers' corporate social responsibility performance, recyclable products, and avoidance of harmful products, whether green, pro-social, or ecologically conscious—these consumers are concerned with the level of consumption input and waste output as well as individual well-being and their effects on environment and people. That all makes sustainable consumption topics appealing and very diverse but difficult to communicate.

Godemann[281] points out that while green marketing often faces criticism, sustainability needs strong communication to reach society—otherwise, people just won't engage with it. Gossen et al.[73] emphasize that marketing can play a key role in driving behavior toward *sufficient consumption*. Bagdare[280] adds that marketing tools have a big impact on shaping how consumers think, decide, and act. They help raise awareness, educate people, shape perceptions, build interest, influence preferences, and even motivate buying decisions.

Reflecting on the modes of sustainability communication, Weder et al.[282] consider: communication *about sustainability* issues as part of the public discourse; communication as a *one-way transmission of a specific sustainability issue*/policy to achieve a specific effect or goal; and communication *for sustainability* or "call-to-action." Fischer et al.[283] highlight that modern marketing increasingly aims to promote sustainable practices using strategies like *nudging* and *social marketing*. Their study emphasizes persuading consumers to prioritize environmental issues and adopt responsible consumption and voluntary simplicity. Amber et al.[13] explained that review of social marketing literature revealed an emphasis on persuading customers to care more about environmental issues and *decrease their consumption*. Greater emphasis is placed on understanding sustainable consumption, defining it, and interpreting it through different types, such as responsible consumption, voluntary simplicity, or anti-consumption.

When we look at what drives most of the consumers—whether it's being green, socially conscious, or eco-friendly—it's clear their concerns go beyond themselves. They care about their own well-being, the planet, and society as a whole. But moving toward sustainable consumption isn't easy, especially when it comes to aligning beliefs with actions. Well-designed marketing campaigns can help close this gap and encourage more sustainable choices. Even so, tackling the complexities of business challenges is no small feat.

45. Use a post-growth marketing mix

The direction of the marketing mix development under the sustainable consumption paradigm is still under development. The traditional four Ps of marketing—product, price, place, and promotion—

referred to as marketing mix, evolved into the *green marketing mix*. Academic ideas on eco-friendly *products* involve discussions on *high-quality products, product longevity, circular production, wasteless product use*, the contrast between short-term solutions like fast fashion and *long-term ones* such as minimalism, as well as *innovations* and new, *emerging markets*.

The discussion about *place*'s development focuses on the Internet's role and *technology evolution*. Studies examine factors such as shopping platform variables, convenience, and website quality. However, a significant question arises regarding sustainable consumption when considering *price* and *promotional strategies*. Academia differentiates between *commercial marketing* and *social marketing* because commercial marketing often faces negative publicity due to its demanding manipulation tactics.

In marketing, stimuli are meticulously designed to create retail environments and interactions that enhance shoppers' motivation to purchase. Pellegrino et al.[80] assert that advertisement customization, promotion, sales, and shopping environment all *increase an individual's impulsive nature*, leading to an urge to buy. Iyer and Muncy[109] highlighted that approximately 60% of in-store purchases are impulsive, with online buyers exhibiting an even greater propensity for impulsivity. Süle[206] confirm that impulsive buying can be triggered by various marketing stimuli such as communication, store atmosphere, and discounts, including the effects of advertising. Discounts available for larger quantities (buy one, get a second free) may result in additional wastage of unnecessary goods with imminent expiration dates. Ah Fook and McNeill[108] give a critique of some sales methods that directly influence impulsive purchases, increased consumer debt, and family conflicts, such as buy-now-pay-later marketing stimuli and advice on using different tools to stay within limits, including planning interventions.

Black Friday events, food festivals, and Christmas promotions represent sales growth initiatives driven by business-to-consumer marketing, facing challenges from the concept of sustainable consumption. Unsurprisingly, businesses increasingly need as much *research, innovation,* and *new technology* as possible to alleviate the strain on natural resources. Dermody et al.[88] repeat that creating and selling *upcycled goods*; *recycling* paper, plastic, glass, and toners; and using recycling baskets, energy-efficient showers, and refillable hygiene product dispensers are essential. These actions support ideas of sustainable production.

Conversely, demand must also align with planetary boundaries. Shobeiri et al.'s[192] findings indicate that *socially conscious consumers* are motivated to take tangible actions, such as *endorsing responsible businesses*, *boycotting irresponsible firms*, embracing *sustainable lifestyles*, and actively *spreading awareness* to drive *societal change*. Dermody et al.[88] pointed out that *marketing messages* must be unlocked from the market to present sustainable consumption beyond buying. Exploration of why consumers voluntarily *resist consumption* or *become frugal* can aid governance, policymakers, and marketing managers in promoting consumer well-being through sustainable consumption. Scholars are urged to delve into *predictors* of sustainable consumption and research methods to uncover *unconscious consumption* behaviors.

New *markets* and *economic products*, such as experiences that could be entirely decoupled from natural resources, are needed. Shobeiri et al.[192] suggested that an *experiential perspective* can effectively support environmentalism and responsible consumption. Pine and Gilmore[172] make a suggestion that rather than viewing consumers solely as purchasers of products and services, *experiential consumption* portrays them as seekers of memorable, unique, and sensory-emotive *experiences*. The issue of overconsumption is particularly critical in today's era, marked by an urgent need for demand control amidst various crises. Businesses must prioritize *eco-friendly products*, *cyclical production*, and *efficient waste management*. Additionally, addressing post-growth needs in the context of resource constraints is essential, emphasizing the *regeneration of natural resources* as fundamental to defining sales and growth limits.

46. Don't use patronizing messaging, but suggest practices and direct benefits

Kakkar et al.[221] assure us that organizations should aim to curtail *harmful environmental consumption* by co-creating *user-centric experiential practices* that demonstrate a non-environmental, *personal impact on their well-being* rather than relying on *patronizing messages on sustainability*. For instance, they recommend implementing collective practices such as "Digital Wellbeing." Huffington Post, for example, encourages employees to use its app "Thrive," which incentivizes them to stay off their phones and focus on work.

Ahmed et al.[229] agree that creating brands' affirmative *environmental image* and the *value of green products* in the minds of consumers is essential. However, it is deemed appropriate to use *practice-based approaches*, which work better in restraining consumption among people than messaging about pro-environmental intentions alone.

Bardey et al.[181] emphasized that consumers desire to shop ethically. I believe many business owners, particularly entrepreneurs closely connected to local communities, seek to engage in beneficial and supportive relationships. Thus, Lu et al.[180] suggest that businesses enhance their skills in *guiding consumers*. Hüttel and Balderjahn[191] suggest the best choice is to *merge concern* for oneself with concern for environmental and climate protection. Ramos-Hidalgo et al.[237] suggest emphasizing benefits of sustainable consumption for *enhancing happiness*. For that reason, Shen et al.[253] suggest businesses must *supply customers with trustworthy information* on the personal benefits of sustainable products. Chang and Chen[252] suggest businesses should *make customers understand* the significance of product information, such as the "clean label" and other product marks. Cao et al.[190] emphasize the need to strengthen the consumption *values related to organic food* consumption.

Connecting sustainable consumption with customers faces a significant challenge. A central problem has been that consumer purchases consistently deviate from their reported sustainability preferences. Scholars have observed that while a substantial percentage of consumers express a desire to purchase greener, healthier, and more sustainable products, their actual buying behavior deviates from these preferences.

According to Liu et al.,[48] the attitude-behavior gap topic has been at the center of academic research since 2006. In their study, they charted the evolution of sustainable consumption research, highlighting that the initial focus was on consumption behavior, public policy, social factors, and economics from 1995–2005, and noting a shift from 2006 toward exploring the environmental impact of consumer behavior, *aiming to bridge the gap between attitudes and behavioral intentions* by deciphering the central factors influencing sustainable consumption.

This situation calls for businesses to *take the lead in supporting their customers*. By addressing this joint challenge, companies can boost mutual trust, stabilize relationships, and pave the way for a more sustainable future we can build together. The current challenges are opportunities for both sides to move beyond passivity and invest in collaborative efforts.

47. Don't build on vulnerabilities

Although research trajectory on sustainable consumption's influence on *consumer well-being* seems established and valuable, the consequences of impulsive buying behavior need further and more detailed research, especially in the area where impulsive buying behavior is named as compensatory for *psychological health and well-being*.

A study on shock events by Ismael and Ploeger[46] showed that *health consciousness* and the impact of COVID-19 significantly and *positively influence intentions to buy green food*. Consumers in their study agreed that organic food consumption provides them with better physical, emotional, and social *well-being*. The study by Cho et al.[65] found that feelings of *boredom* and *nostalgia* led to browsing behavior and *impulse purchases of fitness products*. Another study by Chiu et al.[67] showed that the *perception of COVID-19* positively influenced *fear*, also leading to *impulsive buying behavior of fitness products*. Yanmei Jiang[240] explored the relationships among anticipated emotions, *perceived value*, *perceived threat*, and dining-out intention during the pandemic. *Perceived threat* is a critical situational factor in an individual's evaluation in the context of consumption. *A high perceived threat* makes consumers more conservative, while *a low perceived threat* makes them evaluate products more positively. However, it was found that when consumers have a *higher level of perceived threat* of the pandemic, utilitarian values such as *product price* were not a concern—instead, *comforting yourself* in the dining place and social values like *seeing people* played a more critical role in motivating the intention to dine out. It was explained that consumers needed to *emotionally and socially relieve* their heightened *pressure* and *loneliness* and transform their mood from the pandemic.

Gupta and Mukherjee[104] suggest using the COVID-19 experiences to trigger environmental awareness and concern, aligning with *long-term health* and a *healthy lifestyle*. While infected individuals showed increased motivation for eco-friendly and fitness-related purchases, manufacturers could view them as a potential market segment.[66] However, it's crucial not to capitalize on your *customers' vulnerable moments* but instead invest in long-term relationships through support. In essence, it's beneficial for businesses to refrain from solely focusing on sales growth, mind the potential impact of "environmentally friendly consumerism," and aim to operate within planetary boundaries and limits with a human face.

48. Blacklist sales based on stress, fear, or negative emotions

I previously discussed that when businesses find themselves in difficult circumstances or on the brink of failure, they often become unapologetically defensive. While it is easy to blame them, we must remember our behavior as humans in survival mode. There is no difference, and the reason is simple: behind every business, there are people, not aliens. Therefore, it is not surprising to see survival tactics, but this is not the whole truth about humanity. Collectively, we take pride in the fact that, during tough times, many of us extend helping hands, support those in need, and protect the vulnerable. While we may do harsh things in our struggle for survival, we also perform many beautiful acts, and I believe we survive primarily for the latter reason. The reason is that, no matter what happens, we remember who we truly are and act accordingly by supporting each other.

It is a fundamental human trait—we find true happiness when those around us are well. Consequently, some businesses act differently, embodying our best selves. Why not make it a business rule that, regardless of circumstances, we will support strategies focused on seeking new opportunities rather than mere survival? This approach would help us avoid triggering customers with sophisticated manipulative techniques. While we could understand why marketing targets consumer vulnerabilities, it doesn't mean we should approve or accept such practices. I suggest blacklisting enterprises that use psychological or neurological triggers to induce impulsive purchases.

We should not support offers designed to trigger consumers' impulsive buying intentions, as noted by Chiu et al.[67] We cannot agree with using urgency to encourage customers to place orders immediately, as revealed by Lee and Wan[62] We cannot confirm the necessity of creating attachments to products as described by Cho et al.[65] Most importantly, we should not agree to use fear to increase sales, noting that individuals' fear plays a critical role in impulse purchase decisions, as shown in the study by Chiu et al.[67] We should not target to increase sales of organic products based on the fear of the pandemic, as described in the study of Sajid et al.[66] Even the fear of missing out (FOMO), a seemingly innocent sales driver in good times, should not be addressed, similar to rumination and loss aversion perceptions as drivers of retail sales mentioned by Gupta and Mukherjee.[104]

Addressing missed opportunities from not dining out, as described in the study by Jiang and Lau,[106] or encouraging individuals to engage in compensatory consumption behaviors by incorporating nostalgia in marketing, as suggested by Cho et al.,[65] sounds impractical. Can we find other offers for our customers in difficult times and create storylines beyond simplifying human existence to buying, paying, and grabbing all the last pieces in the world? I trust we can be far more creative in our approach and in our desire to increase sales by all means. Why don't we genuinely believe that our services can help people connect, spend quality time, support special arrangements, and enhance the quality of life? I simply can't believe we are that limited in our imagination.

49. Promote long-term sales, don't stimulate impulsive buying related to material purchases

We already discussed that previous studies have identified a negative correlation between materialism and sustainability. Kilbourne et al.[200] demonstrated that materialism impedes sustainable consumption. They emphasized that materialism is deeply embedded in American society, continuously reinforced through social interactions.

However, another stream of research has shown that materialism can be positively related to sustainability. For example, Kim and Oh[285] found that in the case of luxury goods, the high price of green products influences materialists and plays a role in inducing pro-environmental behavior. Using structural equation model analysis, they found that materialism positively affected the purchase intention for luxury athleisure products. Dermody et al.[88] agree that an exception might exist within sustainable consumption buying behaviors acquiring luxury "green" brands. Yet, they admit that such behaviors are highly controversial if motivated by materialistic, not environmental/humanitarian value systems.

Lee[201] described *materialism* as a consumption orientation that seeks success and happiness by acquiring and possessing material goods. Conversely, a voluntary simplicity lifestyle describes a nonmaterialistic way of living that seeks *mental and spiritual well-being* through *low consumption*, *material simplicity*, and *ecological awareness*. Thus, *voluntary simplicity* should be considered the opposite of materialism. Impulsive buying behavior strongly correlates with materialism but contradicts long-term customer well-being, contributing to multiple crises and exceeding natural resources and planetary boundaries by promoting unlimited consumerism and production. This complicates the implementation of the social concept of sufficiency. However, it could be mitigated by a long-term orientation, which aligns well with materialism. Thus, materially driven consumers may reach their motivating goals by curbing excessive material purchases and focusing efforts toward achieving a greater objective.

50. Innovate as a crazy and search for new opportunities

Enterprises need to *actively innovate*, for sustainability as highlighted by Lu et al.[180] One direction is by allowing *flexibility* for customers to shop anytime and anywhere, as per Lee and Wan.[62] Jiang and Lau[106] highlight the potential for innovation in fostering consumer confidence by *ensuring safety* and providing reliable stock availability and food security information via multiple platforms, which can alleviate consumer anxiety and fear of stock shortages described by Phang et al.[105] Another study by Shaikh et al.[83] also focused on innovations for mitigating operational and safety risks, particularly for women using shared resources like cab-sharing services. Shahpasandi[100] note it should still be *easy for customers to find what they want, pay for it, and receive it on time*. Nguyen et al.[214] add that in the case of green products, there should be even more focus on *increasing their availability*, as well as *decreasing prices*, since the high cost is the main limitation for green food.

Brandão and Cupertino de Miranda[89] encourage *innovation in alternative resources* and emphasize focusing on those that could become increasingly scarce, such as by developing and implementing water management measures like flow meters.

Szmigin et al.[228] propose *innovations in money management*, such as collecting discount vouchers and changing store preferences.

Dozens of innovations proposed in *product design*, such as optimizing mobile apps and incorporating fun elements, utilize gamification according to Um et al.[64] Lu et al.[98] emphasize that streamers can enhance consumer experiences by providing detailed information about services, responding quickly to demand, and maximizing the benefits of visual and voice capabilities. An interesting example provided by Kakkar et al.[221] demonstrates how *gamification transforms psychological need for contentment* into gamified rewards, such as tracking hours away from your phone. Apps like "MyFitnessPal" incentivize individuals to regulate food consumption and encourage physical exercise. Another innovation related to well-being is the inclusion of a dedicated "Digital Wellbeing" mode in Google's Android operating system.

Kim and Oh[285] offer *examples of material innovation*, highlighting Louis Vuitton's introduction of a vegan shoe crafted from 90% recycled biomaterials and Gucci's launch of a vegan sneaker made from wood pulp.

There are multiple suggestions to enhance the quality of services, ranging from menu simplification to easy online ordering for sustainable food providers. Accessibility to appropriate remedies, such as hygiene and safety measures, is crucial for offline restaurants. To increase performance speed and boost interactivity, focus on enhancing the cognitive value of web pages by providing easy navigation, complete information, and suitable delivery options to meet the needs of visitors with specific goals for sustainable Internet service providers. There are suggestions for organic and bio providers to care about their websites including high-definition images, appropriate fonts, colors, and graphics, along with information on organic food (e.g., nutritional content, production processes, environmental friendliness, and animal welfare). Reflecting on our research and this book, I propose critical innovations that could alter history's path toward sustainable consumption: (1) *technological innovations* grounded in eco-friendly and natural principles; (2) *economic product innovations* that could decouple the economy from material purchases, as akin to those suggested by the experience economy; (3) *decentralised networks/infrastructures* that empower people, businesses, and social initiatives to collaborate, *create, build*, and *innovate together*. Truly, the sky is the limit for human creativity, making sensitivity and innovation catalysts crucial for forecasting and seizing opportunities. The future is ours if we dare to think big.

Advocate for a triple win (and help others): key takeaways

1. Mind consumer engagement paradox
2. Evolve business strategy for a triple win: for people, the planet, and prosperity for all
3. Provide customers with trustworthy information
4. Embrace the role of marketing communication in promoting sustainable consumption
5. Use a post-growth marketing mix
6. Don't use patronizing messaging, but suggest practices and direct benefits
7. Promote long-term sales, don't stimulate impulsive buying related to material purchases
8. Blacklist sales based on stress, fear, or negative emotions
9. Don't stimulate impulsive buying related to material purchases
10. Innovate as a crazy and search for new opportunities

12

Custodians of existence and stewards of life equilibrium

Social transformation is inevitable

As discussed earlier, the Sustainable Development Goals envision a sustainable world by 2030, but a report from Soergel et al.[286] shows that just sticking to current trends and policies won't cut it. These researchers say that conventional strategies like green growth and government-led policy transformations may not suffice. They suggest three ways forward: economy-driven innovation, resilient communities, and managing the global commons. Of these, resilient communities, which focuses on big changes in how we use resources, seems to offer the best results for the environment. This matches the book's insights on achieving sustainable development through social sustainable transformations.

However, they also highlight that despite the broad consensus on internationally agreed SDG goals, there are fundamental debates on the strategies to implement them. According to van Driel et al.,[55] a *key criticism* of SDG 12 (sustainable consumption and production goal) is that a gap exists between the ambitious transformation implied by the goal's core headline and the actual targets and indicators adopted. While technical solutions and public policy play vital roles, they are inadequate when considered in isolation from people. In addressing the issue of overconsumption, policy development must recognize impulsive buying influences which are deeply rooted in *personal* and *psychological factors*. Furthermore, nearly half of academic propositions from our sample, utilizing data from a decade of research, highlight the importance of *cultural and educational change* as significant factors needed to achieve sustainable consumption. This necessitates substantial *lifestyle changes, process adjustments*, and *time to cultivate new values*, making discussions on *self-transformation* a priority. Reflecting on SDG 12 as a focal point, I propose exploring business strategies that can drive societal transformation toward sustainable consumption and production patterns.

This book analyzed multiple actionable propositions and examples of tools that could become a new source for *personal transformations* and proposed businesses to become a driving force for the *consumption revolution*. I view shifting from addressing customer needs to empowering them as a competitive advantage that enhances sustainable business practices. This book seeks to contribute additional data and information via the Emotional Capital for the Triple-Win framework, utilizing collected business instruments to address SDG 12 actual targets and indicators gap. This framework addresses the next generation of business leaders, founders, and innovators with 50 science-based innovative strategies to revolutionize consumer behavior. It provides a basis for inner change which can be addressed immediately, broadly, and with excellent outcomes for people, resulting in healthy finances, relationships, and, most importantly, *psychological well-being*. This work is an opportunity and our responsibility for decoupling psychological well-being from overconsumption, where each individual serves a collective goal, and businesses can take an exciting twist. Rather than playing as usual, they could become a *powerful force driving the consumption revolution*.

Serving others reveals our greatest strengths

What personal values do we convey through our leaders and business owners as a society and culture? Most business and management educational programs, including leadership courses, focus on *effectiveness* at the individual level. As a result, we cultivate a growing number of *self-aware, self-reliant*, and *self-confident* people. However, creating conditions where people can thrive is a real alternative. The notion of being the smartest and most confident person in the room does not seem enough, giving a stage to leaders who could *sense others* better and *help them to realize their potential*.

According to Daniel Goleman, the game's rules had already been changed at the beginning of this century. In his book "Working with Emotional Intelligence,"[132] he wrote that we are no longer solely judged by our intelligence, training, and expertise but also by how well we navigate our emotions and relationships. From today's perspective, we may say that our success is directly related to *how well we deal with people first*. We no longer act as parts of the business machine but *thrive in relationships* within socio-ecologica ecosystems. Attributes such as initiative, empathy, adaptability, and persuasiveness emerge as skills illuminating our path to *deeper connections and understanding*. All of them are based on emotional and not intellectual or self-confidence skills, forming a *new leadership demand*.

While individual development is meaningful, we discover *our greatest strengths when we open up and serve others*. When we focus on the well-being of others, we become less prone to doubting our abilities as we pursue a goal greater than ourselves. In such cases, we act out of necessity rather than self-doubt, often achieving the impossible. We have navigated economic crises and pandemics, and despite unmet basic needs, our shared experiences highlight the essence of humanity. These challenges remind us that our evolving personal needs can transform into a commitment to social development by choice. Pro-social behavior, empathy, teamwork, mental health, and community well-being have become integral to our daily lives. *New values* are necessary for fostering *social orientation*. These cannot be adequately expressed through outdated concepts like *collectivism* and *individualism*, which often redistribute power to *dominant individuals* or *closed tribal groups*. As a higher goal, social orientation involves individuals and groups *connecting with and empowering others*.

Where do we find business examples of people who could work countless hours *motivated by making others stronger* and not solely by monetary business results? Fortunately, the solution is already within our grasp. It lies in entrepreneurship, a domain centered on *effectively transferring functional competencies, skills, and resources to empower others*. "The Gift of Sensitivity"[287] book refers to various data sources pointing to 400–600 million entrepreneurs across the globe, which is 5–7% of the world's population. According to Global Entrepreneurship Monitor's survey,[288] which conducted research in 50 different economies worldwide in 2021–2022, entrepreneurial activity increased during the pandemic, but not all entrepreneurs are passionate about enhancing the world's greatness. Some just survive, so how many of them are motivated by money? Thankfully, the answer registered less than 30%. The entrepreneurial mindset is more than a money-making machine.

New managers and leaders are not those who skillfully use yardsticks but ones who can *inspire people* and *help them express their best potential*. What can they learn from entrepreneurs? It was pointed out by Ryan and Deci,[289] young psychologists at the University of Rochester in 1977 who were "thoroughly involved" in studying human motivation. Until they developed the "self-determination theory," psychologists defined motivation as "energy necessary for action," little was known about what gives such energy. The works of Ryan and Deci made a type of *intrinsic motivation* known. When understood, it creates a sense of *purpose and direction*, empowering others to strive for excellence. This is what we call *inspiration*. If we lack emotional connections with others, we simply cannot inspire anybody because we don't care about them and their individual results. People who understand what is needed by others and help them navigate this world better are known for the quality known as *impact*. A mindset that allows them to "sense others" and builds on that is well-known as the *entrepreneurial mindset*.

This unique aspect of entrepreneurship sets it apart from other pursuits. Their *emotional skills*, not academic or traditionally attributed to management ones, predict entrepreneurial success. The core entrepreneurial ability to identify and address "gaps" is rooted in the capacity to discern *places of potential development* and *connect resources to them*. Industrial-era businesses misinterpret the original meaning of "what is needed" for the "needs of others," which gives them an excuse to fuel endless economic production driven by insatiable human needs. However, the multiple crises that result from merely supplying drugs to addicts made the misunderstanding of this concept clear. The initial intent of identifying "gaps" and "what is needed" was to *empower others*, not to fuel *needy consumerism*. We can strengthen the weak by identifying "what is needed" as the *potential development* area. Our task is to remind them who they truly are and make them stronger—my research links *psychological well-being with mitigating impulsive buying*.

We can learn from entrepreneurs, who as small-scale players, receive direct feedback on what is needed and can quickly adapt. They may not be the strongest and are often fragile, but this allows them to continuously *seek support* and *offer it to others*. They must be *sensitive enough* to *recognize opportunities* and *strong enough* to *transform reality*. Global change requires speed, and this is the *force with a mentality ready for it*. Imagine even bigger possibilities of flattening the hierarchical structures of multinational corporations to adopt an entrepreneurial mindset focused on serving others and not by *exploiting needs*. Do you think this idea is utopia? Explore the latest research on *socially inspired innovations* booming in international business studies. Don't rush: approach it wisely.

Lead the consumption revolution by balancing power with responsibility

If *entrepreneurs are catalysts*, who are the *leaders* and *driving forces* for the consumption revolution? Amber et al.[1] point to international corporations, which are leading players in the global economy, significantly influencing social and political life across countries. Dörrenbächer et al.[162] emphasized that when consumers purchase a new car, research upcoming holidays online, or stream their favorite music, they engage with international businesses that play vital roles in the global economic landscape. According to the OECD Statistics and Data Directorate[290] the top 100 internationals generated over $11 trillion in revenues, equivalent to the combined GDP of Germany, France, Italy, and Spain in 2021. Yu et al.[291] highlighted that five international corporations controlled 82% of the world's palladium production, five dominated 90% of the global palm oil trade, 13 harvested 15% of global seafood, and 20 accounted for over a third of carbon emissions from 1965 to 2017. Nippa et al.[292] highlighted that international businesses are major CO_2 emitters, criticized for resisting the shift to clean energy due to profit motives. Yu et al.[291] noted that they contribute to environmental crises through unprecedented *waste generation* and *resource exploitation*, following a cycle of *extracting natural resources in one place, manufacturing* products in another, and *selling them globally*.

Foley et al.[293] describe international businesses as the *global goliaths of modern times*, collectively responsible for significant portions of the world's production, employment, investment, international trade, research, and innovation. Consequently, *resource scarcity*, the *climate crisis, biodiversity loss*, and *social inequalities* could be linked to international corporations' economic and political power. Dörrenbächer et al.[162] pointed to morally and legally dubious activities and the negative impacts of some international corporations' operations. Maksimov et al.[294] noted that among all marketing players, international corporations face increasing pressure from global stakeholders, heightened media scrutiny, community skepticism, and potential spillover effects.

Simultaneously, Amber et al.[1] emphasize that international business structures possess a competitive advantage through access to *innovation clusters, knowledge resources* such as international and host country *experience, technology, marketing expertise, intellectual capital*, and *human capital* at levels surpassing any other business globally. Marano et al.[295] highlight that international enterprises and their global suppliers are increasingly expected to implement sustainability practices throughout their supply chains. Ocelík et al.[296] emphasize their role as critical actors in facilitating a successful transition toward a greener and more equitable future.

They also noted that by moving from exploitative and transactional practices, multinational businesses could evolve into *responsive and transformative forces* in post-growth economies. Therefore, international corporations must go beyond merely addressing traditional issues such as cultural distance, values, long-term orientation, or individualism, as pointed out by Srivastava et al.[298] They should prioritize adaptability and change, serve cross-border collaborations and local communities, implement ethical practices, and commit to sustainable consumption, emphasizing responsible business practices and *fostering meaningful connections with consumers*. In the context of our research, meaningful connections target *empowering customers*, not playing on human vulnerabilities and merely serving needs.

Christopher[299] argues that merely investing in diversity management and effective communication to boost effectiveness is insufficient. This book highlights *entrepreneurs as mindset catalysts* of a consumption revolution. Consequently, international corporations could prioritize resources toward this change. They are well-equipped, with access to myriad consumers, a multicultural workforce, and strong leadership training and marketing strategies. These *corporations could become leaders for a "triple win,"* benefiting people, the planet, and universal prosperity. They are poised to force a new business paradigm shift, *moving from merely serving customer needs to empowering them*. By following these goliaths, every business-related entity could become a *driving force in the consumption revolution*.

Custodians of existence and stewards of life equilibrium

Academic literature highlights how well-being and happiness are tied to sustainable consumption. It has been shown that the main goal of the new *socially driven consumption group* is all about well-being and happiness. It should not be understood as a personal quality: humans naturally desire to stay *connected with others* and remain actively involved in life. For a psychologically healthy individual, it is impossible to find happiness at the expense of others or while the world is in distress. Kusz and Ahmad[300] emphasize that a sense of *social connection* and engagement *promotes our well-being*. In contrast, loneliness and social isolation negatively affect physical health, mental health, and life expectancy. The same applies to our *relationship with nature*, although we have nearly lost this sacred connection due to consumerism, viewing natural resources merely as a means to man-made capital. They are not: *natural capital forms our habitat*, of which we are integral. However, achieving a balance requires a system view: considering social, environmental, and economic pillars as interdependent, not existing at the expense of one another.

A short verdict from considered literature is that absolute majority of factors related to the personal and psychological domains strongly influence impulsive buying behavior. While this varies across product categories, cultures, or age groups, it is evident that impulsive buying can serve as a psychological well-being mechanism. Wamsler[301] highlights that climate change and other sustainability challenges can be understood as a subconscious outcome of how we all live. As such, we have a vast potential right in our hands for personal transformation based on inner development. This argument extends beyond humans. Sustainability was conceived with future generations in mind, providing a framework to maintain and support life conditions. Recognizing this long-term goal, we must accept that *humans are not the center of the universe*, and while happiness and well-being are powerful aims, *they are not the sole purposes of our existence*.

To ensure abundant life is passed on to future generations, *upholding life equilibrium* based on long-term socio-ecological resilience is crucial. We require bees pollinating flowers, fish thriving in rivers, trees silhouetted against sunsets, and crops flourishing in fields. Our existence is intricately tied to ecosystems, making it a *primary goal to maintain the balance necessary for life*. While well-being and happiness are fundamental, they constitute our *adult responsibilities* rather than the ultimate aim of human existence. Our primary goal should be to *support the equilibrium of life*, act as *custodians of existence*, and ensure that the next generation survives and thrives. With that in mind, what could be done with overconsumption, which is killing us? Can we transform impulsive buying behavior into meaningful actions that will help preserve life? What help do we need to heal and transform into stewards of life? What practical steps can businesses take to ensure sustainable consumption understanding and support life balance? This book serves as an inspiration with practical examples from more than 200 research voices all around the world of what could be done by businesses contributing to sustainable consumption. I hope it does work well.

Custodians of existence and stewards of life equilibrium: key takeaways

- Social transformation is inevitable.
- Serving others often reveals our greatest strengths.
- Leading the consumption revolution is possible by balancing power with responsibility.
- Custodians of existence and stewards of life equilibrium are essential roles for the new era. Why not align your business with this mission?

Notes

1. Amber E, Papasolomou I, Thrassou A, Melanthiou Y. A multi-country SLR of sustainable consumption in impulsive buying: Actionable marketing propositions for multinational companies and conceptualization. *International Marketing Research*. 2024 (Manuscript submitted for publication).

2. Lynas M, Houlton BZ, Perry S. Greater than 99% consensus on human caused climate change in the peer-reviewed scientific literature. *ERL*. 2021;16(11):114005.

3. Hagens NJ. Economics for the future – Beyond the superorganism. *Ecol Econ*. 2020;169:106520.

4. Balderjahn I, Appenfeller D. A social marketing approach to voluntary simplicity: Communicating to consume less. *Sustainability*. 2023;15(3):2302.

5. Podoshen JS, Andrzejewski SA. An examination of the relationships between materialism, conspicuous consumption, impulse buying, and brand loyalty. *Journal of Marketing Theory and Practice*. 2012;20(3):319–334.

6. Fisk G. Criteria for a theory of responsible consumption. *Journal of Marketing*. 1973;37(2):24–31.

7. Haider M, Shannon R, Moschis GP. Sustainable consumption research and the role of marketing: A review of the literature (1976–2021). *Sustainability (Basel, Switzerland)*. 2022;14(7):3999.

8. Key TM, Clark T, Ferrell OC, Stewart DW, Pitt L. Marketing's theoretical and conceptual value proposition: Opportunities to address marketing's influence. *AMS Rev*. 2020;10(3–4):151–167.

9. Palminhas JCC. *The degrowth of consumption as an economic strategy: Is sustainable development a fading adage?* ProQuest Dissertations & Theses; 2015.

10. Kilbourne W. Sustainable communication and the dominant social paradigm: Can they be integrated? *Marketing Theory*. 2004;4(3):187–208. doi: 10.1177/1470593104045536.

11. Hickel J, Kallis G, Jackson T, et al. Degrowth can work—here's how science can help. *Nature*. 2022;612(7940):400–403.

12. Lorek S, Spangenberg JH. Sustainable consumption within a sustainable economy–beyond green growth and green economies. *J Clean Prod*. 2014;63:33–44.

13. Amber E, Papasolomou I, Thrassou A, Melanthiou Y. Leveraging SDG12 for marketing communication and consumer trust: Theoretical elucidations and practical recommendations. *Review of Management Literature (RoML)*. In press.

14. Kalaniemi S, Ottelin J, Heinonen J, Junnila S. Downscaling consumption to universal basic income level falls short of sustainable carbon footprint in Finland. *Environ Sci & Policy.* 2020;114:377–383.

15. Sheth JN, Sethia NK, Srinivas S. Mindful consumption: A customer-centric approach to sustainability. *Journal of the Academy of Marketing Science.* 2011;39:21–39.

16. World Bank. *Poverty and shared prosperity 2018: Piecing together the poverty puzzle.* World Bank Publications; 2018.

17. Hornborg A, Martinez-Alier J. Ecologically unequal exchange and ecological debt. *Journal of Political Ecology.* 2016;23(1):328–333.

18. Arrhenius S. On the influence of carbonic acid in the air upon the temperature of the ground. *Philosophical Magazine and Journal of Science.* 1896;41(5): 237–276.

19. OECD. How's life? 2020: Measuring well-being. 2020. Available at: www.oecd.org/en/publications/2020/03/how-s-life-2020_b547d82c.html

20. De Schutter O. Obsession with growth is enriching elites and killing the planet. We need an economy based on human rights. *The Guardian.* Available at: www.theguardian.com/global-development/article/2024/jul/02/obsession-with-growth-is-enriching-elites-and-killing-the-planet-we-need-an-economy-based-on-human-rights-olivier-de-schutter

21. www.linkedin.com/posts/olivier-de-schutter-83990552_growth-is-enriching-an-elite-and-killing-activity-7214182144410054656-aSaV?utm_source=share &utm_medium=member_desktop&rcm=ACoAADRzNpIBoYvQou7PnhLgz RskPN4khMYGqBs

22. Martínez-Alier J, Pascual U, Vivien F, Zaccai E. Sustainable de-growth: Mapping the context, criticisms and future prospects of an emergent paradigm. *Ecol Econ.* 2010;69(9):1741–1747.

23. Sekulova F, Kallis G, Rodríguez-Labajos B, Schneider F. Degrowth: From theory to practice. *J Clean Prod.* 2013;38:1–6.

24. Schumacher EF. *Small is beautiful: Economics as if people mattered. London: Blond & Briggs.* 1973.

25. Douglas AJ. Renewable resources. In: Dordrecht: Springer Netherlands; 1999:512–517. 10.1007/1-4020-4494-1_279.

26. Urton G, Nina Llanos P. *The social life of numbers: A Quechua ontology of numbers and philosophy of arithmetic.* University of Texas Press; 1997.

27. Rockström J, Steffen W, Noone K, et al. A safe operating space for humanity. *Nature (London).* 2009;461(7263):472–475.

28. Persson L, Carney Almroth BM, Collins CD, et al. Outside the safe operating space of the planetary boundary for novel entities. *Environ Sci Technol.* 2022;56(3):1510–1521.

29. Gunderson LH. Ecological resilience – In theory and application. *Annu Rev Ecol Syst.* 2000;31(1):425–439.

30. Holling CS. The resilience of terrestrial ecosystems: Local surprise and global change. *Sustainable Development of the Biosphere.* 1986;14:292–317.

31. Tri HC, Hens L, Phuoc PMT, Hung NT, Phuong TH. A systematic approach to the dilemma between flood vulnerability and resilience: Review and concepts. *Vietnam Journal of Science and Technology.* 2017;55(5): 620–636.

32. Fath BD, Fiscus DA, Goerner SJ, Berea A, Ulanowicz RE. Measuring regenerative economics: 10 principles and measures undergirding systemic economic health. *Global Transitions.* 2019;1:15–27. doi: 10.1016/j.glt.2019.02.002.

33. Folke C, Carpenter SR, Walker B, Scheffer M, Chapin T, Rockström J. Resilience thinking: Integrating resilience, adaptability and transformability. *Ecology and Society.* 2010;15(4).

34. Biggs R, Schlüter M, Schoon ML. An introduction to the resilience approach and principles to sustain ecosystem services in social–ecological systems. *Principles for Building Resilience: Sustaining Ecosystem Services in Social–Ecological Systems.* 2015:1–31.

35. Solow RM. Sustainability: An economist's perspective. *Economics of the Environment: Selected Readings.* 1993;3:179–187.

36. Hobson K. 'Weak' or 'strong' sustainable consumption? Efficiency, degrowth, and the 10 year framework of programmes. *Environment and Planning. C, Government & Policy.* 2013;31(6):1082–1098.

37. Biely K, Maes D, Van Passel S. The idea of weak sustainability is illegitimate. *Environ Dev Sustain.* 2018;20(1):223–232.

38. Hautakangas S. London group on environmental accounting, 23rd meeting | system of environmental economic accounting. Web site. https://seea.un.org/events/london-group-environmental-accounting-23rd-meeting. Updated 2017. Accessed: 13.11.2022.

39. Daly H, Farley J. *Ecological economics.* 2nd ed. Washington: Island Press; 2011:xxvii. www.econis.eu/PPNSET?PPN=1606567128.

40. Helm D. *Natural capital: Valuing the planet.* New Haven: Yale University Press; 2015. 10.12987/9780300213942.

41. Wunderlich S, Gatto KA. Consumer perception of genetically modified organisms and sources of information. *Advances in Nutrition (Bethesda, Md.).* 2015;6(6):842–851.

42. IFIC Foundation. Survey: Nearly half of U.S. consumers avoid GMO foods; large majority primarily concerned about human health impact. *NASDAQ OMX's News Release Distribution Channel.* 2018. Available from: https://search.proquest.com/docview/2059583678.

43. Daly H. *Beyond growth*. 1st ed. Boston: Beacon Press; 1996.

44. Wilderer PA, Kopp H, Schroeder ED. *Global sustainability*. 1. Aufl. ed. Newark: Wiley-VCH; 2006. 10.1002/3527604251.

45. Toth G, Szigeti C. The historical ecological footprint: From over-population to over-consumption. *Ecol Ind*. 2016;60:283–291. doi: 10.1016/j.ecolind.2015.06.040.

46. Ismael D, Ploeger A. The potential influence of organic food consumption and intention-behavior gap on consumers' subjective wellbeing. *Foods*. 2020;9(5):650. 10.3390/foods9050650.

47. Pereira Heath MT, Chatzidakis A. 'Blame it on marketing': Consumers' views on unsustainable consumption. *International Journal of Consumer Studies*. 2012;36(6):656–667. doi: 10.1111/j.1470-6431.2011.01043.x.

48. Liu Y, Qu Y, Lei Z, Jia H. Understanding the evolution of sustainable consumption research. *Sustainable Development*. 2017;25(5):414–430. doi: 10.1002/sd.1671.

49. Amos C, Holmes GR, Keneson WC. A meta-analysis of consumer impulse buying. *Journal of Retailing and Consumer Services*. 2014;21(2):86–97. doi: 10.1016/j.jretconser.2013.11.004.

50. Wang Y, Pan J, Xu Y, Luo J, Wu Y. The determinants of impulsive buying behavior in electronic commerce. *Sustainability*. 2022;14(12). doi: 10.3390/su14127500.

51. Kacen JJ, Hess JD, Walker D. Spontaneous selection: The influence of product and retailing factors on consumer impulse purchases. *Journal of Retailing and Consumer Services*. 2012;19(6):578–588.

52. Husnain M, Rehman B, Syed F, Akhtar MW. Personal and in-store factors influencing impulse buying behavior among generation Y consumers of small cities. *Business Perspectives and Research*. 2019;7(1):92–107.

53. Spiteri Cornish L. Why did I buy this? Consumers' post-impulse-consumption experience and its impact on the propensity for future impulse buying behaviour. *Journal of Consumer Behaviour*. 2020;19(1):36–46.

54. Chan S, Weitz N, Persson Å, Trimmer C. SDG 12: Responsible consumption and production. *A Review of Research Needs. Technical annex to the Formas report Forskning för Agenda*. 2018;2030.

55. van Driel M, Biermann F, Kim RE, Vijge MJ. The impact of the sustainable development goals on global policies on sustainable consumption and production. *Globalizations*. 2024:1–17.

56. Tian P, Zhong H, Chen X, Feng K, Sun L, Zhang N, Shao X, Liu Y, Hubacek K. Keeping the global consumption within the planetary boundaries. *Nature*. 2024;635:625–630.

57. Purvis B, Mao Y, Robinson D. Three pillars of sustainability: In search of conceptual origins. *Sustainability Science*. 2019;14:681–695.

58. Lorek S, Fuchs D. Strong sustainable consumption governance – precondition for a degrowth path? *Journal of Cleaner Production.* 2013;38:36–43.

59. Fischer D, Reinermann J, Mandujano GG, DesRoches CT, Diddi S, Vergragt PJ. Sustainable consumption communication: A review of an emerging field of research. *J Clean Prod.* 2021;300:126880.

60. Markauskaitė R, Rūtelionė A. Causes of consumer materialistic and green value conflict: A systematic literature review. *Sustainability.* 2022;14(9):5021. doi: 10.3390/su14095021.

61. Wei Jie P, Petra H, Syed Arslan S. Impact of internet usage on consumer impulsive buying behavior of agriculture products: Moderating role of personality traits and emotional intelligence. *Frontiers in Psychology.* 2022;13:1–14. 10.3389/fpsyg.2022.951103.

62. Lee D, Wan C. The impact of mukbang live streaming commerce on consumers' overconsumption behavior. *Journal of Interactive Marketing.* 2023;58(2):198–221. doi: 10.1177/10949968231156104.

63. Zafar AU, Qiu J, Shahzad M. Do digital celebrities' relationships and social climate matter? Impulse buying in f-commerce. *Internet Research.* 2020;30(6):1731–1762.

64. Um T, Chung N, Stienmetz J. Factors affecting consumers' impulsive buying behavior in tourism mobile commerce using SEM and fsQCA. *Journal of Vacation Marketing.* 2023;29(2):256–274. 10.1177/13567667221090991.

65. Cho H, Oh G, Chiu W. Compensatory consumption during the COVID-19 pandemic: Exploring the critical role of nostalgia in sport consumer behaviour. *Journal of Marketing Management.* 2021;37(17):1736–1763. doi: 10.1080/0267257X.2021.2001028.

66. Sajid KS, Hussain S, Hussain RI, Mustafa B. The effect of fear of COVID-19 on green purchase behavior in Pakistan: A multi-group analysis between infected and non-infected. *Frontiers in Psychology,* 13, 1–13. 10.3389/fpsyg.2022.826870.

67. Chiu W, Oh G, Eun C. Impact of COVID-19 on consumers' impulse buying behavior of fitness products: A moderated mediation model. *Journal of Consumer Behaviour.* 2022;21(2):245–258.

68. White K, Habib R, Hardisty DJ. How to SHIFT consumer behaviors to be more sustainable: A literature review and guiding framework. *J Market.* 2019;83(3):22–49. 10.1177/0022242919825649.

69. Areias S, Disterheft A, Gouveia JP. The role of connectedness in pro-environmental consumption of fashionable commodities. *Sustainability (Basel, Switzerland).* 2023;15(2):1199. doi: 10.3390/su15021199.

70. Vergragt P, Akenji L, Dewick P. Sustainable production, consumption, and livelihoods: Global and regional research perspectives. *J Clean Prod.* 2014;63:1–12.

71. Dimitrova T, Ilieva I, Angelova M. Exploring factors affecting sustainable consumption behaviour. *Administrative Sciences*. 2022;12(4):155.

72. Figueroa-García EC, García-Machado JJ, Perez-Bustamante Yabar DC. Modeling the social factors that determine sustainable consumption behavior in the community of Madrid. *Sustainability*. 2018;10(8):2811.

73. Gossen M, Ziesemer F, Schrader U. Why and how commercial marketing should promote sufficient consumption: A systematic literature review. *Journal of Macromarketing*. 2019;39(3):252–269. doi: 10.1177/0276146719866238.

74. Testa F, Pretner G, Iovino R, Bianchi G, Tessitore S, Iraldo F. Drivers to green consumption: A systematic review. *Environ Dev Sustainability*. 2021;23:4826–4880.

75. Jakubowska D, Sadilek T. Sustainably produced butter: The effect of product knowledge, interest in sustainability, and consumer characteristics on purchase frequency. *Agricultural Economics/Zemedelska Ekonomika*. 2023;69(1):25–34. 10.17221/294/2022-AGRICECON.

76. Mazhar W, Jalees T, Asim M, Alam SH, Zaman SI. Psychological consumer behavior and sustainable green food purchase. *Asia Pacific Journal of Marketing & Logistics*. 2022;34(10):2350–2369.

77. Khalil MK, Khalil R. Leveraging buyers' interest in ESG investments through sustainability awareness. *Sustainability*. 2022;14(21):14278. doi: 10.3390/su142114278.

78. Fitzpatrick N, Parrique T, Cosme I. Exploring degrowth policy proposals: A systematic mapping with thematic synthesis. *J Clean Prod*. 2022;365:132764.

79. International Foundation for Electoral Systems. Swiss Referendum 2025. ElectionGuide. Available at: www.electionguide.org/elections/id/4556/

80. Pellegrino A, Abe M, Shannon R. The dark side of social media: Content effects on the relationship between materialism and consumption behaviors. *Frontiers in Psychology*. 2022;13:1–15.

81. Folke C, Biggs R, Norström AV, Reyers B, Rockström J. Social-ecological resilience and biosphere-based sustainability science. *Ecology and Society*. 2016;21(3):41.

82. Hüttel A, Balderjahn I. The coronavirus pandemic: A window of opportunity for sustainable consumption or a time of turning away? *J Consumer Aff*. 2022;56(1):68–96. 10.1111/joca.12419.

83. Shaikh A, Mukerjee K, Banerjee S. Cab-sharing services and transformation expectations of consumers: The moderating role of materialism. *Benchmarking: An International Journal*. 2023;30(1):234–255. 10.1108/BIJ-09-2021-0525.

84. Yehuala FS. The nexus between welfare state and subjective well-being: A multi-level assessment. *Interdisciplinary Description of Complex Systems*. 2020;18(2):135–154.

85. Veenhoven R. Well-being in the welfare state: Level not higher, distribution not more equitable. *Journal of Comparative Policy Analysis*. 2000;2(1):91–125. 10.1023/A:1010058615425

86. Maximo M. The difference between welfare and wellbeing and how objective the concept of a good life can be. *International Conference Economic Philosophy*. 1987.

87. https://worldhappiness.report

88. Dermody J, Koenig-Lewis N, Zhao AL, Hanmer-Lloyd S. Critiquing a utopian idea of sustainable consumption: A post-capitalism perspective. *Journal of Macromarketing*. 2021;41(4):626–645. doi: 10.1177/0276146720979148.

89. Brandão A, Cupertino de Miranda C. Does sustainable consumption behaviour influence luxury services purchase intention? *Sustainability*. 2022;14(13):7906–N.PAG.

90. Ramos-Hidalgo E, Diaz-Carrion R, Rodríguez-Rad C. Does sustainable consumption make consumers happy? *International Journal of Market Research*. 2022;64(2):227–248. doi: 10.1177/14707853211030482.

91. Nepomuceno M, Laroche M. When materialists intend to resist consumption: The moderating role of self-control and long-term orientation. *J Bus Ethics*. 2017;143(3):467–483. doi: 10.1007/s10551-015-2792-0.

92. Geiger SM, Keller J. Shopping for clothes and sensitivity to the suffering of others: The role of compassion and values in sustainable fashion consumption. *Environment & Behavior*. 2018;50(10):1119–1144. 10.1177/0013916517732109.

93. Vohs KD, Faber RJ. Spent resources: Self-Regulatory resource availability affects impulse buying. *The Journal of Consumer Research*. 2007;33(4):537–547.

94. Silvera DH, Lavack AM, Kropp F. Impulse buying: The role of affect, social influence, and subjective wellbeing. *The Journal of Consumer Marketing*. 2008;25(1):23–33.

95. Burroughs J, Rindfleisch A. Materialism and well-being: A conflicting values perspective. *Journal of Consumer Research*. 2002;29(3):348–370.

96. Lekavičienė R, Antinienė D, Nikou S, Rūtelionė A, Šeinauskienė B, Vaičiukynaitė E. Reducing consumer materialism and compulsive buying through emotional intelligence training amongst Lithuanian students. *Frontiers in Psychology*. 2022;13:932395.

97. Czarnecka B, Schivinski B, Keles S. How values of individualism and collectivism influence impulsive buying and money budgeting: The mediating role of acculturation to global consumer culture. *Journal of Consumer Behaviour*. 2020;19(5):505–522.

98. Lu X, Sheng T, Zhou X, Shen C, Fang B. How does young consumers' greenwashing perception impact their green purchase intention in the fast fashion industry? an analysis from the perspective of perceived risk theory. *Sustainability*. 2022;14(20):N.PAG. doi: 10.3390/su142013473.

99. Gawior B, Polasik M, el Olmo JL. Credit card use, hedonic motivations, and impulse buying behavior in fast fashion physical stores during COVID-19: The sustainability paradox. *Sustainability.* 2022;14(7):4133. doi: 10.3390/su14074133.

100. Shahpasandi F, Zarei A, Nikabadi MS. Consumers' impulse buying behavior on Instagram: Examining the influence of flow experiences and hedonic browsing on impulse buying. *Journal of Internet Commerce.* 2020;19(4):437–465.

101. Upadhye B, Sivakumaran B, Pradhan D, Lyngdoh T. Can planning prompt be a boon for impulsive customers? Moderating roles of product category and decisional procrastination. *Psychology & Marketing.* 2021;38(8):1197–1219. 10.1002/mar.21490.

102. Princes E. Boosting impulse buying behavior in marketing management: Customer satisfaction perspective. *Polish Journal of Management Studies.* 2019;20(2):403.

103. He J, Liu S, Li T, Mai THT. The positive effects of unneeded consumption behaviour on consumers during the COVID-19 pandemic. *Int J Environ Res Public Health.* 2021;18(12). doi: 10.3390/ijerph18126404.

104. Gupta AS, Mukherjee J. Long-term changes in consumers' shopping behavior post-pandemic: An exploratory study. *International Journal of Retail & Distribution Management.* 2022;50(12):1518–1534. 10.1108/IJRDM-04-2022-0111.

105. Phang IG, Balakrishnan B, Ting H. Does sustainable consumption matter? Consumer grocery shopping behaviour and the pandemic. *Journal of Social Marketing.* 2021;11(4):507–522.

106. Jiang Y, Lau AK. Effect of restaurant consumers' anticipated emotions on perceived value and behavioral intention in the COVID-19 context. *Frontiers in Psychology.* 2022;13: 1013209.

107. Wang S, Liu Y, Du Y, Wang X. Effect of the COVID-19 pandemic on consumers' impulse buying: The moderating role of moderate thinking. *Int J Environ Res Public Health.* 2021;18(21).

108. Ah Fook L, McNeill L. Click to buy: The impact of retail credit on over-consumption in the online environment. *Sustainability.* 2020;12(18):7322. doi: 10.3390/su12187322.

109. Iyer R, Muncy JA. Attitude toward consumption and subjective well-being. *J Consumer Aff.* 2016;50(1):48–67. 10.1111/joca.12079.

110. Shams HA, Hussain S, Feroze T, et al. Stressors, stress and impulsive buying behavior: Moderating role of emotional intelligence. *International Journal of Business and Economic Affairs.* 2021;6(3):164–174.

111. Crawford G, Melewar TC. The importance of impulse purchasing behaviour in the international airport environment. *Journal of Consumer Behaviour: An International Research Review.* 2003;3(1):85–98.

112. Malter MS, Holbrook MB, Kahn BE, Parker JR, Lehmann DR. The past, present, and future of consumer research. *Mark Lett.* 2020;31:137–149.

113. Namazkhan M, Albers C, Steg L. A decision tree method for explaining household gas consumption: The role of building characteristics, sociodemographic variables, psychological factors and household behaviour. *Renewable and Sustainable Energy Reviews.* 2020;119:109542. doi: 10.1016/j.rser.2019.109542.

114. Dennison L, Moss-Morris R, Chalder T. A review of psychological correlates of adjustment in patients with multiple sclerosis. *Clin Psychol Rev.* 2009;29(2):141–153. doi: 10.1016/j.cpr.2008.12.001.

115. Piligrimienė Ž, Žukauskaitė A, Korzilius H, Banytė J, Dovalienė A. Internal and external determinants of consumer engagement in sustainable consumption. *Sustainability.* 2020;12(4):1349.

116. Liao S.-H., Chung Y.-C. The effects of psychological factors on online consumer behavior. *2011 IEEE International Conference on Industrial Engineering and Engineering Management.* 2011:1380–1383. doi: 10.1109/IEEM.2011.6118142.

117. Di Crosta A, Ceccato I, Marchetti D, et al. Psychological factors and consumer behavior during the COVID-19 pandemic. *PloS one.* 2021;16(8):e0256095.

118. Nordlund A. Values, attitudes, and norms: Drivers in the Future Forests context. *Future Forests Working Report.* Framtidens skog, Sveriges lantbruksuniversitet; 2009.

119. Newman A, Donohue R, Eva N. Psychological safety: A systematic review of the literature. *Human Resource Management Review.* 2017;27(3):521–535.

120. Dholakia U, Jung J, Chowdhry N. Should I buy this when I have so much?: Reflection on personal possessions as an anticonsumption strategy. *Journal of Public Policy & Marketing.* 2018;37(2):260–273. 10.1177/0743915618813582.

121. Mandolfo M, Lamberti L. Past, present, and future of impulse buying research methods: A systematic literature review. *Frontiers in Psychology.* 2021;12:687404.

122. Fitness J, Curtis M. Emotional intelligence and the trait meta-mood scale: Relationships with empathy, attributional complexity, self-control, and responses to interpersonal conflict. *Ejournal of Applied Psychology.* 2005;1(1):50–62.

123. Sharma P, Sivakumaran B, Marshall R. Impulse buying and variety seeking: A trait-correlates perspective. *Journal of Business Research.* 2010;63(3):276–283.

124. Nguyen TD, Dadzie CA, Chaudhuri HR, Tanner T. Self-control and sustainability consumption: Findings from a cross cultural study. *Journal of International Consumer Marketing.* 2019;31(5):380–394. doi: 10.1080/08961530.2019.1576152.

125. Zhang Y, Shrum LJ. The influence of self-construal on impulsive consumption. *The Journal of Consumer Research.* 2009;35(5):838–850.

126. Inzlicht M, Werner KM, Briskin JL, Roberts BW. Integrating models of self-regulation. *Annu Rev Psychol.* 2021;72:319–345.

127. Scherbaum S, Frisch S, Holfert A, O'Hora D, Dshemuchadse M. No evidence for common processes of cognitive control and self-control. *Acta Psychol.* 2018;182:194–199. doi: 10.1016/j.actpsy.2017.11.018.

128. Thomas M. To control your life, control what you pay attention to. *Harvard Business Review.* 2018. Available at: https://hbr.org/2018/03/to-control-your-life-control-what-you-pay-attention-to

129. www.linkedin.com/video/live/urn:li:ugcPost:6978740925560717314/

130. Zak P. *Immersion: The science of the extraordinary and the source of happiness.* Lioncrest Publishing; 2022.

131. Baumeister R. *Self-regulation and self-control: Selected works of Roy F. Baumeister.* Routledge; 2018.

132. Goleman D. *Working with emotional intelligence.* NY: Bantam Books; 1998.

133. Mayer JD, DiPaolo M, Salovey P. Perceiving affective content in ambiguous visual stimuli: A component of emotional intelligence. *J Pers Assess.* 1990;54(3–4):772–781.

134. Gendron B. Why emotional capital matters in education and in labour? Toward an optimal exploitation of human capital and knowledge management. 2004. Available at: http://econpapers.repec.org/paper/msewpsorb/r04113.htm

135. Iyer GR, Blut M, Xiao SH, Grewal D. Impulse buying: A meta-analytic review. *Journal of the Academy of Marketing Science.* 2020;48(3): 384–404. 10.1007/s11747-019-00670-w.

136. Zhao Y, Li Y, Wang N, Zhou R, Luo X. A meta-analysis of online impulsive buying and the moderating effect of economic development level. *Inf Syst Front.* 2022;24(5):1667–1688.

137. Seinauskiene B, Mascinskiene J, Petrike I, Rutelione A. Materialism as the mediator of the association between subjective well-being and impulsive buying tendency. *Inžinerinė ekonomika.* 2016;27(5):594–606.

138. Matthews G, Emo AK, Funke G, et al. Emotional intelligence, personality, and task-induced stress. *Journal of Experimental Psychology: Applied.* 2006;12(2):96–107.

139. Cherniss C, Goleman D. *The emotionally intelligent workplace.* Wiley; 2001.

140. Eyel CŞ, Durmaz İBV. The effect of emotional capital on individual innovativeness: A research on Bahcesehir University business administration undergraduate students. *Procedia Computer Science.* 2019;158:680–687.

141. Zembylas M. Emotional capital and education: Theoretical insights from Bourdieu. In: *Bourdieu and education.* Routledge; 2020:41–61.

142. Ahmed S. Affective economies. *Social Text.* 2004;22(2):117–139.

143. Jackson EN. Grief and religion. *The Meaning of Death.* 1959:218–233.

144. Cottingham MD. Theorizing emotional capital. *Theory and Society.* 2016;45:451–470.

145. Nowotny H. Women in public life in Austria. In: *Access to power: Cross-national studies of women and elites,* Epstein CF, Coser RL (eds). Routledge; 1981.

146. Madhavan S, Clark S, Hara Y. Gendered emotional support and women's well-being in a low-income urban African setting. *Gender Soc.* 2018;32(6):837–859. doi: 10.1177/0891243218786670.

147. Reay D. A useful extension of Bourdieu's conceptual framework? Emotional capital as a way of understanding mothers' involvement in their children's education? *Sociol Rev.* 2000;48(4):568–585.

148. Froyum CM. The reproduction of inequalities through emotional capital: The case of socializing low-income black girls. *Qualitative Sociology.* 2010;33:37–54.

149. Gillies V. Working class mothers and school life: Exploring the role of emotional capital. *Gender and Education.* 2006;18(3):281–293.

150. Feeney BC, Lemay Jr EP. Surviving relationship threats: The role of emotional capital. *Person Soc Psychol Bull.* 2012;38(8):1004–1017.

151. Lively KJ, Weed EA. Emotion management: Sociological insight into what, how, why, and to what end? *Emotion Review.* 2014;6(3):202–207.

152. Cottingham MD. *Practical feelings: Emotions as resources in a dynamic social world.* Oxford University Press; 2022.

153. Khazaei M, Holder MD, Sirois FM, Oades LG, Gendron B. Development and assessment of the personal emotional capital questionnaire for adults. *International Journal of Environmental Research and Public Health.* 2021;18(4):1856.

154. Moustakas L. Social cohesion: Definitions, causes and consequences. *Encyclopedia (Basel, Switzerland).* 2023;3(3):1028–1037. doi: 10.3390/encyclopedia3030075.

155. Chan J, To H, Chan E. Reconsidering social cohesion: Developing a definition and analytical framework for empirical research. *Social Indicators Research.* 2006;75(2):273–302. doi: 10.1007/s11205-005-2118-1.

156. Saïd Business School and EY. Transformation leadership: navigating turning points. *Humans@Centre.* 2024. Available at: www.sbs.ox.ac.uk/sites/default/files/2024-04/2024-ey-report.pdf

157. Meadows DH. Places to intervene in a system (an increasing order of effectiveness). *Whole Earth (San Rafael, Calif.)* 1997(91):78.

158. www.statista.com/outlook/emo/online-education/worldwide

159. Maltz E, Pierson K. Maximizing corporate social innovation to enhance social and shareholder value: A systems thinking model of industry transformation. *Journal of Business Research*. 2022;138:12–25.

160. Anand J, McDermott G, Mudambi R, Narula R. Innovation in and from emerging economies: New insights and lessons for international business research. *J Int Bus Stud*. 2021;52:545–559.

161. van der Waal JWH, Thijssens T, Maas K. The innovative contribution of multinational enterprises to the sustainable development goals. *J Clean Prod*. 2021;285:125319. doi: 10.1016/j.jclepro.2020.125319.

162. Dörrenbächer C, Geppert M, Bozkurt Ö. Multinational corporations and grand challenges: Part of the problem, part of the solution? *Critical Perspectives on International Business*. 2024;20(2):153–163. doi: 10.1108/cpoib-01-2024-0008.

163. Sermboonsang R, Tansuhaj PS, Silpakit C, Chaisuwan C. Mindfulness-based transformational learning for managing impulse buying. *Journal of Education for Business*. 2020;95(2):129–137. 10.1080/08832323.2019.1618233.

164. Armstrong Soule CA, Reich BJ. Less is more: Is a green demarketing strategy sustainable? *Journal of Marketing Management*. 2015;31(13–14):1403–1427.

165. Kuanr A, Israel D, Pradhan D, Roy Chaudhuri H. Can we anti-consume our way to sustainability? Finding answers at the intersection of cultural values. *Journal of Consumer Behaviour*. 2021;20(5):1051–1064. 10.1002/cb.1914.

166. Chang HJ, Watchravesringkan K. Who are sustainably minded apparel shoppers? An investigation to the influencing factors of sustainable apparel consumption. *International Journal of Retail & Distribution Management*. 2018;46(2):148–162. 10.1108/IJRDM-10-2016-0176.

167. Mogilner C, Aaker J, Kamvar SD. How happiness affects choice. *The Journal of Consumer Research*. 2012;39(2):429–443.

168. Ortiz Alvarado NB, Rodríguez Ontiveros M, Quintanilla Domínguez C. Exploring emotional well-being in Facebook as a driver of impulsive buying: A cross-cultural approach. *J Int Consumer Market*. 2020;32(5):400–415.

169. Moser, Schoenebeck S, Resnick P. Impulse buying. *Proceedings of the 2019 CHI Conference on Human Factors in Computing Systems*. 2019:1–15.

170. Wang X, Tauni MZ, Zhang Q, Ali A, Ali F. Does buyer-seller personality match enhance impulsive buying? A green marketing context. *Journal of Marketing Theory & Practice*. 2020;28(4):436–446. 10.1080/10696679.2020.1780137.

171. Holbrook MB, Batra R. Assessing the role of emotions as mediators of consumer responses to advertising. *Journal of Consumer Research*. 1987;14(3):404–420.

172. Pine BJ, Gilmore JH. The experience economy: Past, present and future. In: *Handbook on the experience economy*. Edward Elgar Publishing; 2013:21–44.

173. Thøgersen J. Consumer behavior and climate change: Consumers need considerable assistance. *Current Opinion in Behavioral Sciences*. 2021;42:9–14. doi: 10.1016/j.cobeha.2021.02.008.

174. United Nations. The Sustainable Development Goals Report 2022. Available at: https://unstats.un.org/sdgs/report/2022/The-Sustainable-Development-Goals-Report-2022.pdf

175. Rana J, Paul J. Health motive and the purchase of organic food: A meta-analytic review. *International Journal of Consumer Studies*. 2020;44(2):162–171.

176. Rodríguez MS, Vázquez SC, Casas PM, de la Cuerda RC. Neurorehabilitation and apps: A systematic review of mobile applications. *Neurología (English Edition)*. 2018;33(5):313–326.

177. Lu F, Huang X, Wang X. Willingness to pay for mobile health live streaming during the COVID-19 pandemic: Integrating TPB with compatibility. *Sustainability*. 2022;14(23):15932. doi: 10.3390/su142315932.

178. Kago K, Venkataraman P. Possibility of conjunction between altruism and egoism. *Humanities and Social Sciences Communications*. 2023;10(1):1–5.

179. Steg L, Perlaviciute G, Van der Werff E. Understanding the human dimensions of a sustainable energy transition. *Frontiers in Psychology*. 2015;6:805.

180. Lu X, Sheng T, Zhou X, Shen C, Fang B. How does young consumers' greenwashing perception impact their green purchase intention in the fast fashion industry? An analysis from the perspective of perceived risk theory. *Sustainability*. 2022;14(20):N.PAG. doi: 10.3390/su142013473.

181. Bardey A, Booth M, Heger G, Larsson J. Finding yourself in your wardrobe: An exploratory study of lived experiences with a capsule wardrobe. *International Journal of Market Research*. 2022;64(1):113–131. doi: 10.1177/1470785321993743.

182. Ling Xie S, Muhammad Faisal W, Abdul A, Qurat ul S, Zunair A. Do meat anti-consumption opinions influence consumers' wellbeing? The moderating role of religiosity. *Frontiers in Psychology*. 2022;13:1–14.

183. Nguyen TD, Dadzie CA, Chaudhuri HR, Tanner T. Self-control and sustainability consumption: Findings from a cross cultural study. *J Int Consumer Market*. 2019;31(5):380–394.

184. Tariq A, Wang C, Tanveer Y, Akram U, Akram Z. Organic food consumerism through social commerce in China. *Asia Pacific Journal of Marketing and Logistics*. 2019;31(1):202–222. doi: 10.1108/APJML-04-2018-0150.

185. Shahzad MF, Tian Y, Xiao J. "Drink it or not": Soft drink anticonsumption behavior and the mediating effect of behavioral intentions. *Sustainability*. 2019;11(12):3279.

186. Sheth JN, Newman BI, Gross BL. Why we buy what we buy: A theory of consumption values. *Journal of Business Research*. 1991;22(2):159–170.

187. Liu C, Zheng Y, Cao D. Similarity effect and purchase behavior of organic food under the mediating role of perceived values in the context of COVID-19. *Frontiers in Psychology*. 2021;12:1–16.

188. Ladhari R, Pons F, Bressolles G, Zins M. Culture and personal values: How they influence perceived service quality. *Journal of Business Research*. 2011;64(9):951–957. doi: 10.1016/j.jbusres.2010.11.017.

189. Zhang KZ, Xu H, Zhao S, Yu Y. Online reviews and impulse buying behavior: The role of browsing and impulsiveness. *Internet Research*. 2018;28(3):522–543.

190. Cao D, Zheng Y, Liu C, Yao X, Chen S. Consumption values, anxiety and organic food purchasing behaviour considering the moderating role of sustainable consumption attitude. *Br Food J*. 2022;124(11):3540–3562. 10.1108/BFJ-06-2021-0647.

191. Hüttel A, Balderjahn I. The coronavirus pandemic: A window of opportunity for sustainable consumption or a time of turning away? *J Consumer Aff*. 2022;56(1):68–96.

192. Shobeiri S, Rajaobelina L, Durif F, Boivin C. Experiential motivations of socially responsible consumption. *International Journal of Market Research*. 2016;58(1):119–139. 10.2501/IJMR-2016-007.

193. Cho R. Plastic, paper or cotton: which shopping bag is best? *State of the Planet; Columbia Climate School*. Available at: https://news.climate.columbia.edu/2020/04/30/plastic-paper-cotton-bags/

194. White K, Habib R, Hardisty DJ. How to SHIFT consumer behaviors to be more sustainable: A literature review and guiding framework. *J Market*. 2019;83(3):22–49. 10.1177/0022242919825649.

195. Horcea-Milcu A. Values as leverage points for sustainability transformation: Two pathways for transformation research. *Current Opinion in Environmental Sustainability*. 2022;57:101205. doi: 10.1016/j.cosust.2022.101205.

196. Sirgy MJ, Lee D, Yu GB. Shopping-life balance: Towards a unifying framework. *Applied Research in Quality of Life*. 2020;15(1):17–34. 10.1007/s11482-018-9662-8.

197. Asuamah Yeboah S. *Sustaining change: Unravelling the socio-cultural threads of sustainable consumption*. University Library of Munich; 2023.

198. Kacen JJ, Lee JA. The influence of culture on consumer impulsive buying behavior. *Journal of Consumer Psychology*. 2002;12(2):163–176.

199. Hofmann V, Schwayer LM, Stokburger-Sauer NE, Wanisch AT. Consumers' self-construal: Measurement and relevance for social media communication success. *Journal of Consumer Behaviour*. 2021;20(4):959–979.

200. Kilbourne W, Pickett G. How materialism affects environmental beliefs, concern, and environmentally responsible behavior. *Journal of Business Research*. 2008;61(9):885–893.

201. Lee K. How are material values and voluntary simplicity lifestyle related to attitudes and intentions toward commercial sharing during the COVID-19 pandemic? Evidence from Japan. *Sustainability*. 2022;14(13):7812–N.PAG. doi: 10.3390/su14137812.

202. Kasser T. *The high price of materialism*. MIT Press; 2003.

203. Markauskaitė R, Rūtelionė A. Causes of consumer materialistic and green value conflict: A systematic literature review. *Sustainability*. 2022;14(9):5021. doi: 10.3390/su14095021.

204. Wang Y, Pan J, Xu Y, Luo J, Wu Y. The determinants of impulsive buying behavior in electronic commerce. *Sustainability*. 2022;14(12):N.PAG. doi: 10.3390/su14127500.

205. Verain MC, Bartels J, Dagevos H, Sijtsema SJ, Onwezen MC, Antonides G. Segments of sustainable food consumers: A literature review. *International Journal of Consumer Studies*. 2012;36(2):123–132.

206. Süle M. Can conscious consumption be learned? The role of Hungarian consumer protection education in becoming conscious consumers. *International Journal of Consumer Studies*. 2012;36(2):211–220. doi: 10.1111/j.1470-6431.2011.01085.x.

207. Osikominu J, Bocken N. A voluntary simplicity lifestyle: Values, adoption, practices and effects. *Sustainability*. 2020;12(5):1903. doi: 10.3390/su12051903.

208. Chatzidakis A. Guilt and ethical choice in consumption: A psychoanalytic perspective. *Marketing Theory*. 2015;15(1):79–93.

209. Islam T, Pitafi AH, Arya V, et al. Panic buying in the COVID-19 pandemic: A multi-country examination. *Journal of Retailing and Consumer Services*. 2021;59:102357.

210. Benton R. Despair, rigging, anger, and degrowth. *Journal of Macromarketing*. 2022;42(3):345–355.

211. Georgescu-Roegen N. *The entropy law and the economic process*. Harvard University Press; 1971.

212. Kallis G. In defence of degrowth. *Ecol Econ*. 2011;70(5):873–880.

213. Cosme I, Santos R, O'Neill DW. Assessing the degrowth discourse: A review and analysis of academic degrowth policy proposals. *J Clean Prod*. 2017;149:321–334.

214. Nguyen HV, Nguyen C, Hoang T. Green consumption: Closing the intention-behavior gap. *Sustainable development (Bradford, West Yorkshire, England)*. 2019;27(1):118–129. doi: 10.1002/sd.1875.

215. Iwata O. Attitudinal determinants of environmentally responsible behavior. *Social Behavior and Personality: An International Journal*. 2001;29(2):183–190.

216. https://ecovillage.org/

217. Dholakia UM. Temptation and resistance: An integrated model of consumption impulse formation and enactment. *Psychology & Marketing.* 2000;17(11):955–982.

218. Azazz AMS, Elshaer IA. Amid the COVID-19 pandemic, social media usage and food waste intention: The role of excessive buying behavior and religiosity. *Sustainability.* 2022;14(11):6786. doi: 10.3390/su14116786.

219. Oliveira de Mendonça G, Coelho Rocha AR and son D. The minimalist process: An interpretivist study. *Journal of Consumer Behaviour.* 2021;20(5): 1040–1050.

220. Wright C. Minimalism explained. *Exile Lifestyle.* 2010. Available at: https://exilelifestyle.com/minimalism-explained/

221. Kakkar S, Dugar A, Gupta R. Decoding the sustainable consumer: What yoga psychology tells us about self-control and impulsive buying? *South Asian Journal of Business Studies.* 2022;11(3):276–294.

222. European Parliament. Right to repaid: Making repair easier and more appealing to consumers. Press Release. 2024. Available at: www.europarl.europa.eu/news/en/press-room/20240419IPR20590/right-to-repair-making-repair-easier-and-more-appealing-to-consumers

223. Webb S. Why eBay is showing secondhand fashion on the runway. *Vogue Business.* September 12, 2024. Available at: www.voguebusiness.com/story/sustainability/why-ebay-is-showing-secondhand-fashion-on-the-runway-london-new-york

224. Lang C, Zhang R. Second-hand clothing acquisition: The motivations and barriers to clothing swaps for Chinese consumers. *Sustainable Production and Consumption.* 2019;18:156–164. doi: 10.1016/j.spc.2019.02.002.

225. Dermody J, Koenig-Lewis N, Zhao AL, Hanmer-Lloyd S. Critiquing a utopian idea of sustainable consumption: A post-capitalism perspective. *Journal of Macromarketing.* 2021;41(4):626–645. doi: 10.1177/0276146720979148.

226. Eckhardt GM, Bardhi F. The sharing economy isn't about sharing at all. *Harvard Business Review.* 2015. Available at: https://hbr.org/2015/01/the-sharing-economy-isnt-about-sharing-at-all

227. Chakraborty S, Sadachar A. "Why should I buy sustainable apparel?" Impact of user-centric advertisements on consumers' affective responses and sustainable apparel purchase intentions. *Sustainability.* 2022;14(18):11560–N.PAG. doi: 10.3390/su141811560.

228. Szmigin IT, O'Loughlin DM, McEachern M, et al. Keep calm and carry on: European consumers and the development of persistent resilience in the face of austerity. *European Journal of Marketing.* 2020;54(8):1883–1907. doi: 10.1108/EJM-04-2018-0253.

229. Ahmed RR, Streimikiene D, Qadir H, Streimikis J. Effect of green marketing mix, green customer value, and attitude on green purchase intention: Evidence from

the USA. *Environ Sci Pollut Res Int.* 2023;30(5):11473-11495. doi: 10.1007/s11356-022-22944-7.

230. Oh J, Chul Y. Theory-based approach to factors affecting ethical consumption. *International Journal of Consumer Studies.* 2014;38(3):278-288.

231. Rayner L, Easthope G. Postmodern consumption and alternative medications. *Journal of Sociology.* 2001;37(2):157-176.

232. Spinelli G, Nelson-Becker H, Ligossi R. Consumer competence strategies, spiritually inspired core values and locus of control: What are the links? *Sustainability.* 2019;11(17):4787. doi: 10.3390/su11174787.

233. Horley J. A longitudinal examination of lifestyles. *Soc Indicators Res.* 1992;26:205-219.

234. Pícha K, Navrátil J. The factors of lifestyle of health and sustainability influencing pro-environmental buying behaviour. *J Clean Prod.* 2019;234:233-241. 10.1016/j.jclepro.2019.06.072.

235. Höfer R. *Sustainable solutions for modern economies.* Vol 4. Royal Society of Chemistry; 2009.

236. Urh B. Lifestyle of health and sustainability – the importance of health consciousness impact on LOHAS market growth in ecotourism. *Quaestus.* 2015(6):167.

237. Ramos-Hidalgo E, Diaz-Carrion R, Rodríguez-Rad C. Does sustainable consumption make consumers happy? *International Journal of Market Research.* 2022;64(2):227-248. doi: 10.1177/14707853211030482.

238. https://youtu.be/o-RBDl1Uf20?feature=shared

239. Trzebiński J, Cabański M, Czarnecka JZ. Reaction to the COVID-19 pandemic: The influence of meaning in life, life satisfaction, and assumptions on world orderliness and positivity. In: *Loss and trauma in the COVID-19 era.* Routledge; 2024:44-57.

240. Yanmei Jiang L. Effect of restaurant consumers' anticipated emotions on perceived value and behavioral intention in the COVID-19 context. *Frontiers in Psychology.* 2022;13:1-20.

241. Tang Q, Zhang K, Huang X. Indulgent consumption signals interpersonal warmth. *Journal of Marketing Research (JMR).* 2022;59(6):1179-1196. 10.1177/00222437221097089.

242. Ramadan Z, Farah MF, Bou Saada R. Fooled in the relationship: How Amazon Prime members' sense of self-control counter-intuitively reinforces impulsive buying behavior. *Journal of Consumer Behaviour.* 2021;20(6):1497-1507. 10.1002/cb.1960.

243. Peluso AM, Pichierri M, Pino G. Age-related effects on environmentally sustainable purchases at the time of COVID-19: Evidence from Italy. *Journal of Retailing and Consumer Services*. 2021;60:102443.

244. Qi X, Ploeger A. Explaining Chinese consumers' green food purchase intentions during the COVID-19 pandemic: An extended theory of planned behaviour. *Foods*. 2021;10(6):1200. 10.3390/foods10061200.

245. Salazar HA, Oerlemans L, van Stroe-Biezen S. Social influence on sustainable consumption: Evidence from a behavioural experiment. *International Journal of Consumer Studies*. 2013;37(2):172–180.

246. Shahzad MF, Tian Y, Xiao J. "Drink it or not": Soft drink anticonsumption behavior and the mediating effect of behavioral intentions. *Sustainability*. 2019;11(12):3279. doi: 10.3390/su11123279.

247. Ghaffar A, Islam T, Khan H, Kincl T, Sharma A. A sustainable retailer's journey to sustainable practices: Prioritizing the customer and the planet. *Journal of Retailing and Consumer Services*. 2023;74:103388.

248. Hamdan E, Abdullah SNF. *Key opinion leaders: Influencers of the digital age*. Bulletin. Universiti Teknologi MARA, Negeri Sembilan; 2023.

249. Liegey V, Nelson A. *Exploring degrowth*. Pluto Press; 2023.

250. Areias S, Disterheft A, Gouveia JP. The role of connectedness in pro-environmental consumption of fashionable commodities. *Sustainability*. 2023;15(2):1199. doi: 10.3390/su15021199.

251. https://visitayianapa.com/rucms/pages/?a=240

252. Chang M, Chen H. Understanding consumers' intentions to purchase clean label products: Evidence from Taiwan. *Nutrients*. 2022;14(18):N.PAG. doi: 10.3390/nu14183684.

253. Shen X, Xu Q, Liu Q. Predicting sustainable food consumption across borders based on the theory of planned behavior: A meta-analytic structural equation model. *PLoS ONE*. 2022;17(11):1–22. 10.1371/journal.pone.0275312.

254. Ladhari R, Souiden N, Dufour B. The role of emotions in utilitarian service settings: The effects of emotional satisfaction on product perception and behavioral intentions. *Journal of Retailing and Consumer Services*. 2017;34:10–18. doi: 10.1016/j.jretconser.2016.09.005.

255. Billore S, Anisimova T. Panic buying research: A systematic literature review and future research agenda. *International Journal of Consumer Studies*. 2021;45(Early View Articles):777–804.

256. Verplanken B, Herabadi A. Individual differences in impulse buying tendency: Feeling and no thinking. *European Journal of Personality*. 2001;15(S1):S71–S83.

257. Pereira Heath MT, Chatzidakis A. 'Blame it on marketing': Consumers' views on unsustainable consumption. *International Journal of Consumer Studies.* 2012;36(6):656–667. doi: 10.1111/j.1470-6431.2011.01043.x.

258. Alcott B. The sufficiency strategy: Would rich-world frugality lower environmental impact? *Ecol Econ.* 2008;64(4):770–786.

259. Awais M, Samin T, Gulzar MA, Hwang J, Zubair M. Unfolding the association between the big five, frugality, E-mavenism, and sustainable consumption behavior. *Sustainability.* 2020;12(2):490. doi: 10.3390/su12020490.

260. Frank P, Fischer D, Stanszus L, Grossman P, Schrader U. Mindfulness as self-confirmation? An exploratory intervention study on potentials and limitations of mindfulness-based interventions in the context of environmental and sustainability education. *J Environ Educ.* 2021;52(6):417–444.

261. Ares G, de Saldamando L, Giménez A, et al. Consumers' associations with wellbeing in a food-related context: A cross-cultural study. *Food Quality and Preference.* 2015;40:304–315. doi: 10.1016/j.foodqual.2014.06.001.

262. Waters L, Algoe SB, Dutton J, et al. Positive psychology in a pandemic: Buffering, bolstering, and building mental health. *The Journal of Positive Psychology.* 2022;17(3):303–323.

263. Diener E, Thapa S, Tay L. Positive emotions at work. *Annual Review of Organizational Psychology and Organizational Behavior.* 2020;7(1):451–477.

264. Roşu M, Ianole-Călin R, Dinescu R, Bratu A, Papuc Ră, Cosma A. Understanding consumer stockpiling during the COVID-19 outbreak through the theory of planned behavior. *Mathematics.* 2021;9(16):1950. 10.3390/math9161950.

265. Schomburgk L, Hoffmann A. How mindfulness reduces BNPL usage and how that relates to overall well-being. *European Journal of Marketing.* 2023;57(2):325–359.

266. Brown KW, Kasser T, Ryan RM, Linley PA, Orzech K. When what one has is enough: Mindfulness, financial desire discrepancy, and subjective well-being. *Journal of Research in Personality.* 2009;43(5):727–736.

267. Six Seconds. Why "six seconds"? The inside story & neuroscience behind our intriguing name. Available at: www.6seconds.org/2019/06/19/why-six-seconds-about-our-intriguing-name/

268. Nguyen TN, Lobo A, Greenland S. Pro-environmental purchase behaviour: The role of consumers' biospheric values. *Journal of Retailing and Consumer Services.* 2016;33:98–108.

269. Johnston TC, Burton JB. Voluntary simplicity: Definitions and dimensions. *Academy of Marketing Studies Journal.* 2003;7(1):19–36.

270. Seyfang G. Sustainable consumption, the new economics and community currencies: Developing new institutions for environmental governance. *Reg Stud.* 2006;40(7):781–791.

271. Chao DY, Lin TM, Ma W. Enhanced self-efficacy and behavioral changes among patients with diabetes: Cloud-based mobile health platform and mobile app service. *JMIR diabetes.* 2019;4(2):e11017.

272. Bandura A, Adams NE. Analysis of self-efficacy theory of behavioral change. *Cognitive Therapy and Research.* 1977;1(4):287–310.

273. Halper LR, Vancouver JB. Self-efficiency's influence on persistence on a physical task: Moderating effect of performance feedback ambiguity. *Psychol Sport Exerc.* 2016;22:170–177. https://doi.org/10.1016/j-psychsport.2015.08

274. Vrontis D, Makrides A, Christofi M, Thrassou A. Social media influencer marketing: A systematic review, integrative framework and future research agenda. *International Journal of Consumer Studies.* 2021;45(4):617–644. doi: 10.1111/ijcs.12647.

275. Walker CC, Druckman A, Jackson T. Welfare systems without economic growth: A review of the challenges and next steps for the field. *Ecol Econ.* 2021;186:107066.

276. Magids S, Zorfas A, Leemon D. When companies connect with customers' emotions, the payoff can be huge. consider these examples: After a major bank introduced a credit card for millennia is that was designed to. *Harv Bus Rev.* 2015;93(11):68–76.

277. Magids S, Zorfas A, Leemon D. The new science of customer emotions: A better way to drive growth and profitability. *Harv Bus Rev.* 2015. Available at: https://hbr.org/2015/11/the-new-science-of-customer-emotions

278. Wang Y, Pan J, Xu Y, Luo J, Wu Y. The determinants of impulsive buying behavior in electronic commerce. *Sustainability (Basel, Switzerland).* 2022;14(12):7500.

279. Djordjevic A, Cotton D. Communicating the sustainability message in higher education institutions. *International Journal of Sustainability in Higher Education.* 2011;12(4):381–394.

280. Bagdare S. Marketing communications for sustainable consumption: A conceptual framework. *International Journal of Marketing & Business Communication.* 2018;7(4):45–49.

281. Godemann J. Communicating sustainability. Some thoughts and recommendations for enhancing sustainability communication. *The Sustainability Communication Reader: A Reflective Compendium.* 2021:15–29.

282. Weder F, Karmasin M, Krainer L, Voci D. Sustainability communication as critical perspective in media and communication studies—An introduction. *The Sustainability Communication Reader: A Reflective Compendium.* 2021:1–12.

283. Fischer D, Reinermann J, Mandujano GG, DesRoches CT, Diddi S, Vergragt PJ. Sustainable consumption communication: A review of an emerging field of research. *J Clean Prod.* 2021;300:126880.

284. Richins ML, Dawson S. A consumer values orientation for materialism and its measurement: Scale development and validation. *Journal of Consumer Research.* 1992;19(3):303–316.

285. Kim Y, Oh KW. The effect of materialism and impression management purchase motivation on purchase intention for luxury athleisure products: The moderating effect of sustainability. *Journal of Product & Brand Management.* 2022;31(8):1222–1234.

286. Soergel B, Rauner S, Daioglou V, et al. Multiple pathways towards sustainable development goals and climate targets. *Environmental Research Letters.* 2024;19(12):124009.

287. Amber E. *The gift of sensitivity: The extraordinary power of emotional engagement in life and work.* Practical Inspiration Publishing; 2023.

288. Global Entrepreneurship Monitor. 2021/2022 Global report: Opportunity amid disruption. 2022. Available at: www.gemconsortium.org/report/gem-20212022-global-report-opportunity-amid-disruption

289. Ryan RM, Deci EL. *Self-determination theory: Basic psychological needs in motivation, development, and wellness.* Guilford Press; 2017.

290. OECD Statistics and Data Directorate. Unlocking new insights into multinational enterprises with the power of open-source data. oecdstatistics.blog Web site. https://oecdstatistics.blog/2023/05/10/unlocking-new-insights-into-multinational-enterprises-with-the-power-of-open-source-data/. Updated 2023. Accessed September 26, 2024.

291. Yu H, Bansal P, Arjaliès D. International business is contributing to environmental crises. *J Int Bus Stud.* 2023;54(6):1151–1169.

292. Nippa M, Patnaik S, Taussig M. MNE responses to carbon pricing regulations: Theory and evidence. *J Int Bus Stud.* 2021;52:904–929.

293. Foley CF, Hines JR, Malatoni RJ, Wessel D. Multinational activity in the modern world. In: *Global goliaths: Multinational corporations in the 21st century economy*, Foley CF, Wessel D, Hines JR (eds). Brookings; 2021.

294. Maksimov V, Wang SL, Yan S. Global connectedness and dynamic green capabilities in MNEs. *J Int Bus Stud.* 2019:1–18.

295. Marano V, Wilhelm M, Kostova T, Doh J, Beugelsdijk S. Multinational firms and sustainability in global supply chains: Scope and boundaries of responsibility. *J Int Bus Stud.* 2024:1–16.

296. Ocelík V, Kolk A, Ciulli F. Multinational enterprises, industry 4.0 and sustainability: A multidisciplinary review and research agenda. *J Clean Prod.* 2023;413:137434. doi: 10.1016/j.jclepro.2023.137434.

297. Ocelík, V., Kolk, A., & Ciulli, F. (2023). Multinational enterprises, Industry 4.0 and sustainability: A multidisciplinary review and research agenda. *Journal of Cleaner Production, 413,* 137434.10.1016/j.jclepro.2023.137434

298. Srivastava S, Singh S, Dhir S. Culture and international business research: A review and research agenda. *International Business Review.* 2020;29(4):101709. doi: 10.1016/j.ibusrev.2020.101709.

299. Christopher I. The impact of multi-culture on international business. *Vilnius University Proceedings.* 2023;37:28–33.

300. Kusz H, Ahmad A. Preserving engagement, nurturing resilience. *Clin Geriatr Med.* 2020;36(4):601–612. doi: 10.1016/j.cger.2020.06.004.

301. Wamsler C. Education for sustainability: Fostering a more conscious society and transformation towards sustainability. *International Journal of Sustainability in Higher Education.* 2020;21(1):112–130.

Index

Note: page numbers in *italic* type refer to Figures; those in **bold** type refer to Tables.

A
Abdullah, SNF 142
access economy 131
Acne Studios 126
actionable business propositions 23
active emotional practices for social cohesion 86–87
active impact (Five Dimensions of Emotional Capital model) 89, 97, 133–147
activism values 119–120
Adams, NE 163
adaptability, systems approach 17
addictive behavior 78
  see also impulsive buying behavior
affective economies 82
Agenda 21 53
agriculture 20
A-growth 10
Ah Fook, L 68, 159, 174
Ahmad, A 191
Ahmed, RR 134, 137, 138, 160, 172, 176
Ahmed, S 82
Airbnb 92, 131
Alcott, B 152
Alion 136
altruism 106, 143
Amazon Prime 139
Amber, E 11, 37, 54–55, 57, 58, 93, 173, 188, 189–190

Amos, C 22
Anand, J 92–93
Andrzejewsi, SA 10, 66, 102
animal welfare 107, 124
Anisimova, T 150
anti-consumption 4, 11, 28, 32, 43, **46–47**, 51, 53, 56, *56*, 57–58, 95, 107, 108, 112, 117, 123, 124–125, 132, 135, 138–139, 140, 141, 147, 151, 163, 164, 173
  influence of social networks on 141
  meat consumption 125, 135, 151
  soft drinks 108
anti-industrialism 121
anti-materialism 125
Appenfeller, D 10, 111
Areias, S 42, 120, 134, 138, 144, 146, 172
Ares, G 153
Armstrong Soule, CA 101–102
Arrhenius, Svante 13
Asia 27, *27*, 111–112
Asuamah Yeboah, S 112, 141
attention management 74–75
attitude-behavior gap 22, 58, 95, 177
attitudes 70–71, *71*, **72**, 73, 160–161
avoidance behavior 141
Awais, M 152, 158
Azazz, AMS 125, 135

B

B Corp certification 128
Babauta, Leo 126
Bagdare, S 172, 173
Balderjahn, I 6, 10, 59, 109, 111, 153, 176
Bandura, A 163
Bardey, A 126, 127, 137, 146, 176
Bardhi, F 131
Batra, R 103
Baumeister, R 75, 146
"being more human" approach 138–140
beliefs 70–71
benevolence 119, 123
Benton, R 121
Bhutan 64
Biely, K 20, 21
Biggs, R 18
Billmore, S 150
biodiversity loss 9, 190
bioeconomy 20–21
biotechnologies, negative social feedback against 20
BlackRock 92
BNPL (buy-now-pay-later) schemes 158–160, 174
Bocken, N 119, 123–124
BOSH 145
Bourdieu, P 83
Brabantia 128–129
brand avoidance 122, 125
Brandão, A 65, 143, 153–154, 163–164, 171, 181
brands 23, 96, 176
 brand loyalty 67
 superfans 133–134
Brexit 9
Burroughs, J 66, 102
Burton, JB 161–162
business strategy for the triple-win approach 169–170
businesses
 for-profit businesses, sustainable consumption challenges 10–11
 origins of 5
 and social change 92
 survival tactics 178–179
 see also international corporations
"buy local" **46**

C

Canada 27
Cao, D 109, 150, 151, 164, 171, 176
capacities to feel 86
capital, as a factor of production 14
capsule wardrobes 127, 146
cashless payment 67
Caucasians, buying behavior 112
celebrities 142
Chakraborty, S 132, 167
Chan, J 85
Chan, S 23
Chang, HJ 102, 136–137, 161, 164, 168
Chang, M 145–146, 170, 171, 172, 176
Chao, DY 163
Chatzidakis, A 22, 30, 118, 119, 120, 151–152
Chen, H 145–146, 170, 171, 172, 176
China
 mHealth 105–106
 online buying behavior 113
 organic food 142
 soft drinks consumption 141
 study of sustainable consumption and impulsive buying behavior 27, 28
 US-China trade dispute 9
Chiu, W 34, 68, 150, 179

Cho, H 33, 67, 138, 145, 150, 177, 179
Cho, Renée 110
Christopher, I 191
Chul, Y 134, 160, 163, 165
Chung, Y-C 71
circular design 128–129
circular economy 14, 20, 123, 127, 129, 145
circular production 174
Clean Tech 20
climate change 11, 13, 21, 140
  consumer behavior 170, 171
  international corporations 190
  and personal responsibility 118
clothing 132, 146
  second-hand 129–130, 132
CO_2 emissions, international corporations 190
Coca Cola 22
cognitive control 74, 75
collaborative creation 138
collective compass 113–115
collectivism 115, 164, 187
commercial marketing 174
commons-orientated people power 144
communities
  local 136–137, 176
  resilient 185
compassion 120, 143
compensatory consumption 150
connectedness 144
conscious consumption 51, 58
consumer behavior
  alterations in 23
  see also impulsive buying
consumer debt 66, 102, 114
  finance planning and education 158–160
consumer engagement paradox 167–169
consumer responsibility, sustainable consumption studies 30–31
consumer self-efficacy 163–164
consumer transformation 90–91
consumer trust 139–140
  trustworthy information 170–172
consumerism 5, 11, 104, 144
consumers
  consumer social responsibility 135
  demographic criteria 134
  personal responsibility 118
  young 134
consumption
  decreasing consumption 11, 13, 53, 56, 59, 65, 122, 147
  studies identifying need for **31**, 31–33, **33**, 35, **36**, 37–38
  individual behavioral changes 30–31
  micro, meso and macro-level 30, 84
  see also green consumerism/consumption; overconsumption; responsible consumption; sustainable consumptions
"consumption engineering," marketing as 10
consumption revolution 6, 9–19, **17**, 186
  Emotional Capital for the Triple-Win framework applications 90–94, *94*, **95**
  leadership of 189–191
consumption values 109
corporate social responsibility 10, 172
Cosme, I 121
Cottingham, Marci 83, 84, 86
COVID-19 pandemic 9, 33–34, 35, 51, 55, 108, 120–121, 138, 140

emotional impact and impulsive buying behavior 68, 71, 168, 177–178
health and self-care 105–106
survival mode 149–150
Zhong-Yong thinking (moderate thinking) 155–156
Crawford, G 69
crises, and shifting priorities 9–10
cultural change 6, 90–91, 96
cultural values shift 114–115
Cupertino de Miranda, C 65, 143, 153–154, 163–164, 171, 181
Curtis, M 73
custodians of existence 192
Cyprus 136
Czarnecka, B 66, 112–113, 159

D
Daly, H 20, 21, 58, 63
De Schutter, O 13
decarbonization goals 9
decentralised networks/ infrastructures 182
Deci, EL 188
degrowth 4, 10, 51, 53, 57, 64, 92, 117, 121, 144, 145, 152
definitions of 14
growth-degrowth nexus 12–14
demand, and planetary boundaries 175
demarketing 101–102
demographic criteria 134
Dennison, L 70
Dermody, J 64, 113, 118, 131, 144, 146, 162, 175, 180
Dholakia, J 73, 102, 122, 125, 130, 156
Di Crosta, A 71
Diener, E 154
"Digital Wellbeing" 176, 182
Dimitrova, T 43, 70–71

Dörrenbächer, C 93, 189, 190
Douglas, AJ 14
downshifting 43
Durmaz, İBV 82
dynamic characteristics of systems 17

E
Easthope, G 135
Eckhardt, GM 131
eco-friendly products 174
and the COVID-19 pandemic 120–121
ecological economics 63
ecological equilibrium 18
ecological lifestyles 136
ecological resilience 16–17, **17**
economic growth 3, 9, 23
growth-degrowth nexus 12–14, 164
economic pillar of sustainability 15–16, 21
economically driven consumption (triple-win model of sustainable consumption) 41, 52, 52, 54, 54–56
economics, and consumer behavior 26–27
"eco-villages" 122–123
education 90–91
educational changes 6, 96
online education market 92
ego depletion theory 75
egoism 106, 160
Elshaer, IA 125, 135
emerging markets 174
emotion
survival mode, and overconsumption 149–150
see also negative emotions
Emotional Capital for the Triple-Win framework 81, 98, 186

50 innovative business strategies 95–97, *97*
business advocacy for 167–183
emotional capital 6
  concept development 82–84
  as a tripartite concept 84–87
  emotional competencies 81–82
  Five Dimensions of Emotional Capital model 87–88, *88*
    active impact 89, 97, 133–147
    empowerment 90, 97, 149–162
    leadership by example 90, 97, 167–183
    sustainable awareness 88–89, 97, 101–115
    triple-win mindset 89, 97, 117–132
  practical applications for consumption revolution 90–94, *94*, **95**
emotional engagement 75
emotional intelligence 81–82, 152, 157, 187
  and impulsive buying behavior 69, 76–78
emotional management 84, 86–87, 149, 151
  "taking a pause" 157
emotional regulation 76, 152–153
emotional skills 81–82, 86–87, 188
emotional strategies 54–55
emotion-based knowledge 86–87
empathy 82
empowerment 153, 189, 191
  Five Dimensions of Emotional Capital model 90, *97*, 149–162
engineering resilience 16, 17, **17**, 18
entrepreneurship 187–188, 189, 191
environmental capital 64

environmental damage 9, 11
environmental pillar of sustainability 15–16, 21
environmental studies, and consumer behavior 26–27, 29, 29–30
environmental sustainability attitudes 124, 125
environmental values 105
environmentally driven consumption (triple-win model of sustainable consumption) 41, 52, *52*, 56, 56–58
environmentally-friendly consumerism 102
environmentally-friendly products 32–33, **36**, 37–38, 53, 110
ePowerFun 129
equilibrium of life 192
ethical consumption **45–46**, 51, 58, 165
ethics 134
EU (European Union)
  recycling 145
Europe
  sustainable consumption and impulsive buying behavior 27, **27**
European Commission 128
exchange of goods 146
experience economy 4, 92, 175, 182
experiential testimonies 137–138
Eyel, CŞ, 82

F
Faber, RJ 66, 102
factors of production 14
Fairphone 145
Fairtrade **46**
fake reviews 171

families, influence of 140–142
Farley, J 20
fashion 126, 132, 137, 142, 143, 144, 146
  capsule wardrobes 127, 146
  fast fashion 67, 174
  second-hand clothing 129–130, 132
fasting 125
Fath, BD 18
"feature-frugal approach" 126, 127
Feeney, BC 83
Figuero-García, EC 43
finance planning and education 158–160
financial institutions, "sustainability" and "social responsibility" claims 136
financial management, innovations in 181
First International Conference on Economic DeGrowth for Ecological Sustainability and Social Equity 121
Fischer, D 30, 43, 53, 173
Fisk, George 10
Fitness, J 73
Fitzpatrick, N 51
Five Dimensions of Emotional Capital model *see* Emotional Capital for the Triple-Win framework
flow experience 142
Foley, CF 190
Folke, C 18, 58
food 118, 171
  food-sharing 130–131
  GMO (genetically modified food) 20–21, 172
  green food 51, 140, 161, 181
  healthy food consumption 51, 54, 107, 125, 140, 141, 151
  mukbang 143
  organic 22, 107, 108, 109, 142, 150, 151, 154, 161, 170, 176, 179, 182
for-profit businesses 10–11
for-profit businesses, sustainable consumption challenges 10–11
Frank, P 153, 156
Frankenstein food (GMO/ genetically modified food) 20–21
Frayme Mylo™ 110
freecycling 130–131, 146
friends, influence of 140–142
Fromm, Erich 121
Froyum, CM 84
frugality **46–47**, 51, 56, 57, 65, 123, 124, 152, 158, 175
Fuchs, D 30, **49**, 118–119, 122, 124

G
"Gaia" TV channel 137
gamification 181
Gatto, SK 20
Gawior, B 66–67, 108–109, 159, 167
GDP, as measure of national well-being 13, 23
Geiger, SM 65–66, 120, 143
Gendron, B 77, 82, 85
Genos International 75
Georgescu-Roegen, N 121
Germany 27
Ghaffar, A 141–142
Gillies, V 83
Gilmore, JH 103, 175
"global asymmetric resource flows" 12
global commons 185
Global Ecovillage Network 122

Global Entrepreneurship Monitor 188
GMO (genetically modified food) 20–21, 172
GNH (Gross National Happiness), Bhutan 64
Godemann, J 172–173
Goldsmith, Edward 121
Goleman, D 77, 81–82, 187
Goodman, Paul 121
Gossen, M 43, 95–96, 173
gratification
  immediate 74
  see also impulsive buying behavior
Grebitus, Carola 117–118
green consumerism/consumption 10, 11, 32–33, **36**, 37–38, 42, 43, **45**, 50–51, 53, 54–55, 124, 134, 139, 151–152, 160, 172
green demarketing 101–102
green economy 10, 20
Green Growth 10
green marketing mix 174
green revolution 20
greenwashing 10, 54–55, 66, 139
grocery bags 110
growth-degrowth nexus 12–14
  see also economic growth
Groyum, CM 83, 84
Gucci 182
guilt 134
Gunderson, LH 16, 17, 21
Gupta, AS 68, 140, 150, 178, 179

H
Hagens, NJ 9
Haider, M 10, 43–44, **44–50**, 50, 67, 122, 131
Halper, LR 163–164
Hamdan, E 142

happiness 114
Harvard Business Review 74
He, J 67, 151, 162
"Headspace" app 137
health
  health benefits of sustainable consumption 107–108
  and self-care 105–106
hedonism 160, 163–164
  hedonic values 109, 142, 143, 149, 164, 168
Helm, D 20
Herabadi, A 151
Hickel, J 10–11
Hires, Daniel 138
Hobson, K 19, 124
Höfer, R 135
Hoffmann, A 155, 158–159
Hofman, V 113
Holbrook, MB 103
Hollong, CS 16
Horcea-Milcu, A 111
HoReCa (hotel, restaurant, and café catering) sector 33–34, 55
Horley, JJ 135
Hornberg, A 12
Huatakangas, S 20
Hughes, Lucy 110–111
human capital 64
Humans@Centre report, 2024 86
humility 136
Husnain, M 22
Hüttel, A 59, 65, 109, 153, 176

I
IFIC Foundation 20
Illich, Ivan 121
impact
  active impact (Five Dimensions of Emotional Capital model) 89, 97, 133–147
  impact values 119–120

impulsive buying behavior 3, 4, 5, 10, 51, 87, 108, 113, 150, 174
 awareness of 101–102
 education on the consequences of 102–103
 emotional and psychological factors 67–68, 69, 70–73, **71**, **72**, 167, 185–186, 192
 emotional impact of 66, 102, 125
 emotional intelligence 69, 76–78
 emotional strategies to promote 54–55
 factors influencing 69, *70*, 70–73, **72**
 fast fashion 143
 financial instruments 158–160
 non-stimulation of 180
 and overconsumption 185–186
 planning prompt 157–158
 scale of 22
 self-control 73–76
 social climate 142
 social impact of 53
 and sustainable consumption 23, 25, 117
  consumer responsibility 30–31
  emergence of publications on 25–27, *26*
  global study of 27, 27–28
  interdisciplinary approach to 29, 29–30
  positive influence of impulsive buying 33–35, **34–35**
  product changes 35, **36**, 37–38
  reduced consumption **31**, 31–33, **32**, 35, **36**, 37–38
 "taking a pause" 156–158
 vulnerabilities, of consumers 177–178
 well-being 66–69, 91
 see also addictive behavior

India 27, 125
individual actions 109–111
individual behavior changes 53
individualism 115, 164, 187
 cultural polarization of 111–113
indulgent consumption 51
industrialization 21
influencers 141, 142, 143
 see also opinion leaders
information
 informed choices 109–111
 trustworthy 170–172, 176
inner development 91
inner transformation 53, 58
innovation 92–93, 169–170, 174, 175, 181–182, 185
"insatiable human needs" 63
inspiration 188
international corporations 189–190
 and post-growth economies 190–191
 see also businesses
International Journal of Consumer Studies 117–118
intrinsic motivation 188
investment choices 136
Inzlicht, M 74
Ismael, D 22, 154, 161, 177
Issey Mayake 126
Iwata, O 122
Iyer, GR 103, 125, 164, 174
Iyer, R 68

J
Jackson, EN 83
Jakubowska, D 51, 107
Japan 12, 126
Jensen, Anabel 157
Jiang, Y 68, 168, 179, 181
Johnston, TC 161–162
JPMorgan 92

K

Kacen, JJ 112
Kacen, Y 22
Kago, K 106
Kakkar, S 127, 137, 176, 181
Kalaniemi, S 11, 118
Kallis, G 121
Kasser, T 114
Keller, J 65–66, 120, 143
Key, TM 10
Khalil, MK 51, 139
Khalil, R 51, 139
Khazaei, M 84–85
Kilbourne, W 10, 113–114, 180
Kim, Y 180, 182
Klarna 158
knowledge communities 60, 137–138, 142, 143–144
Köhler, Stefan 129
Kohr, Leopold 121
Korea 27
Kuanr, A 102, 112, 122, 124–125, 137–138, 144, 162, 163
Kusz, H 191

L

labor, as a factor of production 14
Ladhari, R 108, 149
Lamberti, L 73
land, as a factor of production 14
Lang, C 130
Laroche, M 65, 114, 125, 152–153
Lau, AK 68, 168, 179, 181
leadership 136
  Five Dimensions of Emotional Capital model 90, **97**, 167–183
  transformational 86
Lee, D 33, 137, 143, 179, 181
Lee, JA 112, 114
Lee, K 132, 180
Lekavičienė, R 66, 67, 69, 77, 78, 102–103
Lemay, EP Jr 83
"less is more" 126, 146
leverage points 91
Liao, S-H 71
Liegey, V 144
life equilibrium 192
life expectancy 191
lifestyles 135–136
  and anti-consumption 124–125
  lifestyle changes 11, 13, 73, 95, 96, 109, 186
  sustainable 175
"Limits to Growth" (Club of Rome, 1972) 12
Ling Xie, S 107, 124, 125, 135, 140, 141, 142, 151
Liu, C 108, 160, 177
Liu, Y 30, 43, 119
Lively, KJ 84
LOHAS (Lifestyle of Health and Sustainability) 135
long-term change, systems approach 17
long-term orientation 114, 152, 180
long-term sales 180
Lorek, S 11, 30, **49**, 53, 118–119, 122, 124
Louis Vuitton 182
Lu, F 106, 135, 139, 143, 167, 168, 170, 171, 176, 181
Lu, X 66
luxury consumption 51
Lynas, M 9

M

Madhavan, S 83
Magids, S 168
Maksimov, V 190
Malter, MS 70, 103

Maltz, E 92
Mandolfo, M 73
Marano, V 190
MarinaTex 111
Markauskaité, R 32, 51, 53, 139, 153
Market Forces 136
marketing 54–55
   as "consumption engineering" 10
   emotions 76–77, 168
   impulsive buying behavior 91–92
   neuromarketing and emotion-based techniques 168
   oppressive techniques 118
   post-growth marketing mix 173–175
   study of sustainable consumption and impulsive buying behavior 29, 29
marketing communication 55–56, 175
   avoidance of patronizing messaging 176–177
   social media 141–142
   sustainable consumption 172–173
marketing stimuli 72, **72**, 174
Martínez-Alier, J 12, 13–14
materialism 11, 60, 112, 113–114, 115, 142, 143, 162, 164, 180
   emotional and psychological factors 67–68, 69
   global phenomenon 113
   negative consequences of 102–103
   positive relationship to sustainability 180
   susceptibility to 78
   well-being 65, 66
Matthews, G 78
Maximo, M 64

Mayer, JD 77
Mazhar, W 51, 106, 160, 162, 164
McCann, Deiric 75
McNeill, L 68, 159, 174
Meadows, DH 91
meat consumption 125, 135, 140, 151
Melewar, TC 69
mHealth 105–106
Middle East 27, 27
mindfulness 153, 154–156
   mindful consumption 11, 43, **47–48**, 51, 58–59, 102, 155
minimalism 4, 11, 56, 56, 57, 58, 61, 95, 107, 117, 123, 126–127, 132, 146, 158, 174
Mishan, EJ 121
moderate thinking 155–156
modesty 65, 136
Mogilner, A 102
money management, innovations in 181
Morris, William 121
Moser, C 103
motivation 82, 188
mukbang 143
Mukherjee, J 68, 140, 150, 178, 179
multiple equilibria, systems approach 17
Muncy, JA 68, 125, 164, 174
Muslim dietary practices 125
mycelium 110
"MyFitnessPal" app 181

N
Namazkhan, M 70
National Endowment for Financial Education 22
natural capital 14–15, 18, 175, 191
natural resources 4, 12

resource depletion 9, 21, 190
Navrátil, J 135
negative emotions 120–121, 140, 178–179
  survival mode, and overconsumption 149–150
Nelson, A 144
Nepomuceno, M 65, 114, 125, 152–153
Newman, A 73, 101, 150
NextGEN 122
Nguyen, TD 74, 102, 107, 119, 122, 160, 172, 181
Nippa, M 190
Nordlund, A 72, 91
norms, and impulsive buying behavior 70–71, 72, 73
North America 27, 27
Nowotny, Helen 83
nudging 173

O
Obama, Barack 146
Ocelik, V 190
OECD 13, 189
Oh, J 134, 160, 163, 165
Oh, KW 180, 182
Oliveira de Mendonça, G 126
online shopping 69, 77, 142
open-access journals 28
opinion leaders 141, 142–143
organic food 22, 107, 108, 109, 136, 142, 150, 151, 154, 161, 170, 176, 179, 182
Ortiz Alvarado, NB 103
Osikuminu, J 119, 123–124
Oslo Symposium, 1994 42
"Our Common Future" (Brundtland Commission, 1987) 12
overconsumption 4, 5, 10–11, 58, 68, 75, 87, 96, 104, 125, 175
  education about emotional reasons for 103–104
  impulsive buying behavior 185–186
  "overconsumption detonator" 22
  survival mode 149–150
overpopulation 4
oxytocin 75

P
Pakistan 141
Palmihas, JCC 10
panic buying, COVID-19 pandemic 68, 120–121, 150, 151, 161
paper recycling 145, 175
Patagonia 102, 110
Paul, J 105
peer groups, influence of 140–142
Pellegrino, A 57, 142, 174
Peluso, AM 140
perceived threat 177–178
perceptions, and impulsive buying behavior 72, 73
Pereira Heath, AT 22, 30, 118, 119, 151–152
personal responsibility 118, 162
personal values 105–106, 108–109
Persson, L 15
Phang, IG 68, 107, 150, 181
Picha, K 135
Pierson, K 92
Piligrimienė, Z 70
Pine, BJ 103, 175
place, post-growth marketing mix 174
planetary boundaries 4, 9, 13, 15, 19, 175
planning prompt 157–158
plastics 15, 110–111
Ploeger, A 22, 140, 154, 161, 177
Podoshen, JS 10, 66, 102
pollution 15, 21, 140

population growth 21–22
"post-development" framework 14, 121, 152
post-purchase dissatisfaction 66, 74, 102
poverty reduction, and economic growth 12
"Poverty and Shared Prosperity Report 2018" (World Bank) 12
power, and responsibility 189–191
price 181
  post-growth marketing mix 174
Princes, E 67
priorities, changing of 9–10
product certification 170, 171
product design 127, 181
product innovations 182
production
  factors of 14
  large-scale 13, 23
products
  new 169–170
  packaging and labelling 170, 171, 176
  post-growth marketing mix 174
  trustworthy information about 170–172
pro-environment behavior 144–147
pro-environment identity 170
pro-environmental self-identity 161–162
promotion, post-growth marketing mix 174
pro-social behavior 60, 65, 143–144
"prosperity without growth" 10, 51
Purvis, B 30

Q
Qi, X 140
Quechua indigenous thought 14–15

R
Ramadan, Z 139
Ramos-Hidlago, E 65, 134, 136, 154, 176
Rana, J 105
Rayner, L 135
Reay, D 83
reclaiming 157
recycling 15, 130, 145, 146, 161–162, 175
reflection 157
regeneration, of natural capital 15, 175
Reich, BJ 101–102
rejection 157
relationship management 82
religion, and consumption 125, 135
renewable resources 14
repairing 128, 145, 146, 162
resilience 58
  ecological equilibrium approach 18
  ecological resilience 16–17, **17**
  engineering resilience 16, 17, **17**, 18
  socio-ecological resilience 18, 19
resource productivity 21
responsibility, and power 189–191
responsible consumption 10, 43, **44**, 51, 58
restriction 157
retailers 10, 67
  membership programs 139–140
reusing 15, 145, 146, 161–162
Rindfleisch, A 66, 102
Rio Principles, 1992 53
Rockström, J 15
Rodríguez, MS 105
role models 142
Roşu, M 160–161
Ruskin, John 121

Rūtelione, A 32, 51, 53, 139, 153
Ryan, RM 188

S
Sadachar, A 132, 167
Sadilek, T 51, 107
Sajid, KS 34, 120–121, 137, 150, 168, 179
Salazar, HA 141
Salovey, P 77
Scandinavian culture, and minimalism 126
Scherbaum, S 74
Schomburgk, L 155, 158–159
Schumacher, EF 14, 121
Schwarts Model 119
SCR (social corporate responsibility) 50, 122
SDG 12 (United Nations Sustainable Development Goal 12) 6, 23, 93, 185, 186
second-hand items 127, 162
 clothing 129–130, 132
Sekulova, F 14, 121
self-awareness 60, 82, 153
self-care 105–106
self-confidence 163
self-control 71, 71, 114, 152, 155, 158
 and impulsive buying behavior 73–76
self-direction 119, 123
self-efficacy 125, 153, 163–164
self-expression 164
self-gratification 165
self-help 136
self-identity 73
 pro-environmental 161–162
self-interest 106
self-management 82
self-monitoring 77, 78
"self-organization" 16
self-regeneration 16, 19, 21
self-regulation 78, 82, 155
self-reliance 161–162
self-sufficient lifestyle 112
self-transcendence 91
self-transformation 60, 91, 144, 145–146, 186, 192
Sermboonsang, R 101, 155
serving others 186–189
Seyfang, G 162
Shahpasandi, F 67, 125, 157, 181
Shahzad, MF 108, 141
Shaikh, A 60, 65, 132, 134, 143, 144, 181
Shams, HA 69, 77
shared experiences 138, 143
shared responsibility 117–119
sharing consumption 37, **48–49**, 51, 58
sharing economy 4, **48–49**, 60, 65, 92, 117, 131–132, 143–144
Sharma, P 73, 77, 78, 103
Shen, X 147, 176
Sheth, IS 11, **48**, 108
Shobeiri,S 109, 137, 175
Shrum, LJ 74
Silvera, DH 66, 103
simplicity 126
 see also voluntary simplicity
simulation 119
Sirgy, MJ 111–112, 159
Six Seconds 157
slow consumption 43, 123
Smith, Adam 10
social inequalities, and international corporations 190
social isolation 191
"Social Life of Numbers, The" (Orton) 14–15
social marketing 173, 174
social media 141–142

social networks 140–142
social orientation 187
social pillar of sustainability 15–16, 20
Social Refrigerator 130
social relationships 83
social sciences 29, *29*
social skills 82
social stability, customers who care about 133–135
social status 66, 106
social transformation 85, 185–186
social values 91, 143, 168
socially driven consumption (triple-win model of sustainable consumption) 41, 51–52, *52*, 53, 58–60, *59*
socially driven transformation 53
socially responsible consumers 172
socio-ecological resilience 18, 19
socio-environmental system 96
Soergel, B 185
soft drinks 108, 141
Solow, RM 19
South America 27, *27*
South Asia 12
Spangenberg, JH 11, 53
spirituality 125, 135
Spiteri Cornish, L 22, 33, 74, 102, 103, 118, 154
Srivastava, S 190
standard of living measurements 12
State of the Planet, Columbia Climate School 109–110
Steg, L 106, 152, 162
Stiglitz-Sen-Fitoussi Commission 13
stimulation 123, 180
strong sustainability 18, 19, 21, 104
strong sustainable consumption approach 19

sub-Saharan Africa 12
success 114
sufficiency 11, 13, **49–50**, 51, 56, 57, 87, 95, 117, 122–123, 142, 152, 173, 180
Süle, M 118, 174
superfans 133–134
survival mode, and overconsumption 149–150
survival tactics, of businesses 178–179
sustainability
 economic pillar 15–16, 21
 environmental pillar 15–16, 21
 social pillar 15–16, 20
 strong sustainability 18, 19, 21, 104
 systems approach to 15–18, **17**
 weak sustainability 18–19, 20, 21
sustainable awareness (Five Dimensions of Emotional Capital model) 88–89, 97, 101–115
sustainable consumption 3–4, 5, 23, 41, 152, 176
 customers who care about 133–135
 enhancing customers' sustainable attitudes 160–161
 general sustainable consumption 50–51, 54
 health benefits of 107–108
 impulsive buying behavior 23, 25–27, 117
 consumer responsibility 30–31
 emergence of publications on 25–27, *26*
 global study of 27, *27*–28
 interdisciplinary approach to 29, *29*–30
 positive influence of impulsive buying 33–35, **34–35**

product changes 35, **36**, 37–38
reduced consumption **31**,
31–33, 32, 35, **36**, 37–38
marketing communication
172–173
multiverse of 50–52
optimal solution for 41–42
personal values 108–109
positive emotions 153–154
scope and definitions of 42–44,
44–45, 50
social networks 140–142
strong and weak 19, 25, 43, 124
triple-win model 41, 52, 52–54
economically driven
consumption 41, 52, 52, 54,
54–56
environmentally driven
consumption 41, 52, 52, 56,
56–58
socially driven consumption 41,
51–52, 52, 53, 58–60, 59
sustainable degrowth 121
sustainable development 15
sustainable development policies
10
"sustainable luxury" 164
sustainable products 3, 23
sustainable responsibility 118
Sweden 118
Switzerland 54–55
systems approach to sustainability
15–18, **17**
Szigeti, C 21–22
Szmigin, T 132, 181

T
"taking a pause" 156–158
Tariq, A 107, 142, 161, 170
technological advancements 20–21,
169–170, 175, 182
Testa, F 50

Thøgersen, J 171
Thomas, Maura 74
Thoreau, Henry David 121
thriftiness 136
"Thrive" app 176
Tian, P 29–30
Tolstoy, Leo 121
Toth, G 21–22
trait models of impulsivity 103
transcendence 91
transformation, systems approach
to 17
"transition towns" 122
transparency 171
Tri, HC 17
triple-win approach (people,
planet, and prosperity for
all) 4, 7
business strategy for 169–170
triple-win mindset
Five Dimensions of Emotional
Capital model 89, 97,
117–132
triple-win model of sustainable
consumption 41, 52, 52–54
economically driven consumption
41, 52, 52, 54, 54–56
environmentally driven
consumption 41, 52, 52, 56,
56–58
socially driven consumption 41,
51–52, 52, 53, 58–60, 59
trust 167
Trzebiński, J 138

U
Uber 92, 131
Uhr, B 135–136
Um, T 33, 181
uncertainty 120–121, 138–139
United Kingdom 27
United Nations 144

Special Rapporteur on Extreme Poverty and Human Rights 13
United States 12, 22, 27
materialistic culture 114, 180
US-China trade dispute 9
universalism 119, 124
unneeded consumption 51
Upadhye, B 67, 102, 157–158
upcycling 130, 146, 175
Urton, Gary 14–15
U.S. Department of Agriculture, Agricultural Marketing Service 20
utilitarian values 109, 143, 149, 164, 178

V
values
  activism values 119–120
  consumption values 109
  environmental values 105
  hedonic values 109, 142, 143, 149, 164, 168
  impact values 119–120
  impulsive buying behavior 68, 70–71, 72, 73
  lifestyle 135–136
  personal values 105–106, 108–109
  serving others 186–189
  social values 91, 143, 168
  utilitarian values 109, 143, 149, 164, 178
van der Waal, JWH 93
van Driel, M 23, 185
Vancouver, JB 163–164
Veenhoven, R 64
Venkataraman, P 106
Verain, MC 118
Vergragt, P 42–43
Verplanken, B 151

Vohs, KD 66, 102
voluntary simplicity 4, 11, 28, 37, 43, 46, **47**, 51, 53, 56, 56, 57, 61, 65, 87–88, 95, 112, 114, 119–120, 122, 123–124, 132, 136, 145, 152, 158, 162, 163, 173, 180
vulnerabilities, of consumers 177–178

W
Walker, CC 168
Wamsler, C 192
Wan, C 33, 137, 143, 179, 181
Wang, S 68, 73, 76, 113, 122, 142, 150, 155–156, 159, 171
Wang, X 103
warmth, interpersonal 140
warranties, extended 145
waste 117, 127–131, 174, 190
  zero-waste living 123, 127–131
Watchravesringkan, K 102, 136–137, 161, 164, 168
Waters, L 154
weak sustainability 18–19, 20, 21
Weder, F 173
Weed, EA 84
WeForest 128
Wei Jie, P 33, 60, 76–77, 137, 141, 142, 143, 167, 168
welfare state 64
welfare, value of well-being over 104–105
well-being 18, 35, 63–64, 65–66, 79, 153–154, 186, 187, 191
  education about 104–105
  impulsive buying behavior 66–69, *70*, 70–73, *71*, **73**, 73–78, 79, 91
  innovations for 181–182
  reducing consumption 11, 59

sustainable consumption 65–66
welfare state 64
Well-being Framework, OECD 13
Western Europe 12
Westerners, self-concept 111–112
wezpomoz.pl 130
White, K 38, 111, 131, 138–139, 142
Wilderer, PA 21
"window of vitality" 18
"Wise Shopping App" 158
women, emotional capital and social relationships 83
World Happiness Report 64
Wright, Colin 126
Wunderlich, S 20

Y
Yanmei Jiang, L 138, 150, 177–178
Yehuala, FS 63–64

Yohjii Yamamoto 126
young consumers 134
Yu, H 189–190

Z
Zafar, AU 33, 141, 142
Zak, Paul 75, 133
Zembylas, M 82
zero-waste living 123, 127–131
Zhang, KZ 109
Zhang, R 130
Zhang, Y 74
Zhong-Yong thinking (moderate thinking) 155–156
Zipcar 131
Zuckerberg, Mark 146

A quick word from Practical Inspiration Publishing...

We hope you found this book both practical and inspiring – that's what we aim for with every book we publish.

We publish titles on topics ranging from leadership, entrepreneurship, HR and marketing to self-development and wellbeing.

Find details of all our books at: www.practicalinspiration.com

Did you know...

We can offer discounts on bulk sales of all our titles – ideal if you want to use them for training purposes, corporate giveaways or simply because you feel these ideas deserve to be shared with your network.

We can even produce bespoke versions of our books, for example with your organization's logo and/or a tailored foreword.

To discuss further, contact us on info@practicalinspiration.com.

Got an idea for a business book?

We may be able to help. Find out more about publishing in partnership with us at: bit.ly/PIpublishing.

Follow us on social media...

- @PIPTalking
- @pip_talking
- @practicalinspiration
- @piptalking
- Practical Inspiration Publishing